# Mathematical Foundations for Communication Engineering

# MATHEMATICAL FOUNDATIONS
## *for*
# COMMUNICATION ENGINEERING

**Volume 1**
**Determinate Theory of**
**Signals and Waves**

**Kenneth W. Cattermole**
*Professor of Telecommunications*
*Department of Electronic Systems Engineering*
*University of Essex*

A HALSTED PRESS BOOK

**JOHN WILEY & SONS**
**New York**

Published in the U.S.A.
by Halsted Press, a Division of
John Wiley & Sons, Inc., New York

**Library of Congress Cataloging in Publication Data**

Cattermole, Kenneth W. (Kenneth William)
  Mathematical foundations for communication
engineering.

  Bibliography: v. 1, p.
  Contents: Determinate theory of signals and waves —
v.  2. Statistical analysis and finite structures.
  1. Signal theory (Telecommunication)    2. Tele-
communication —Mathematics.    I. Title.
TK5102.5.C338    1985    621.38′01′51    85-878
ISBN 0-470-20176-2 (v. 1)
ISBN 0-470-20177-0 (v. 2)

Printed in Great Britain

# Preface

The main purpose of a preface is to tell the reader what the book is about: it is also the one place where the author may drop the scholarly style and appear as himself. I propose to do both by explaining how this book came to be written.

As a young engineer, I worked for several years on the development of microwave radio systems. My main personal innovation was in the theory of phase distortion and the techniques of phase measurement and equalisation, which took me fairly deeply into frequency-modulation theory. I was also interested in other aspects of the project, and studied several microwave topics including the theory of reflective antennas. Perhaps naively, I was astonished to find that the analyses of frequency modulation and of circular antennas — apparently quite different things — both introduced Bessel functions, which at that time were new to me. I tried, with no immediate success, to understand why the same mathematical functions should appear in such diverse physical problems. I read (not without difficulty) Watson's famous textbook. I looked into the origin of Bessel functions: on finding that the astronomer F. W. Bessel had used them to model periodic perturbations of nearly-uniform planetary motions, the connection with f.m. became apparent — but why the antennas?

That was over thirty years ago. Further experience has only deepened my conviction that virtually all the applied mathematics I have encountered has an underlying unity. I gradually realised that Fourier series, Fourier integrals, Laplace transforms, z-transforms (which I innocently re-invented while trying to analyse an early version of time-division telephony) and generating functions are all 'really' the same thing. Discrete and continuous signals or distributions can be subsumed under a common theory. Signal analysis in time, space, or space–time is much the same.

To a mathematician whose mind inhabits abstract space, I suppose all this is completely trite. To an analytically-inclined engineer, it was

v

a discovery. And I find that to successive cohorts of engineering students, it is still an enlightenment. The fact is that most engineering teaching has not made full use of this unity. Signal analysis, wave propagation, statistical estimation, digital signal processing, coding theory are presented by different teachers using different textbooks. Yet to someone who needs them all — and I would contend that a communication engineer does — they are most easily intelligible together.

There will never be one encyclopaedic textbook: but the time is ripe for a unified treatment of the mathematical foundations of these and cognate topics. This book is my version, as of now. The form of words implies both that there could be other reasonable versions, and that my own might well change. I think, however, that my present material constitutes an essential nucleus, with which in time still further topics may be integrated.

My general theme is, then, the common theoretical substratum underlying diverse problems and practices. The common features of Chapters 2–4 are the analysis of patterns in time and space, primarily by means of the Fourier transform and its derivatives; and the use of probabilistic methods. These techniques are conventional in signal theory, but it is illuminating to go beyond the conventional range of application. Chapter 5, on finite mathematics, shows that superficially different applications such as digital signal processing and error control coding have a common basis in the theory of Galois fields. It also shows that Galois field theory is linked to familiar signal theory in ways not apparent from the usual algebraic treatment: notably, the Galois field has a Fourier transform, in terms of which coding becomes much like filtering.

Two features of the book are indissolubly linked. To accommodate a wide range of topics at moderate length, it has been essential to adopt a fairly terse presentation based on powerful and general methods. This might be thought to demand of the reader that elusive quality known as 'mathematical maturity'. On the contrary, I would say that this is one of the qualities that the book may assist the reader to develop, because of the second feature. My experience in teaching both graduate and undergraduate courses has been that most engineering students can grasp abstract ideas and general methods very readily, if these are presented in the right context and with varied instances of application. Some highly abstract and general concepts are introduced, but examples and illustrations are interspersed very frequently. What might be 'difficult mathematics' will, I hope, become a familiar operation to be thought of in physical rather than abstract terms. Such an approach to abstractions opens the way both to their appreciation and their use.

The book should be intelligible to students of electrical engineering or allied subjects, at universities or polytechnics, from the second year of honours degree courses onwards: and to practicing engineers whose education has extended to degree, C.E.I. Part II or H.N.D. level. It is suitable for the solitary reader, who is advised to read it with pencil and paper handy for working out exercises as they occur. Teachers of engineering should find it suitable for use as a student textbook, or in their private reading as a source of problems, illustrations and a somewhat new slant on what may be a familiar subject. It is likely that many experienced engineers or teachers will know some of the topics very well but be less familiar with others. For them the book offers a convenient means of broadening their knowledge; its unified approach leads to explicit and implicit mutual relevance, so that familiarity with part of the subject can assist comprehension of the remainder.

After the foregoing remarks, it is hardly necessary to say that the book is not based on any syllabus or course, even of my own University, as it exists at the time of writing: it presents the direction in which I think that courses should be, and are, evolving.

The division into two volumes is mainly a matter of expediency: the work was conceived as a whole, but a single volume would be uncomfortably large. However, the reader may be assured that Volume 1 makes sense on its own. It gives a comprehensive treatment of determinate signal and wave theory, together with self-contained introductions to random signals and to finite transforms. Volume 2 gives a comprehensive treatment of probability and random processes, and of finite groups and fields, in each case with some significant applications. It has been written as a sequel to Volume 1, and is best read in conjunction with it.

The source material derives about equally from the industrial and the academic halves of my career; but the book was wholly written during my time as Professor of Telecommunications in the Department of Electronic Systems Engineering at the University of Essex. Among the many colleagues who have helped to shape the Essex telecommunications group, those who have most influenced my thinking on some of the topics included here are Dr. Don Pearson and Dr. John O'Reilly. To these good friends, to many other colleagues and students, and to previous writers on whose work I have drawn, I owe my best thanks.

October 1984                                      Kenneth W. Cattermole

# Notations and conventions

Fourier transformation is indicated by the arrow symbol $\Rightarrow$.

Corresponding functions in original and transform domains are usually allotted corresponding lower-case and capital letters, thus: $g(t) \Rightarrow G(f)$.

Woodward's notation for repetition is used, thus:

$$\text{rep}_X f(x) = \sum_{n=-\infty}^{\infty} f(x-nX)$$

Vectors and matrices are in bold type, usually lower-case and capital respectively, thus: $\mathbf{x}$, $\mathbf{A}$.

Random variables are usually denoted by capital letters, and values in their sample spaces by corresponding lower-case letters. Thus, $X$ may have a probability density $f(x)$.

Definitions, theorems and equations are numbered sequentially in each section. Within a section only the sequence number is used, but in citing material from other sections a full reference is given. For example, the central limit theorem is Theorem 5 in Section 4.2, and is cited as Theorem 4.2.5 elsewhere.

# Contents

# Contents of Volume 2

## Statistical Theory and Finite Structures

# Chapter 1

# Modelling of signals and systems

## 1.1 THE SCOPE OF COMMUNICATION ENGINEERING

We will not attempt any initial definition of such key words as signal, or information, or communication. Anyone interested in the subject will have some intuitive concept, which will become progressively refined and extended as he studies it in greater depth. The concepts, in fact, are clarified by the use we make of them. We will first survey some of the things that communication engineers do, and then develop the analytical methods which are common to several of these activities. Among the items of concern are the following:

*Communication terminals*, which take messages of significance to a human user — speech, pictures, written messages, etc. — and convert them into electrical signals which in some way represent the message content. Conversely, the electrical signals must be converted bsck to some form of visible or audible display, intelligible to a human recipient. We need to have a language in which messages and signals can be described in detail; enough detail to specify significant features and to design equipment which will preserve them. For engineering purposes, the description must be of objective properties rather than semantics or human connotations. Our messages are presented to the input terminal, and displayed by the output terminal, as a distribution of energy in space, or time, or both. It is the patterns and the fluctuations which convey meaning: the arrangement of light and dark areas in a visual image, the fluctuation of sound pressure in speech, the sequence of symbols in a text. We can characterise these patterns by such measures as the fineness of fluctuation in the speech sounds, the probability that certain intensities of light or sound occur. We can establish by experiments in perception the range of a parameter — for example, of speech frequency — significant to the user. The terminal equipment can then be designed to accept, and to display, the full repertoire of patterns which are significant and which occur with non-trivial probability.

*Communication media and channels.* The signals representing messages are conveyed from place to place by means of terrestrial and submarine cables, radio links, communication satellites, waveguides, beams of light, etc. The language of patterns and distributions which we can use to describe messages and signals is equally suitable for the channels which carry them. The range of frequencies which can be conveyed, the range of intensities, the probability of channel fluctuations such as radio fades, are examples of significant parameters. During its transit our signal will inevitably be corrupted by admixture with unwanted and irrelevant perturbations which are usually called noise or interference. We can no more give an objective definition of noise than one can define a weed by botanical classification. Noise, like weeds, is something that we wish to eliminate in favour of something else which we prefer. Our noise may be someone else's signal — in which case it is usually called crosstalk. Or it may be the unintended concomitant of human action — such as an electrical surge induced by a passing train. Or it may be the result of random motions of the elementary particles of which our material structures are composed: a fundamental random fluctuation usually called thermal noise. Whatever the source of noise, it can be described in the same language as signals and channels. It has a distribution of amplitude, of frequency, of temporal fluctuation. The relationship between the signal and the noise emerging from a channel — often quoted as a single parameter, the ratio of their long-term mean powers — is an important measure of a channel quality; though a single parameter is meaningful only against a great deal of background knowledge of the signal and its significant features.

The properties of channels depend in part on the spatial distribution of energy, say the radiation pattern from a laser or a radio antenna. We shall see that the methods of analysing spatial distributions have a lot in common — more than is usually recognised — with the methods of analysing temporal patterns and distributions.

*Communication systems* By this term we mean the totality of terminals, media etc. by means of which a message is conveyed from one user to another. It is something more than the sum of our preceding items, in two distinct senses. Firstly, we have spoken of (say) a telephone terminal as converting speech to electrical signals, and vice versa. In practice, a signal representing a single voice signal will not usually be conveyed very far in that form. It may be combined with other signals representing voice signals from other users, control signals for use in the telephone network (holding, clearing, dialling signals for example), and special signals unknown to the user but important for the operation of the transmission equipment (for regulating gain, indicating faults, etc.). This complex of signals must be conveyed, without mutual interference, over a common medium; which requires further apparatus. Many communication systems, and not only in the public telephone service, have complicating features of this kind which are imperceptible to the user but important for the engineers.Secondly, it is essential that the several items of equipment — the means of converting between messages and signals, the means of multiplexing (i.e. sharing equipment and medium between many signal channels), of providing amplification at intermediate points, etc. — should be designed in a unified and compatible manner. Again the language of signals and channels is useful in characterising the mutual interference between signals, the relationship of the signal to its channel, the temporal distribution of events such as overloads or failures, etc.

*Communication networks*    Only a small proportion of present-day telecommunication takes place over a simple point-to-point link, i.e. between two stations having a connecting channel dedicated to their exclusive use. Most communication is established, in whole or in part, by the use of facilities which are at any time shared between many users and are potentially available to many others. The prime example is, of course, the public telephone network. Any subscriber can be connected via a network of lines and switches to any one of several million other subscribers on his national telephone service; and to a large proportion of the 400 million or so telephone subscribers throughout the world by means of an international network which constitutes one of the finest examples of international cooperation yet achieved. Many other examples could be drawn from private telephone systems, telegraph and telex services, broadcasting, data communications, specialised international communications for aviation, meteorology, navigation, satellite operations etc. of the sharing of facilities between many users, and the provision of a service to any one user by means of a multiplicity of apparatus and media widely dispersed.

In a switched communication network, the technical problems in our preceding categories are supplemented by two others. Part of the connection is accomplished by using a channel to which other users have access, and which is made available to a caller on demand. It would be uneconomic, and probably in some cases physically impossible, to provide enough channels for all potential users to be accommodated at once. So a caller may find that at a time of peak demand he is blocked, i.e. cannot obtain the required connection because all the channels are in use at some point on the route. A statistical theory of traffic fluctuations is now highly developed, and the number of channels provided at each point is based on an estimate of peak demand and a judgement of the tolerable blocking probability. The topological structure of a switched network is interwoven with traffic theory, and has perhaps more in common with signal theory than is usually recognised: for example, the first significant discovery about the minimum number of switches required in a network was based on information–theoretic reasoning.

When a connection is made, it utilises several links in tandem, each a more or less random selection from many available channels; the route chosen may in fact be one of several available routes. Thus the transmission quality of the connection — the losses and other impairments suffered by the signal — is a random variable whose distribution is dependent on many more factors than would be relevant to a single link or a dedicated equipment. Again, there is a statistical model in terms of which the quality of the network can be estimated, and with whose aid the specification of individual channels or equipment can be rationally determined.

*Data processing*   We can distinguish (i) telecommunications, in which information unmodified other than by the exigencies of an imperfect channel is conveyed to a distance, (ii) data storage, in which information again without intentional modification is retained over a period of time for later access, (iii) data processing, in which information is deliberately modified by some process of computation, selection or rearrangement. While extreme cases of telecommunication, storage or processing are identifiable as such, there are many mixed systems in which the several technologies are used together; moreover physically different operations have a common theory. Thus one can apply communication-switching ideas to the problem of storage access: signal theory to the question of packing density in stores: computing processes to the filtering or detection of signals: storage and computing operations to communication switching. An important class of signal coding operations is required because computers, unlike human users, are always liable to be misled by mutilated messages: and is accomplished by a branch of computing technology. Many of these 'overlap' areas are of both theoretical and practical importance to the communication engineer.

*Observational systems* The techniques of communication engineering are widely used to detect both natural phenomena and human artefacts. Radio astronomy was in origin an offshoot of radio communication. Radar was invented by physicists probing the ionosphere. The detection of signals impaired by noise is a problem common to communication, radar, astronomy, seismology and many other activities: advances primarily inspired by each of those named have been used in all the others. Signal theory is now widely applied in optical instrumentation, where its use is perhaps the most important development of recent years. The uncertainty principle, a basic postulate of physics concerning the observability of things, is readily understood as signal theory.

The community of theory behind apparently diverse techniques is well illustrated by the problem of resolving a spatial distribution of waves, for example to construct a highly directional radio telescope. We may construct a large single directional antenna: use an elaborate fixed array of small antennas whose signals are combined electronically: or record the signals received over a period of time by a few scanning antennas and perform computations on this data to extract significant correlations. Similar correlations may be extracted by modulating signals on to light beams which are then diffracted in a suitable way. The basic ideas behind these techniques are very similar and they can be understood from a common viewpoint.

## 1.2 DETERMINATE MODELS

An information-bearing signal is, of its nature, unpredictable in detail: to estimate the overall performance of a communication system, we must consider a class of signals, and usually this is done by taking statistical measures. But in analysis and measurement of channels, design and testing of subsystems, it is much more convenient to postulate model signals of determinate form. Moreover, it is best to choose certain specific elementary signals: sine waves and ideal impulses. Neither of these corresponds precisely to a real signal: the one is infinitely long in duration and narrow in bandwidth, the other infinitely wide in bandwidth and short in duration. But they lend themselves to analysis of real systems: they are linked by a linear transform, in a way which is implied by our verbal description: and in a linear system, the response to any signal may be expressed as the superposition of responses to elementary components.

The fact that the ideal elementary signals are not physically realisable is, at first sight, an impediment to rigorous analysis. The best available approach, adopted in this book, seems to be to treat the ideal signals as the limiting case of realisable signals: pulses of progressively shorter length tend toward an ideal impulse of zero duration but non-zero effect. We introduce this concept at the beginning, and derive everything else from it. The relationship between our two ideal signals — the impulse and the sine wave — is the genesis of the Fourier transform. This linear integral transform is taken as the main tool of analysis, and the progenitor of related discrete and continuous transforms. Given the concept of the impulse, we can subsume continuous and discrete signals under a common theory. On this basis, Chapter 2 gives a unified theory of one-dimensional signal analysis; principally by demonstrating general theorems, but also by exhibiting many specific examples.

The conventional theory of waveforms and spectra can be expressed in one dimension quite satisfactorily; but there are many problems in communication theory which require analysis in 2, 3, 4 or even more dimensions. Obvious examples are the analysis of spatial patterns such as visual images, and the combination of space and time as in wave motion. (A less obvious case takes us towards statistical theory: namely the joint treatment of two or more samples from a one-dimensional signal.) The cardinal feature of our treatment is that many apparently diverse matters are all amenable to the same form of analysis, based on a multi-dimensional Fourier transform. Any problem involving movement — scanning, wave motion, diffraction from a moving structure — can be solved by a change of axes in transform space. Maxwell's equations — the most general constraint on electromagnetic signals — can be given a simple formulation in the transform domain. Discrete transforms, like continuous ones, generalise readily to several dimensions. The principal operations and relationships — convolution, transformation, asymptotic behaviour, etc. — transfer easily from one to several dimensions, assisting both intuition and rigorous analysis.

## 1.3 STATISTICAL MODELS

A statistical model is appropriate for any phenomenon which is unpredictable in detail but is nevertheless subject to some regularity. There are two ways in which such characteristics arise.

Firstly, a system is normally subject to random natural phenomena: additive electrical noise, quantum effects in optics, fading of radio channels. These are inescapable, and set ultimate bounds to the performance of a communication channel. Random though they are, they exhibit statistical regularities: mean noise power, for instance, may be fairly steady. These effects are a staple of communication theory.

Secondly, an event affecting a system may be open to human choice: the seizure of a channel at a certain time, the sending of a specific message. The repertoire of possible actions is well-defined, and there may also be substantial statistical regularity. Very often, the system is accessible to large numbers of potential users, and may be loaded by many users simultaneously. It is fundamental to statistical theory that the combined effect of many small independent sources exhibits some characteristic statistical regularity: this principle opens the way to statistical analysis of many phenomena which, to their active agents, may not appear to be random at all.

For these reasons, it is usual to model as random processes (i) communication signals of many kinds (ii) noise and other perturbations of the channels which carry the signals (iii) the occupancy of channels and groups of channels by active traffic.

The statistical problems of communication engineering can be very complex. For example, compound randomness is the norm rather than the exception. That is to say, a process of primary interest may be described by a statistical distribution which itself has one or more randomly varying parameters. Consider for instance the signal passing through the transponder of a satellite communication system. It is the sum of a random number of signals, each of which can be modelled as a random process. There are many other such examples. The problems are often multi-dimensional; even in dealing with a single signal, we use correlation and spectral properties which depend on the joint distribution of two or more samples of the random process. The effects of interest are commonly the sum of many contributions each with its own source of fluctuation: for instance the overall properties of a communication link depend on the sum of impairments and perturbations introduced by each of many tandem amplifiers, line or radio paths, noise sources, etc.

These problems require powerful statistical methods, but fortunately such are accessible via some mathematical approaches which have much in common with other areas of communication theory. The basic probabilistic concept is that of expectation, which grows out of the familiar technique of averaging. Any statistic is the expectation of some function of a random variable $X$. The expectations of functions such as $z^X$ or $e^{j\theta X}$ are related to the probability distribution of $X$ as linear transforms: and the most useful statistical transforms are similar to the familiar transforms of signal theory. The characteristic function is effectively the Fourier transform: the probability generating function is the $z$-transform. Operations on the random variables have their counterparts in the transform domain: for instance, addition of independent random variables corresponds to multiplication in any of the principal transform domains. On this basis we build up a theory of probability which embraces all the common distributions and operations.

A random process can be thought of as the evolution in time (or occasionally in some other index variable) of a random variable. The temporal dimension transforms into a frequency domain, much as it does for determinate functions. Many real phenomena of interest, notably signals and noise, can be modelled as covariance-stationary random processes, described by the joint statistics of a pair of samples. These bivariate statistics are readily analysed by transform methods, which give rise quite naturally to the orthogonal-function expansions which enable the most difficult problems, such as non-linear random analysis, to be tackled.

Signals and noise are continuous random processes; another class of random phenomena are modelled as point processes, which consist of a series of discrete events. We deal with both types, and also show the relationship between them via the concept of the filtered point process.

Statistical techniques of estimation and decision have their most obvious and vivid realisation in the problem of signal detection: that is, the recovery (with high probability) of a signal which is confused by admixture with random noise. The foundations of statistical decision theory are contentious, and indeed somewhat confused. The approach adopted here is based on R. A. Fisher's concept of likelihood, which seems to be both non-contradictory in its foundations and compatible with much engineering practice.

The aim of communication is the conveyance of information. What is information? The best value-free definition has been found to be probabilistic: the conveyance of a message changes our knowledge of some event to which the message refers, and the change is expressed quantitatively as a change in the probability distribution of states of affairs. Our final statistical model is the very abstract one implied by Shannon's theory of information, and before that by Boltzmann's theory of entropy.

# Chapter 2

# Time and frequency: the one-dimensional analysis of signals

## 2.1 INTRODUCTORY

All communication signals have a pattern or structure both in space and in time. A signal is bounded in time and in frequency, which are reciprocal aspects of the same dimension. It is bounded in space, being confined to a guiding medium such as a cable or being distributed according to the radiation pattern of an antenna preferentially in a limited solid angle. (The 'isotropic radiator' is of course a convenient fiction.) It fluctuates, and it moves.

A complete theory of communication signals must therefore extend into at least four dimensions: three spatial, and one temporal. It may well need more, if we are representing a multi-dimensional phenomenon (such as a moving image) by another multi-dimensional phenomenon (an electromagnetic wave). It is common practice to separate these dimensions, and up to a point this is a legitimate simplification. It is part of our theme, however, that (i) some problems are inherently multi-dimensional and best considered as such, (ii) even when we can separate the dimensions (say the spatial and temporal properties) the best methods of analysis are much the same in each aspect, and can usefully be presented in a unified manner.

We begin with a one-dimensional analysis of signals, partly because it gives a complete solution of the 'separable' problems and partly as the simplest introduction to signal analysis. We couch it in terms of time and frequency, because most readers will have some familiarity with the concepts of a 'waveform' and a 'spectrum', considered as properties of a signal in the form of a voltage or current at some point in a line or network.

A practical waveform has both duration in time and extension in frequency. It is convenient to tnalyse signals and systems in terms of idealised elementary signals which have either infinitesimal duration or infinitesimal bandwidth; that is, the unit impulse and the sine wave, respectively. This is not only a mathematical convenience; the results which we derive in this way are closely related to observable properties of real systems. Practical test instruments generate useful approximations to these elementary waveforms, which can be used as driving signals. We can observe the resulting waveform on an oscilloscope, or measure the amplitude and frequency of harmonic components with a wave analyser. Thus we find the response of a network to a sine wave which, though it does not go on for ever, lasts long enough for transient effects to become imperceptibly small. We see its response to a pulse which, though not infinitely brief, is much shorter in period than the natural oscillations of the network.

An arbitrary signal can be expressed as a sum or integral of elementary signals. By the principle of superposition, the response of a linear network is the sum of its responses to the elementary components into which the driving signal can be analysed. Thus both signals and linear systems can be described in terms of either time or frequency functions. The relationship between these two is the most important tool of signal analysis.

## 2.2 PULSES, IMPULSES AND CONVOLUTIONS

### Pulses

A pulse is generally taken to be a waveform which is localised or concentrated at a certain epoch in time. We adopt a formal

*Definition 1*: a waveform $g(t)$ is a pulse if its infinite integral is finite and non-zero, and if the integral of its absolute value exists.

Thus, a pulse of current conveys a finite non-zero charge. A concentration about the central epoch is ensured by the second condition, which implies that either (i) the pulse is bounded in time, or (ii) it vanishes rapidly enough at infinity: specifically, $g(t) = O(t^{-2})$*.

EXAMPLES  The rectangular pulse

$$\left. \begin{array}{ll} \text{rect } t = 1 & |t| < \tfrac{1}{2} \\ = 0 & \tfrac{1}{2} < |t| \end{array} \right\} \tag{1}$$

---

* We shall use the standard notations $O$ and $o$, meaning respectively 'a term of order at most' and 'a term of order less than'. Thus, $g(t) = O(t^{-2})$ means that $|g(t)| < K|t|^{-2}$ for some finite $K$, if $|t|$ is large enough; $f(t) = o(t^{-2})$ would imply that $|f(t)| < \varepsilon|t|^{-2}$ for any positive $\varepsilon$, however small, for large enough $|t|$.

is bounded in time. The Gaussian pulse

$$\phi(t) = e^{-\pi t^2} \tag{2}$$

(named after the Gaussian or normal probability distribution) vanishes rapidly enough at infinity, being $o(t^{-k})$ for any $k$.

EXERCISE Show that the following waveforms satisfy the definition of a pulse: $\text{rect}\,(t - \frac{1}{2}), \frac{1}{2}e^{-|t|}, \pi^{-1}\,(1 + t^2)^{-1}$. Show that the following do not satisfy the definition: $t^{-1}\sin t$, $\sin(2\pi t)\,\text{rect}\,t$.

## Impulses

The ideal impulse which we adopt as an elementary signal can be visualised as a pulse of infinitesimal duration but of unit integral; a current impulse conveys unit charge in a period which is so small that its exact value is immaterial. Formally, we define the impulse as the limit of a sequence.

*Definition 2*: the unit impulse is

$$\delta(t) = \underset{a \to \infty}{\text{Limit}}\; ag(at) \tag{3}$$

where $g(t)$ is a pulse of unit integral.

Some terms of two such sequences are shown in Figure 2.2.1. As the width diminishes, the peak amplitude rises. In the limit the width is 'zero' and the amplitude 'infinity'; we must not take this form of words as a definition, infinite amplitudes being rather intractable. The integral of any term in the sequence is unity, and so

$$\int_{-\infty}^{\infty} \delta(t)dt = 1 \tag{4}$$

Also, since $g(t) = O(t^{-2})$ it follows that for any $t$ other than zero $ag(at) = O(a^{-1})$ as $a \to \infty$. In the limit

$$\delta(t) = 0, \qquad t \neq 0 \tag{5}$$

An impulse cannot be said to have an amplitude, in the normal sense of the word. However, there is a measure by which we distinguish impulses of different strengths, namely the infinite integral, often called the moment (strictly, the zero-order moment). The unit impulse has unit moment, from (4). An impulse of moment B can

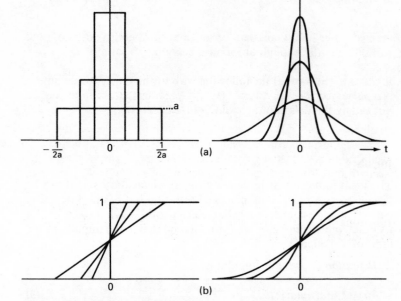

*Figure 2.2.1 Definition of an impulse. (a) Sequences tending to δ(t); (b) Integrals of above sequences*

be written $B\delta(t)$ and defined by

$$B\delta(t) = \underset{a \to \infty}{\text{Limit}} \, Bag(at) \qquad (6)$$

which of course reduces to (3) for a unit impulse.

The concept of an impulse as confining a significant physical quantity within an infinitesimal extent is similar to that of a point-mass, point-charge, etc. which has long been used in physics. While it has been used sporadically in mathematics, a systematic mathematical formulation is more recent*. A mathematician would probably take as foundation a relationship which, given our definition of an impulse, we shall prove as:

*Theorem 1* (the sifting theorem): let $f(t)$ be a function which is either

---

* Like most recent writers on such topics, I have been profoundly influenced by the books of Laurent Schwartz and M. J. Lighthill (see bibliography). Even though the present treatment differs substantially from theirs, it would not have been possible without their guiding light.

bounded, or diverges only at isolated singular points. Then

$$\int_{-\infty}^{\infty} \delta(x-t)f(x)dx = f(t) \tag{7}$$

That is to say, considered as a weighting function, $\delta(t)$ picks out a spot value of $f(t)$. This is intuitively plausible, since the impulse itself is zero at all but a spot value of its argument. The proof is a little complex, so we shall approach it in easy stages. A newcomer to the subject might well study only the first partial proof immediately, and return to the second and third parts after completing the chapter.

*First partial proof of Theorem 1*   This proof is confined to functions $f(t)$ with derivatives of all orders. Such functions can be expanded in Taylor series about any point:

$$f(x) = \sum_{i=0}^{\infty} \frac{(x-t)^i}{i!} f^i(t) \tag{8}$$

Let the impulse be defined by a sequence of rectangular pulses (Figure 2.2.2). Then we wish to show that

$$\underset{a \to \infty}{\text{Limit}} \int_{-\infty}^{\infty} a\,\text{rect}\,(ax-at)f(x)dx = f(t) \tag{9}$$

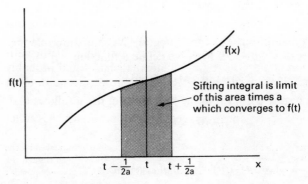

*Figure 2.2.2 Sifting integral*

The integral in (9) can be evaluated using the series (8),

$$a \int_{t-1/2a}^{t+1/2a} f(x)dx = a \sum_{i=0}^{\infty} f^i(t) \frac{\{1-(-1)^{i+1}\}}{(2a)^{i+1}(i+1)!}$$

$$= f(t) + \frac{f''(t)}{24a^2} + O(a^{-4}) \tag{10}$$

which converges to $f(t)$ as $a \to \infty$.

*Second partial proof of Theorem 1*   Many functions of interest cannot be represented by Taylor series; for example, any function which is bounded in time. The next proof covers all functions $f(t)$ which are bounded in magnitude (so having a maximum range $M_1$) and once differentiable (so having a maximum slope $M_2$). It also permits the impulse to be defined by any sequence satisfying Definition 2. This is not just an elegant piece of mathematics: it has a vital physical significance, namely that in the analysis of signals and systems by impulse methods the exact form of pulse is immaterial provided that it is short enough.

Consider a sifting integral (7) with the impulse replaced by a pulse $ag(at)$:

$$\psi(a,t) = \int_{-\infty}^{\infty} ag(ax-at)f(x)dx \tag{11}$$

This differs from $f(t)$ by an amount

$$\psi(a,t) - f(t) = \int_{-\infty}^{\infty} ag(ax-at)\{f(x)-f(t)\}dx$$

(using the fact that the pulse has unit integral). We shall show that this difference vanishes as $a \to \infty$. First we define a function

$$\theta(x) = \min\{M_1, M_2|x|\} \tag{12}$$

illustrated in Figure 2.2.3. From the properties of $f(t)$, it follows that

$$|f(x) - f(t)| \leqslant \theta(x-t)$$

and so

$$|\psi(a,t) - f(t)| \leqslant \int_{-\infty}^{\infty} a|g(ax)|\theta(x)dx$$

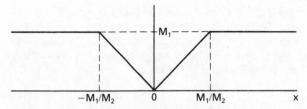

*Figure 2.2.3 The function θ(x) of Equation 2.2.12*

The comparison function $\theta(x)$ has slope discontinuities at $|x| = M_1/M_2 \equiv K$, so the last integral must be evaluated separately for various intervals of $x$. Firstly,

$$\int_K^\infty a|g(ax)|\theta(x)dx = M_1 \int_K^\infty a|g(ax)|dx$$

$$= M_1 \int_{aK}^\infty |g(x)|dx$$

Since $g(x) = O(x^{-2})$ the indefinite integral is $O(x^{-1})$; for given finite $K$, the definite integral is $O(a^{-1})$ and vanishes in the limit. Secondly,

$$\int_0^K a|g(ax)|\theta(x)dx = M_2 \int_0^K ax|g(ax)|dx$$

$$= a^{-1}M_2 \int_0^{aK} x|g(x)|dx$$

Now $xg(x)$ is $O(x^{-1})$ so its indefinite integral is $O(\log x)$ and for given finite $K$ its definite integral is $O(\log a)$. The whole expression is therefore $O(a^{-1}\log a)$ and vanishes in the limit. The negative intervals may be evaluated in a similar way.

It follows that the integral (11) converges to $f(t)$ as $a \to \infty$, and so the sifting theorem is proved for a wider category of functions. It remains to be proven for functions containing discontinuities or impulses. Discontinuities must be deferred until we have defined the value of a function at a point of discontinuity (Definition 7, below). Impulses, however, can be dealt with by the following method, which exemplifies very well the power of the 'sequence' approach.

*Third partial proof of Theorem 1*    We will take $f(t) = \delta(t)$; the proof is easily extended to functions containing impulses of arbitrary strength and location. To interpret an integral containing two impulses, we represent each impulse by a sequence of Gaussian pulses (Equation 2). The sifting integral becomes

$$\int_{-\infty}^{\infty} \delta(x-t)\delta(x)dx = \underset{\substack{a \to \infty \\ b \to \infty}}{\text{Limit}} \int_{-\infty}^{\infty} a\phi(ax-at)b\phi(bx)dx \qquad (13)$$

Writing out the integral in full, it is

$$\int_{-\infty}^{\infty} ae^{-\pi a^2(t-x)^2}be^{-\pi b^2 x^2}dx$$

Some rearrangement of the exponent of the integrand gives

$$abe^{-\pi c^2 t^2} \int_{-\infty}^{\infty} e^{-\pi(ab/c)^2(x-c^2 t/b^2)^2}dx = ce^{-\pi c^2 t^2}$$

where $c^{-2} = a^{-2} + b^{-2}$. Letting $a$ and $b$ tend to infinity,

$$\int_{-\infty}^{\infty} \delta(x-t)\delta(x)dx = \underset{c \to \infty}{\text{Limit}} \, c\phi(ct) = \delta(t) \qquad (14)$$

which is the result required to justify the sifting integral.

EXERCISE    Establish the second proof of Theorem 1 by substituting $g(t) = \pi^{-1}(1+t^2)^{-1}$ and evaluating the integrals. (This function vanishes at infinity as slowly as is permitted by Definition 1.)

## Impulse response

*Definition 3*: let a driving waveform $\delta(t)$ be applied to a linear network or system. The output waveform educed is a characteristic of the network, and is called its impulse response.

The impulse response of a stable system must be integrable. For a lumped network it decays exponentially as $t \to \infty$, a simple example being shown in Figure 2.2.4. Also, in a causal system the output cannot anticipate the input, so the impulse response must be zero for $t < 0$; however, the method which follows is not restricted to this case,

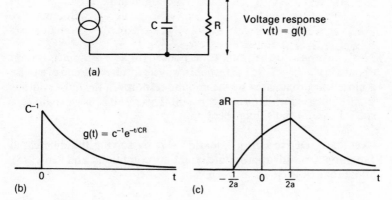

*Figure 2.2.4 A lumped network and its impulse response*

as we often utilise idealised waveforms which can only be approximated in practice when combined with a delay.

Given a practical network, it is usually much easier to calculate its impulse response than the response to a pulse of non-zero width. For example, the CR network of Figure 2.2.4 satisfies the differential equation

$$C\frac{dv}{dt}+\frac{v}{R}=i \tag{15}$$

A current impulse $i(t)=\delta(t)$ gives the capacitor a unit charge in infinitesimal time; so the impulse response for $t>0$ is a solution of

$$C\frac{dv}{dt}+\frac{v}{R}=0$$

with initial condition $v(0)=C^{-1}$. This is

$$g(t)=C^{-1}e^{-t/CR}, \qquad t>0 \tag{16}$$

The simplest pulse of non-zero duration is a rectangular one. Putting $i(t)=a\,\text{rect}\,(at)$ in Equation (15) leads to

$$v(t)=aR(1-e^{-t/CR-1/2aCR}), \qquad -\frac{1}{2a}\leqslant t\leqslant\frac{1}{2a}$$

$$=aR(e^{1/2aCR}-e^{-1/2aCR})e^{-t/CR}, \qquad \frac{1}{2a}\leqslant t \tag{17}$$

whose form is sketched in Figure 2.2.4(c). Expanding the second line of (17) in power series,

$$v(t) = C^{-1}e^{-t/CR}\left\{1 + \frac{1}{24(aCR)^2} + O\{(aCR)^{-4}\}\right\} \qquad (18)$$

This converges to the impulse response (16) as $a \to \infty$: it is within about 1% if $aCR > 2$. So the response waveform after the end of a pulse is closely approximated by the impulse response, if the pulse width is small compared with the time constant. This result is, as we shall see, a special case of the sifting theorem.

EXERCISE   Derive $v(t)$ of Equation (17) by solving the differential Equation (15) with appropriate boundary conditions, and verify (18). Show that $v(0) \to \frac{1}{2}C^{-1}$ as $a \to \infty$.

### Time response

The importance of the impulse, and the impulse response, lies in the fact that waveforms and time responses in general can be expressed in the same terms.

*Theorem 2* (signal representation): let $h(t)$ be a waveform which is bounded, or diverges only at isolated singular points. Then it can be represented by the integral

$$h(t) = \int_{-\infty}^{\infty} \delta(t - x)h(x)dx \qquad (19)$$

*Proof*   The waveform can be considered as the sum of a large number of non-overlapping narrow pulses (Figure 2.2.5a). Each constituent pulse of width $dx$, centred on the epoch $t = x$, has moment $h(x)dx$ and can be approximated by the impulse $\delta(t - x)h(x)dx$. The entire waveform is the sum of such terms, which in the limit as $dx \to 0$ becomes the integral (19). The validity of the passage to the limit is established by the identity of the representation integral (19) with the sifting integral (7), proven in connection with Theorem 1. In fact, Theorems 1 and 2 amount to different interpretations of the same equation; each aspect has been stated explicitly because each is necessary to an intuitive understanding of signal theory.

*Theorem 3* (time response): let a driving signal of waveform $h(t)$ be applied to a linear network or system whose impulse response is

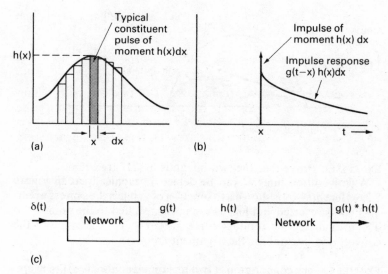

*Figure 2.2.5 Waveform dissection and convolution*

$g(t)$. Then the output waveform educed is

$$\int_{-\infty}^{\infty} g(t-x)h(x)dx \tag{20}$$

*Proof* Let the driving waveform be dissected into constituent pulses, as in the proof of Theorem 2. Each constituent pulse educes a response of the form $g(t)$ with the appropriate epoch and amplitude, namely $g(t-x)h(x)dx$ (Figure 2.2.5b). By the principle of superposition, the output waveform is the sum of such terms, namely the integral (20). The validity of the passage to the limit is assured by our proof of Theorem 1, provided that the driving waveform satisfies the restrictions of Theorem 2 and that the impulse response is integrable (as the impulse response of a stable system must be).

Integrals of the form (20) are so common that it is worth having a special name and notation for them.

*Definition 4*: the convolution of two functions $g(t)$, $h(t)$ is

$$\int_{-\infty}^{\infty} g(t-x)h(x)dx = \int_{-\infty}^{\infty} g(x)h(t-x)dx \equiv g(t)*h(t) \tag{21}$$

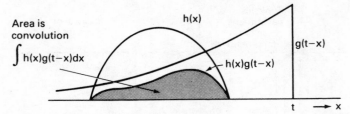

*Figure 2.2.6 Graphical convolution*

EXERCISE    Prove that the two integrals in (21) are equal.

A convolution integral can be depicted graphically as in Figure 2.2.6. Here $g(t-x)$ is shown as a function of $x$; it has the same shape as $g(x)$ but is reversed and has its time origin shifted to the point $x=t$. The area under the product curve $h(x)g(t-x)$ is the value of the convolution integral for the argument $t$.

EXAMPLE    The convolution of two rectangular pulses is a trapezium, as shown in Figure 2.2.7(a).

EXERCISE    Find the convolution of a rectangular pulse rect $t$ with (i) an equal rectangular pulse (ii) a trapezium rect $(t/a)$*rect $(t/b)$ with $a>b>1$ (iii) a half sine wave cos $(\pi t)$ rect $t$, as shown in Figure 2.2.7(b).

The response of a CR network to a rectangular pulse (Figure 2.2.4), which we found by solution of the differential equation (15), can be obtained as the convolution of the impulse response (16) with a rectangular pulse. There are three intervals of $t$ to consider (Figure 2.2.8), in one of which the response is zero.

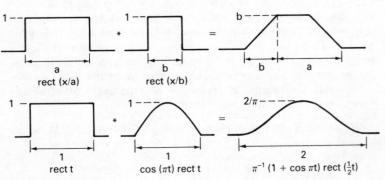

*Figure 2.2.7 Convolutions*

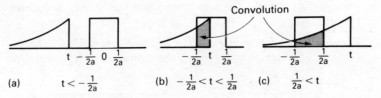

*Figure 2.2.8 Response of CR network to square pulse*

EXERCISE  Evaluate the convolution integral for the intervals of $t$ indicated in Figure 2.2.8 at (ii) and (iii): show that the result agrees with Equation (17). Is it a coincidence that a term in $1/24a^2$ appears in both Equations (10) and (18)?

### The unit step

The impulse response of the $CR$ network, like many other waveforms, has a discontinuity. It is convenient to have a name and a notation for a simple discontinuous waveform:

*Definition 5*: (a) the unit step $U(t)$ assumes the values

$$U(t)=0 \qquad t<0$$
$$\phantom{U(t)}=1 \qquad 0<t \tag{22}$$

(b) the unit step is

$$U(t)=\underset{a\to\infty}{\text{Limit}} \int_{-\infty}^{t} ag(ax)dx \tag{23}$$

where $g(t)$ is a pulse of unit integral.

The second definition accords with our treatment of the unit impulse. Indeed, the step is the integral of the impulse:

$$U(t)= \int_{-\infty}^{t} \delta(x)dx \tag{24}$$

Figure 2.2.1 shows sequences converging to a unit step. The first definition is well-known and is for most purposes equivalent. Nevertheless, the definition as the limit of a sequence is more reliable in dealing with tricky problems; our rule will be, when in doubt resort to the sequence.

The unit step is sometimes used as an elementary signal for testing or specifying a network. The response educed by a step is the subject of Theorem 4.

*Theorem 4* (step response): if the impulse response of a linear network or system is $g(t)$, then its step response is the integral of $g(t)$.

*Proof*   From Theorem 3 the output is the convolution

$$U(t)*g(t) = \int_{-\infty}^{\infty} U(t-x)g(x)dx = \int_{-\infty}^{t} g(x)dx \qquad (25)$$

which is the required result.

Thus we gain essentially the same information from the step and impulse responses, whether measured or calculated; it is a matter of convenience which to use in a particular case.

An integral with a variable limit may conveniently be expressed as a convolution with a discontinuous function, for example:

$$\int_{-\infty}^{t} g(x)dx = g(t)*U(t) \qquad (26)$$

$$\int_{t-\frac{1}{2}c}^{t+\frac{1}{2}c} g(x)dx = g(t)*\text{rect}(t/c) \qquad (27)$$

These are illustrated in Figure 2.2.9. The latter, considered as a function of $t$, is a running mean; it will occur frequently in signal analysis.

EXERCISE   Calculate the step response of the *CR* network of Figure 2.2.4 (i) by solving the differential equation (15) with appropriate

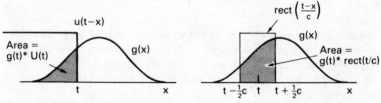

*Figure 2.2.9 Integrals as convolutions*

boundary conditions, (ii) by integrating the impulse response; and show that the results agree.

EXERCISE   A network is driven by a rectangular pulse rect $t$, and the output waveform is $h(t)$. What would be its response to a driving signal consisting of two impulses, $\delta(t+\frac{1}{2})-\delta(t-\frac{1}{2})$?
A related discontinuous function which we shall use is the signum.

*Definition 6*: the signum function sgn $t$ assumes the values

$$\text{sgn } t = -1 \qquad t<0$$
$$= +1 \qquad 0<t \tag{28}$$

Equivalently, using either definition of the unit step

$$\text{sgn } t = U(t) - U(-t) \tag{29}$$

EXERCISE   (i) Express $U(t)$ in terms of sgn $t$ (ii) Find another expression for $t$ sgn $t$.
The sifting integral, Equation (7) or (19), has been justified only for differentiable functions. What would happen if it were applied to a discontinuous function such as $U(t)$? Formally, this gives

$$U(t) = \int_{-\infty}^{\infty} \delta(x-t)U(x)dx$$

which is clearly satisfied for the continuous intervals $t \neq 0$. At the discontinuity, it implies that

$$U(0) = \int_{-\infty}^{\infty} \delta(x)U(x)dx$$

Now this is quite meaningless if we think of $\delta(x)$ as 'infinite amplitude at $x=0$'. It can be interpreted as the limit of a sequence in either of two ways. Taking a sequence for $\delta(t)$

$$U(0) = \underset{a \to \infty}{\text{Limit }} a \int_{-\infty}^{\infty} g(ax)U(x)dx \tag{30}$$

The result is no longer independent of pulse shape; but any pulse with even symmetry leads to $U(0)=\frac{1}{2}$ (Figure 2.2.10a). Alternatively, we can take a sequence for $U(t)$, with the same result (Figure 2.2.10b).

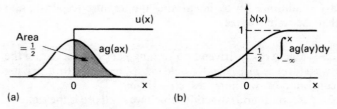

*Figure 2.2.10 Evaluation of discontinuous functions*

*Definition 7*: the value of a discontinuous function at the point of discontinuity is the mean of the limiting values immediately above and below.

This convention is more arbitrary than our other definitions, but it turns out that some convention is necessary if one is to use discontinuous functions without inconsistency, and this one is simple.

EXAMPLES $U(0) = \frac{1}{2}$, $2 \, \text{rect}(\frac{1}{2}) = 1$, $\text{sgn}(0) = 0$

*The proof of Theorem 1 completed* The partial proofs given covered (i) functions all of whose derivatives exist (ii) bounded functions whose first derivative exists (iii) functions containing impulses. If we now adhere to Definition 7, and take $g(t)$ as an even function in Definitions 2 and 5, then the sifting integral applies also to functions with simple discontinuities. Further categories of singularity can be shown to be admissible, but we shall not labour their proof, having covered the waveforms of greatest interest for signal theory.

The general result may be stated in the language of convolution:

$$h(t) = \delta(t) * h(t) \tag{31}$$

for any function $h(t)$ of interest. We recall, too, that this equation can be interpreted in the sense of Theorem 1 or of Theorem 2, that is, either sifting or signal representation.

## Time shift

We shall frequently use waveforms of similar shape but occurring at different epochs in time. Moreover, time delay is a common physical phenomenon. Delay can be expressed analytically by subtraction of a constant from the argument of a function.

To manipulate delayed functions we need:

*Theorem 5* (shifting): if either component of a convolution be shifted along the time scale, the resultant is shifted by an equal amount.

*Proof* The time response of a linear system is the convolution of the impulse response $g(t)$ with the driving signal $h(t)$. Clearly, if the input is delayed by $\tau$ relative to some reference epoch, the output will be delayed equally.

EXERCISE Give alternative proofs of Theorem 5 by (i) considering a network with adjustable propagation delay (ii) making appropriate substitutions in the convolution integral.

EXAMPLE Applying Theorem 5 to equation (31) gives:

$$h(t-\tau) = h(t) * \delta(t-\tau) \tag{32}$$

This apparently trite result is remarkably useful.

## 2.3 SINE WAVES AND THE FOURIER TRANSFORM

The second idealised elementary waveform is the simple harmonic or sine wave, which we shall normally write in the exponential form

$$e^{j2\pi ft} = \cos 2\pi ft + j\sin 2\pi ft \tag{1}$$

It is a periodic function. The parameter $f$ is the frequency, i.e. the number of cycles per second or Hertz (Hz). It is also common usage to write $\omega = 2\pi f$; this is the angular frequency in radians per second. Another usage is the complex frequency $s$; when only real frequencies are in question, $s$ can be considered equivalent to $j\omega$.

A general sinusoidal wave has two other parameters, as well as frequency: its amplitude $|A|$ and its phase $\theta$, which may be combined in a single complex parameter $A$:

$$Ae^{j\omega t} = \{|A|e^{j\theta}\}e^{j\omega t} = |A|e^{j(\omega t + \theta)} \tag{2}$$

Using the exponential form, positive and negative frequencies are distinct, so our frequency scale must extend on either side of zero. A real wave requires terms at $\pm f$, for example

$$\cos \omega t = \tfrac{1}{2}e^{j\omega t} + \tfrac{1}{2}e^{-j\omega t}$$

An important property of a sinusoid is that its derivatives are sinusoidal,

$$\left(\frac{d}{dt}\right)^n e^{j(\omega t + \theta)} = (j\omega)^n e^{j(\omega t + \theta)} \tag{3}$$

Thus it emerges naturally in the solution of linear differential equations. In particular, if a linear network or system be driven with a sine wave, its output is a sine wave of the same frequency though in general of different amplitude and phase.

*Definition 1*: let a driving wavform $Ae^{j2\pi ft}$ be applied to a linear network or system, the consequent output being $Be^{j2\pi ft}$. The ratio of complex amplitudes $B/A$, considered as a function of frequency, is characteristic of the network and is called its frequency response.

EXAMPLE    The frequency response of the $CR$ network in Figure 2.2.4 may be found from its differential equation (2.2.15). Let $i(t) = e^{j2\pi ft}$, and postulate $v(t) = Ge^{j2\pi ft}$. Then

$$C(j2\pi fGe^{j2\pi ft}) + R^{-1}(Ge^{j2\pi ft}) = e^{j2\pi ft}$$

whence

$$G(f) = \frac{R}{1 + j2\pi fCR} \tag{4}$$

This is a complex quantity which could be expressed as the sum of real and imaginary parts, or in terms of modulus and phase,

$$G(f) = |G(f)|e^{-j\beta(f)}$$

where

$$|G(f)| = R\{1 + (2\pi fCR)^2\}^{-1/2}$$

$$\beta(f) = \tan^{-1}(2\pi fCR)$$

*Definition 2*: a filter is a network whose frequency response is localised in or concentrated around a limited frequency interval. It has a passband, i.e. a frequency interval within which attenuation is small and $|G(f)| \approx 1$: and a stop band, i.e. a frequency interval within which the attenuation is high and $|G(f)| \ll 1$.

The passband and stopband may not be sharply distinct; there is normally a transition or 'cut-off' region in which $G(f)$ changes substantially. A filter may be low-pass (having a passband which includes zero frequency) or bandpass (having a passband which does not extend down to zero frequency). Complementary to these are high-pass and band-stop filters.

**The Fourier transform**

Since the impulse response and the frequency response are each characteristic of a linear system, there ought to be a relationship between them.

*Theorem 1* (the Fourier transform): the impulse response $g(t)$ and the frequency response $G(f)$ of a linear system are related by the integral equation

$$G(f) = \int_{-\infty}^{\infty} g(t)e^{-j2\pi ft}dt \qquad (5)$$

*Proof*  Let a sine wave $e^{j2\pi ft}$ be applied as driving signal. The output is, by Theorem 2.2.3, the convolution

$$e^{j2\pi ft}*g(t) = \int_{-\infty}^{\infty} e^{j2\pi f(t-x)}g(x)dx$$

$$= e^{j2\pi ft} \int_{-\infty}^{\infty} e^{-j2\pi fx}g(x)dx$$

and from Definition 1 the coefficient of $e^{j2\pi ft}$ is the frequency response $G(f)$.

*Definition 3*: the frequency function $G(f)$ is said to be the Fourier transform* of $g(t)$, and the relationship will be written

$$g(t) \Rightarrow G(f)$$

or

$$G(f) \Leftarrow g(t)$$

EXERCISE  By carrying out the integration, show that

$$U(t)e^{-\lambda t} \Rightarrow (\lambda + j2\pi f)^{-1} \qquad (6)$$

Compare with the impulse response and frequency response of the *CR* network, Figure 2.2.4, which have been given above.

EXAMPLE  The Fourier transform of an impulse is a constant.

$$\delta(t) \Rightarrow 1 \qquad (7)$$

---

* Named after J. B. Fourier (1768–1830) who, in the course of investigating heat conduction, developed analytical methods which have subsequently been used in electromagnetic theory and elsewhere.

For proof, substitute in equation (5) and consider it as a sifting integral. Alternatively, consider a degenerate network in which the output is identical with the input.

EXERCISE    Show that

$$\text{rect } t \Rightarrow \frac{\sin \pi f}{\pi f} \equiv \text{sinc } f \qquad (8)$$

This function occurs so often that the special notation is worth while. It is illustrated in Figure 2.3.1.

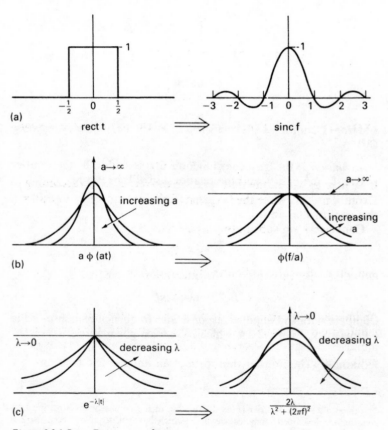

Figure 2.3.1 Some Fourier transforms

EXAMPLE   The Gaussian pulse, Equation (2.2.2), is its own Fourier transform. Using the substitution $y = t + jf$

$$e^{-\pi t^2} \Rightarrow \int_{-\infty}^{\infty} e^{-\pi t^2} e^{-j2\pi ft} dt$$

$$= e^{-\pi f^2} \int_{-\infty}^{\infty} e^{-\pi y^2} dy = e^{-\pi f^2} \tag{9}$$

Theorem 2 (similarity): if $g(t) \Rightarrow G(f)$, then

$$g(t/T) \Rightarrow |T| G(fT) \tag{10}$$

Proof

$$\int_{-\infty}^{\infty} g(t/T) e^{-j2\pi ft} dt = |T| \int_{-\infty}^{\infty} g(t/T) e^{-j2\pi (fT)(t/T)} d(t/T)$$

$$= |T| G(fT)$$

EXAMPLE   Applying the similarity theorem to the Gaussian pulse $\phi(t) = e^{-\pi t^2}$

$$a\phi(at) \Rightarrow \phi(f/a)$$

If we now let $a \to \infty$, the time function converges to $\delta(t)$ according to Definition 2.2.2, while the frequency function converges to $\phi(0) = 1$; this confirms (7) above.

Conversely, on substituting $b = a^{-1}$ so that

$$\phi(t/b) \Rightarrow b\phi(bf)$$

and letting $b \to \infty$, we obtain a new result

$$1 \Rightarrow \delta(f) \tag{11}$$

An impulse in the frequency domain must be interpreted as a filter of infinitesimal bandwidth. As we might expect after the derivation of impulses in Section 2.2, a variety of filters yield similar results in the limit.

EXERCISE   Show that

$$e^{-\lambda|t|} \Rightarrow \frac{2\lambda}{\lambda^2 + (2\pi f)^2} \tag{12}$$

(compare Equation 6). By taking limits as $\lambda \to \infty$ and $\lambda \to 0$ confirm Equations (7) and (11).

*Theorem 3* (shifting): if $g(t) \Rightarrow G(f)$, then

$$g(t - \tau) \Rightarrow e^{-j2\pi f \tau} G(f) \tag{13}$$

$$G(f - F) \Leftarrow e^{j2\pi Ft} g(t) \tag{14}$$

*Proof* Each of these results follows from a linear substitution in the defining equation (5). For the first one, substitute $x = t - \tau$ obtaining

$$\int_{-\infty}^{\infty} g(t - \tau)e^{-j2\pi ft} dt = e^{-j2\pi f\tau} \int_{-\infty}^{\infty} g(x)e^{-j2\pi fx} dx$$

$$= e^{-j2\pi f\tau} G(f)$$

For the second one, substitute $y = f - F$; the detail is left as an exercise.

EXAMPLES Applying the shifting theorem to impulses in the time and frequency domains,

$$\delta(t - \tau) \Rightarrow e^{-j2\pi f\tau} \tag{15}$$

$$\delta(f - F) \Leftarrow e^{j2\pi Ft} \tag{16}$$

The first of these follows directly from substitution in Equation (5), but the second is less obvious.

*Delay* Electromagnetic waves travel at a finite speed. Consider a long path which is distortionless except for a propagation delay of $\tau$ seconds. Its impulse response is $\delta(t - \tau)$. By Equation (15) its frequency response is a phase lag of $2\pi f\tau$ radians; this is immediately intelligible if we think of the delay as $f\tau$ periods.

*Echo* Signals may by design or accident be propagated via two paths of differing length. The impulse response will have two constituents of similar form but relatively displaced. From (13) it follows that

$$g(t) + hg(t - \tau) \Rightarrow G(f)\{1 + he^{-j2\pi f\tau}\} \tag{17}$$

i.e. the frequency response of a system with echo is undulatory (Figure 2.3.2). Conversely, an undulatory frequency response may be interpreted in terms of echos.

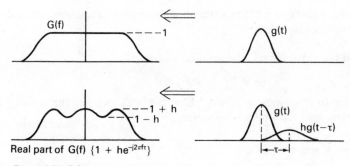

Real part of G(f) {1 + he$^{-j2\pi ft}$}

*Figure 2.3.2 Echo*

*Low-pass to band-pass transformation* Filters may be constructed whose passbands are of similar shape but centred on different frequencies. By Equation (14), their impulse responses are related.

Consider a low-pass filter $G(f)$ with impulse response $g(t)$. We define a related band-pass filter centred on a frequency $F$; since a real filter will respond both to positive and negative frequencies, there are passbands around $\pm F$. The filter function and its impulse response are

$$\tfrac{1}{2}G(f-F)+\tfrac{1}{2}G(f+F)\Leftarrow g(t)\cos(2\pi Ft) \tag{18}$$

That is, the impulse response is a sine wave at the mid-frequency $F$ whose amplitude varies with time, fitting within an envelope $g(t)$ as shown in Figure 2.3.3. As the filter bandwidth is reduced, the envelope

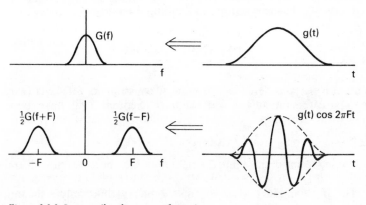

*Figure 2.3.3 Lowpass/bandpass transformations*

becomes prolonged; in the limit, an infinitesimal bandwidth yields a continuous sine wave.

EXERCISE    A filter has the impulse response

$$e^{-\pi(t-\tau)^2/b^2}\cos 2\pi f(t-\tau)$$

Deduce its frequency response. (Hint: use both forms of the shifting theorem, and the similarity theorem.)

**Inverse Fourier transform**

We have derived several general theorems and specific transform pairs $g(t)$, $G(f)$ from the defining Equation (5), and it would be possible to go on and obtain many more results. However, they would all be of the type 'given something about $g(t)$, find something about $G(f)$'. A more significant extension of the theory is to find an inverse expression giving $g(t)$ in terms of $G(f)$. Many of the examples we have seen fall into complemntary pairs, such as Equations (13) and (14) or (7) and (11); this suggests that the inverse relationship must be similar in form to the direct one, which is indeed the case.

> *Theorem 4* (inverse Fourier transform): the impulse response $g(t)$ and the frequency response $G(f)$ of a linear system are related by the integral equation
>
> $$g(t)= \int_{-\infty}^{\infty} G(f)e^{j2\pi ft}df \qquad (19)$$
>
> *Proof*   $G(f)$ can be written as a sifting integral
>
> $$G(f)= \int_{-\infty}^{\infty} \delta(f-x)G(x)dx$$

This can be considered as the sum of constituents $\delta(f-x)\,G(x)dx$ (compare the time-domain dissection, Theorem 2.2.2). Using the transform (16)

$$\delta(f-x)G(x)dx \Leftarrow e^{j2\pi xt}G(x)dx$$

Summing terms of this kind, the right hand side becomes the integral (19).

The direct and inverse transforms (5) and (19) differ only in the sign of the exponent in the integrand. Thus for any relationship established by means of one, there is a similar relationship in the other direction. The two results may differ by a change of sign, or they may be identical in form; for instance, transforms of even functions are the same in each direction.

EXAMPLE

$$\text{rect } t \Rightarrow \text{sinc } f \qquad \text{(Equation 8, above)}$$

$$\text{rect } f \Leftarrow \text{sinc } t \qquad \qquad (20)$$

EXERCISE   A rectangular low-pass filter cuts off at frequency $F$. Show that its impulse response is oscillatory and has zeros at $t = n/2F$ ($n = 1, 2, 3 \ldots$).

## The spectrum

*Theorem 5* (signal representation): let $h(t)$ be a waveform which is bounded, or diverges only at isolated singular points. Then it can be represented by the integral

$$h(t) = \int_{-\infty}^{\infty} H(f) e^{j2\pi ft} df \qquad (21)$$

where

$$H(f) = \int_{-\infty}^{\infty} h(t) e^{-j2\pi ft} dt \qquad (22)$$

*Proof*   By the principle of superposition, any number of sinusoids of arbitrary amplitudes and frequencies may be added. The first integral (21) sums constituent sine waves of frequency $f$ and anplitude $H(f)df$, and for any given $H(f)$ it defines a waveform which we can call $h(t)$. Convergence of such an integral is assured by the identity of form with the Fourier integral in Theorem 4. On making this identification, the second integral (22) follows from Theorem 1.

An independent proof could be given by establishing, from (21) alone, the transform $\delta(t - x) \Rightarrow e^{-j2\pi fx}$. Then in the dissection of a waveform according to Theorem 2.2.2, we can transform each constituent pulse

$$\delta(t - x)h(x)dx \Rightarrow e^{-j2\pi fx}h(x)dx$$

Summing terms of this kind gives the integral (22).

*Definition 4*: the frequency function $H(f)$ in Theorem 5 is called the spectrum of the signal whose waveform is $h(t)$.

*Relationship of Theorems 1, 4 and 5* The similarity between Theorem 5 and the previous theorems might make it seem redundant. This is not so, because although the relationships asserted are similar they are predicated of different entities. The frequency response is a property of a linear network or system. The spectrum is a property of a signal. Compare, for instance, the low-pass to bandpass transformation described above, and the process of modulation (described below).

The link between signal and system properties lies in the fact that the spectrum of an impulse is uniform. Thus, an input signal $\delta(t)$ contains all sinusoids $e^{j2\pi ft}$ in equal measure. The spectrum of the output signal educed is therefore equal to the frequency response of the system.

*Modulation* An amplitude-modulated wave is often used to convey a message waveform in a frequency band whose location is determined by a carrier frequency $F$. The modulated wave (Figure 2.3.4) is the product of the waveform $h(t)$ with a real sinusoid, and its spectrum follows from the shifting theorem:

$$h(t)\cos 2\pi Ft = \tfrac{1}{2}h(t)(e^{j2\pi Ft} + e^{-j2\pi Ft})$$
$$\Rightarrow \tfrac{1}{2}H(f-F) + \tfrac{1}{2}H(f+F) \tag{23}$$

Commonly, though not invariably, the message spectrum $H(f)$ is of low-pass form, in which case the product spectrum is centred on $F$. Alternatively, if the message spectrum is centred on a frequency $F_1$, it is translated to $F_2 = F + F_1$ or $F_3 = F - F_1$; either of the latter can be selected by a filter. Thus a signal representing a message can be assigned to any spectral interval of suitable bandwidth.

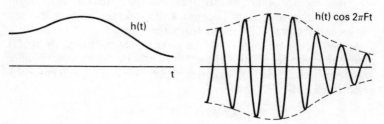

*Figure 2.3.4 Amplitude modulation*

EXERCISE   Apply the relation (23) to $h(t) = \cos \alpha t$, and compare your result with the trigonometric identity

$$\cos \alpha t \cos \beta t = \tfrac{1}{2} \cos (\alpha + \beta)t + \tfrac{1}{2} \cos (\alpha - \beta)t$$

## Transmission channels

We have defined the frequency response of a network or system (Definition 1) and the spectrum of a signal (Definition 4). If a signal is to pass through a transmission channel without any impairment, the channel must convey impartially all frequency components present in the signal.

> *Definition 5*: a distortionless channel, with respect to any given signal, has equal loss (or gain) and equal delay at all frequencies in the signal spectrum.

That is, its frequency response is of the form $Ae^{-j2\pi ft}$, where $A$ and $\tau$ are real and constant over the frequency range concerned. If the input signal is $h(t)$, then the output is $Ah(t - \tau)$.

Such a channel is an ideal to which practical channels can only approximate, since neither realizable signals nor realizable channels have a sharply defined extent in the frequency domain. A channel is usually a filter, in the sense of Definition 2; and the signal spectrum has similar properties. We shall see later how the channel characteristics must be related to the signal in order to minimise the inevitable distortion according to various criteria, or to retain certain specific signal properties.

It is convenient to distinguish: (i) amplitude distortion, i.e. variation of $A$ with frequency in a linear system (ii) delay distortion, i.e. variation of $\tau$ with frequency in a linear system (iii) non-linear distortion, i.e. departures from linearity which invalidate the principle of superposition. Delay requires careful definition if it is not constant.

> *Definition 6*: the group delay $\tau(f)$ is $(2\pi)^{-1}$ times the derivative of phase shift at the frequency $f$. That is, if $G(f) = |G(f)|e^{-j\beta(f)}$ then

$$\tau(f) = \frac{1}{2\pi} \frac{d\beta}{df}$$

The significance is that a narrow-band signal centred on a frequency $f_0$ is delayed by $\tau(f_0)$. The phase characteristic can be expanded in Taylor series around $f_0$:

$$\beta(f) = \beta_0 + 2\pi\tau_0(f - f_0) + \dots$$

the first term being phase shift at $f_0$, the second the delay, and higher-order terms the delay distortion which over a sufficiently narrow band is negligible. A narrow-band signal

$$h(t)e^{j2\pi f_0 t} \Rightarrow H(f - f_0)$$

is modified by the phase characteristic to

$$e^{-j\beta_0}\{H(f - f_0)e^{-j2\pi\tau_0(f-f_0)}\}$$
$$\Leftarrow h(t - \tau_0)e^{j(2\pi f_0 t - \beta_0)}$$

which exhibits the delay $\tau_0$.

It is often possible to correct for linear distortion by means of an added linear network; and delay distortion may in principle be corrected without change of amplitude characteristic. Consequently, it is common practice to idealise a linear channel by neglecting delay distortion, and we shall sometimes do this.

### Convolution

*Theorem 6* (convolution): if $g(t) \Rightarrow G(f)$ and $h(t) \Rightarrow H(f)$, then

$$g(t)*h(t) \Rightarrow G(f)H(f) \tag{24}$$

$$g(t)h(t) \Rightarrow G(f)*H(f) \tag{25}$$

*Proof*   The first part follows from consideration of two networks in tandem (Figure 2.3.5). If they be specified by their impulse response, the impulse response of the combination is $g(t)*h(t)$, by Theorem 2.2.3. If they be specified by their frequency response, the frequency response of the combination is $G(f)H(f)$.

The second part is then to be expected, given the near-reciprocity of the Fourier transform. A direct proof is also available, as follows. From Theorem 4, express each of $g(t)$ and $h(t)$ as Fourier integrals;

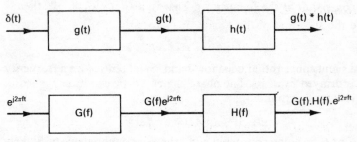

*Figure 2.3.5 Tandem networks*

then

$$g(t)h(t) = \int\limits_{-\infty}^{\infty} \int\limits_{-\infty}^{\infty} G(x)H(y)e^{j2\pi(x+y)t}dxdy$$

With the substitution $f = x + y$ this becomes

$$\int\limits_{-\infty}^{\infty} \int\limits_{-\infty}^{\infty} G(x)H(f-x)e^{j2\pi ft}dxdf$$

which is recognisable as the inverse transform of

$$\int\limits_{-\infty}^{\infty} G(x)H(f-x)dx = G(f)*H(f)$$

*Corollary* Any number of factors, taken in any order, may be multiplied together: so the same is true of convolution.

EXAMPLE A very short pulse is applied to a two-stage amplifier, each stage of which has the frequency response $(\lambda + j2\pi f)^{-1}$. What is the output waveform?

The impulse response of each stage is $U(t)e^{-\lambda t}$, from Equation (6). Assuming that the 'very short pulse' has negligible duration compared with the time constant $1/\lambda$ we calculate the impulse response of the complete amplifier by convolution:

$$U(t)e^{-\lambda t} * U(t)e^{-\lambda t} = U(t)te^{-\lambda t} \tag{26}$$

EXERCISE Derive the spectrum of a triangular pulse,

$$\{1 - |t|\} \operatorname{rect}(\tfrac{1}{2}t) \Rightarrow (\operatorname{sinc} f)^2 \tag{27}$$

*Non-linear distortion* As a special case of Equation (25) we can find the spectrum of the square of a waveform,

$$h(t)h(t) \Rightarrow H(f)*H(f)$$

and, repeating the procedure as many times as necessary, the spectrum of an arbitrary power

$$[h(t)]^n \Rightarrow [H(f)]^{*n} \tag{28}$$

where the starred exponent means convolution of $n$ similar factors.

A nominally linear system commonly has small departures from linearity, which distort the signal. Consider a device whose instantaneous output amplitude $y$ is related to the instantaneous input amplitude $x$ by the transfer characteristic

$$y = a_1 x + a_2 x^2 + a_3 x^3 + \ldots \tag{29}$$

If the input signal has waveform $x(t)$ with spectrum $X(f)$, the output waveform follows immediately from (29), and the output spectrum is

$$Y(f) = a_1 X(f) + a_2 [X(f)]^{*2} + a_3 [X(f)]^{*3} + \ldots \tag{30}$$

The right-hand terms after the first are distortion products of second order, third order, etc.

EXAMPLE    A sinusoid $2 \cos \alpha t$ has the spectrum

$$X(f) = \delta(f - \alpha) + \delta(f + \alpha)$$

This spectrum and its self-convolutions are shown in Figure 2.3.6. Such convolutions are easily derived using Theorem 2.2.5 and the relation $\delta(f) * \delta(f) = \delta(f)$. The Figure also shows the spectrum of $2 \cos \alpha t + 2 \cos \beta t$ and its self-convolutions.

EXERCISE    Justify the second- and third-order spectra in Figure 2.3.6(b) by writing

$$2 \cos \alpha t + 2 \cos \beta t \Rightarrow X_1(f) * X_2(f)$$

where

$$X_1(f) = \delta(f - \tfrac{1}{2}\alpha - \tfrac{1}{2}\beta) + \delta(f + \tfrac{1}{2}\alpha + \tfrac{1}{2}\beta)$$
$$X_2(f) = \delta(f - \tfrac{1}{2}\beta + \tfrac{1}{2}\alpha) + \delta(f + \tfrac{1}{2}\beta - \tfrac{1}{2}\alpha)$$

and using the self-convolutions of Figure 2.3.6(a). Deduce the $n$th-order spectrum, for any $n$. Show that if any signal spectrum extends up to a maximum frequency $F$, the $n$th-order products extend up to $nF$. Form the squares and cubes of sinusoidal signals using trigonometric identities, and compare with Figure 2.3.6.

## Differentiation and integration

Theorem 7 (differentiation): if $g(t) \Rightarrow G(f)$, then

$$g'(t) \Rightarrow j2\pi f G(f) \tag{31}$$
$$G'(f) \Leftarrow -j2\pi t g(t) \tag{32}$$

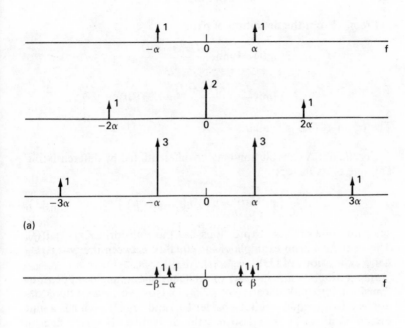

(a)

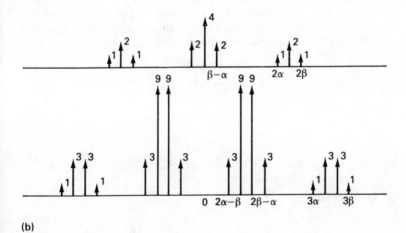

(b)

*Figure 2.3.6 Self-convolutions of spectra. (a) $2\cos\alpha t$; (b) $2\cos\alpha t + 2\cos\beta t$*

*Proof* From the definition of $g'(t)$,

$$g'(t) = \underset{\tau \to 0}{\text{Limit}} \frac{g(t+\tau) - g(t)}{\tau}$$

$$\Rightarrow \underset{\tau \to 0}{\text{Limit}} \frac{e^{j2\pi f\tau} G(f) - G(f)}{\tau} = j2\pi f G(f)$$

The proof of (32) is similar.

*Corollary* A convolution may be differentiated by differentiating any one of its factors:

$$\frac{d}{dt}\{g(t)*h(t)\} = g'(t)*h(t) = g(t)*h'(t) \tag{33}$$

since any one of these expressions has the transform $j2\pi f G(f)H(f)$. Theorem 2.2.4 is an example of the equality between the two right-hand expressions of (33).

Integration, being inverse to differentiation, might appear to transform into multiplication by $(j2\pi f)^{-1}$. However, integration does not lead to a unique result. Consider $U(t)$ and $\frac{1}{2}\,\text{sgn}\,t$: each has a unit discontinuity at $t=0$ and so has the derivative $\delta(t) \Rightarrow 1$. Which, if either, has the transform $(j2\pi f)^{-1}$? From Theorem 2, if $g(t) \Rightarrow G(f)$ then $g(-t) \Rightarrow G(-f)$. So if $g(t) \Rightarrow (j2\pi f)^{-1}$ it follows that $g(t) + g(-t)$ has the transform zero and is itself zero. This condition is satisfied by only one waveform with a unit discontinuity, namely $\text{sgn}\,t$. We conclude that

$$\tfrac{1}{2}\,\text{sgn}\,t \Rightarrow (j2\pi f)^{-1} \tag{34}$$

$$U(t) \Rightarrow (j2\pi f)^{-1} + \tfrac{1}{2}\delta(f) \tag{35*}$$

*Theorem 8* (integration): if $g(t) \Rightarrow G(f)$, then

$$\int_{-\infty}^{t} g(x)dx \Rightarrow \frac{G(f)}{j2\pi f} + \tfrac{1}{2}\delta(f)G(0) \tag{36}$$

or, equivalently

$$\int_{-\infty}^{t} g(x)dx - \tfrac{1}{2}\int_{-\infty}^{\infty} g(x)dx \Rightarrow \frac{G(f)}{j2\pi f} \tag{37}$$

---

* There is some popular confusion on this point, and many reputable sources quote $U(t) \Rightarrow (j2\pi f)^{-1}$. However, this version leads to contradictions and cannot be justified.

*Proof* Using Equations (2.2.26) and (35),

$$\int_{-\infty}^{t} g(x)dx = g(t)*U(t)$$

$$\Rightarrow G(f)\left\{\frac{1}{j2\pi f}+\tfrac{1}{2}\delta(f)\right\}$$

which is equivalent to (36). The second form (37) follows on expressing $G(0)$ as a Fourier integral. Integration in the frequency domain can be treated similarly.

Waveforms with discontinuities or slope discontinuities can be transformed easily, by transforming their derivatives.

EXAMPLE With $g(t)$ as shown in Figure 2.3.7(a),

$$g'(t) \Rightarrow -e^{j2\pi fT}+2-e^{-j2\pi fT}=2(1-\cos 2\pi fT)$$

$$g(t) \Rightarrow \frac{1-\cos 2\pi fT}{j\pi f}$$

EXERCISE Find the transform of the trapezoidal pulse, Figure 2.3.7(b), by transforming its second derivative. Check that your result agrees with the transform of the convolution of two rectangles.

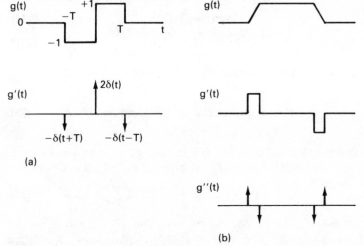

*Figure 2.3.7 Discontinuous function examples*

## Power and energy

The power and energy of a signal are important physical quantities. In the present context, it is common to normalise a signal by considering it as a voltage or current applied to a load of unit resistance; then the instantaneous power dissipated equals the squared amplitude, and the total energy dissipated is the time integral of this quantity. It is less obvious, but very significant, that a similar integral can be taken in the frequency domain; the total energy is the sum of the energy in the various frequency components.

*Theorem 9* (Parseval's theorem): let a real waveform $g(t)$ have a spectrum $G(f)$; then

$$\int_{-\infty}^{\infty} \{g(t)\}^2 dt = \int_{-\infty}^{\infty} |G(f)|^2 df \tag{38}$$

provided that the integrals exist.

*Proof*  By Theorem 6, $\{g(t)\}^2 \Rightarrow \{G(f)\}^{*2}$; that is to say,

$$\int_{-\infty}^{\infty} \{g(t)\}^2 e^{-j2\pi ft} dt = \int_{-\infty}^{\infty} G(x)G(f-x)dx$$

On putting $f=0$ and replacing the dummy variable $x$ by $f$,

$$\int_{-\infty}^{\infty} \{g(t)\}^2 dt = \int_{-\infty}^{\infty} G(f)G(-f)dx \tag{39}$$

From the definition integral (5), $G(f)$ and $G(-f)$ are related by

$$G(\pm f) = \int_{-\infty}^{\infty} g(t)\cos 2\pi ft \,.\, dt \mp j \int_{-\infty}^{\infty} g(t)\sin 2\pi ft \,.\, dt \tag{40}$$

so that if $g(t)$ is real then $G(-f)$ is the complex conjugate of $G(f)$. It follows that $G(f)G(-f)=|G(f)|^2$, substitution of which in (39) proves the theorem.

EXERCISE  Find the energy in the pulse $e^{-\pi a^2 t^2}$, and show by integration in the time and frequency domains that it satisfies Theorem 9.

If the integral is difficult to evaluate in one domain, it may be easier in the other.

EXERCISE    Use Theorem 9 to find $\displaystyle\int_{-\infty}^{\infty} (\operatorname{sinc} t)^2 dt$.

·The energy in an impulse or a sinusoid is infinite. However, a real sinusoid $A\cos(2\pi Ft + \theta)$ has a finite energy per cycle,

$$\int_0^{1/F} \{A\cos(2\pi Ft + \theta)\}^2 dt = \frac{A^2}{2F} \tag{41}$$

and so has a definable mean power $\frac{1}{2}A^2$. This concept is extended to other periodic waveforms in the next section.

## The Laplace transform

There are several other integral transforms related to the Fourier transform; the most widely used is the Laplace transform.

*Definition 7*: Let $g(t)$ be a real function defined for $t \geqslant 0$, and $s = \sigma + j\omega$ a complex variable with positive real part $\sigma$. Then the *Laplace transform* of $g(t)$ is

$$\bar{G}(s) = \int_0^{\infty} g(t)e^{-st} dt$$

Formally, it is similar to the Fourier integral (5); but there are two important differences.

(i)    The 'frequency' variable $s$ is complex; the imaginary axis of $s$ corresponds to real frequencies. We can think of the Laplace integral as a superposition of elements in the form of decaying sinusoids

$$e^{-st} = e^{-\sigma t} e^{-j\omega t}$$

rather than the strictly periodic sinusoids of the Fourier integral.

(ii)    The 'time' variable is confined to the positive interval $t \geqslant 0$. To ensure that an impulse at $t = 0$ has an unambiguous Laplace transform we must in this context take $g(t)$ in Definition 2.2.2 as a pulse located on the positive side of the time origin.

*Example*  The Laplace transform of a damped complex sinusoid is

$$e^{-\alpha t - j\beta t} \overset{\mathcal{L}}{\Rightarrow} \frac{1}{s + \alpha + j\beta} \tag{42}$$

Compare the special case $\beta = 0$ with the Fourier transform (6).

EXERCISE   Show that the Laplace transform of a real sinusoid is

$$e^{-\alpha t}(a\cos\beta t + b\sin\beta t) \overset{\mathcal{L}}{\Rightarrow} \frac{a(s+\alpha) + b\beta}{(s+\alpha)^2 + \beta^2} \tag{43}$$

Most of the useful properties of the Fourier transform have their counterparts; for example, if $g(t) \Rightarrow \bar{G}(s)$ then

$$g'(t) \overset{\mathcal{L}}{\Rightarrow} s\bar{G}(s) \tag{44}$$

which is the basis for some important applications. The property most obviously lacking, however, is reciprocity.

EXERCISE   Derive the Laplace-transform counterparts of the similarity, differentiation and convolution theorems (Theorems 2, 7 and 6 respectively).

There is an inversion theorem for the Laplace transform, analogous to Theorem 4. Since $s$ is a complex variable, the inverse transform requires a contour integral in the complex plane. We shall not develop this topic here*.

The Laplace transform, because of the exponential damping $e^{-\sigma t}$ in its integrand, has a domain of convergence in the classical sense even for non-integrable functions like $U(t)$; whereas the older literature of the Fourier transform is dominated by convergence problems. Given the modern theory of generalised functions (on which we have drawn in our treatment of the impulse $\delta(t)$ and related topics) these problems have virtually disappeared. On the whole, we shall employ the Fourier transform in this book. There are however certain applications in which the time variable $t$ is essentially non-negative, or for which the concept of a complex frequency $s = \sigma + j\omega$ is useful. For these the Laplace transform is eminently suitable.

---

* The theory is given in many standard works. My personal favourite is Van der Pol and Bremmer (1). These authors define a two-sided integral which can be specialised to either the Fourier or the usual Laplace transform. There is also a brief but useful treatment of this approach in Bracewell (1) Chapter 11; this book is recommended for its general coverage of Fourier theory.

*Linear lumped networks*   Consider a linear system which is (i) causal, in the sense that its impulse response does not begin until the impulse is applied (ii) stable, in the sense that the response to any integrable input is integrable (iii) definable in terms of linear differential equations. By the first two properties, the impulse response $g(t)$ has a Laplace transform. We can use the relationship (44) to transform the differential equations to algebraic equations. As an elementary example, the $CR$ network of Figure 2.2.4 with differential Equation (2.2.15) has an impulse response defined by

$$Cg'(t) + R^{-1}g(t) = \delta(t)$$

which transforms into

$$Cs\bar{G}(s) + R^{-1}\bar{G}(s) = 1$$

Thus

$$\bar{G}(s) = \frac{1/C}{s + 1/CR} \overset{\mathscr{L}}{\Leftarrow} C^{-1}e^{-t/CR}$$

in agreement with the direct solution of Equation (2.2.16). The frequency response of the network is found by evaluating $\bar{G}(s)$ at real frequencies; it is

$$\bar{G}(j2\pi f) = \frac{R}{1 + j2\pi f\, CR}$$

in agreement with Equation (4) and with the Fourier transform (6). This example readily generalises to the important class of *linear lumped networks* made up of resistors, capacitors and inductors. The voltage/current relationships for the inductor and capacitor

$$v(t) = Li'(t), \qquad v(t) = \frac{1}{C}\int i(t)dt \qquad (45)$$

transform into

$$\bar{V}(s) = sL\bar{I}(s), \qquad \bar{V}(s) = \frac{1}{sC}\bar{I}(s) \qquad (46)$$

giving two familiar expressions $sL$, $1/sC$ for the *impedance* or voltage/current ratio of the components. The transfer function of any lumped network is a ratio of polynomials in $s$

$$\bar{G}(s) = \frac{\sum\limits_{j=0}^{m} a_j s^j}{\sum\limits_{k=0}^{n} b_k s^k} \equiv \frac{A(s)}{B(s)} \qquad (47)$$

in which usually $n > m$. (If it is not, a constant or polynomial can be extracted, leaving a fractional part for which this is true.) The numerator and denominator can be factorised into $m$ and $n$ linear factors, respectively,

$$\bar{G}(s) = \frac{K \prod_{j=1}^{m} (s - \delta_j)}{\prod_{k=1}^{n} (s - \gamma_k)} \tag{48}$$

where the $\delta_j$ and $\gamma_k$ are the *zeros* and *poles* respectively; note that

$$\bar{G}(\delta_j) = 0, \qquad \bar{G}(\gamma_k) \to \infty \tag{49}$$

The inverse transform of this $\bar{G}(s)$ is readily found, and gives a general expression for the impulse response of a linear lumped network.

*Theorem 10*: Let a lumped network (or equivalent dynamical system) have the transfer function $\bar{G}(s) = A(s)/B(s)$ as above, and let $B(s)$ have distinct roots $\gamma_k$ $(k = 1, 2, \ldots n)$. Then the frequency response of the network is

$$\bar{G}(j2\pi f) = \sum_{k=1}^{n} \frac{C_k}{j2\pi f - \gamma_k} \tag{50}$$

and the impulse response is

$$g(t) = \sum_{k=1}^{n} C_k e^{\gamma_k t} \tag{51}$$

where the coefficients are

$$C_k = \{(s - \gamma_k)\bar{G}(s)\}_{s = \gamma_k} \tag{52}$$

*Proof* depends on expansion of $G(s)$ into partial fracrions

$$\bar{G}(s) = \sum_{k=1}^{n} \frac{C_k}{s - \gamma_k} \tag{53}$$

If such an expansion exists, then the coefficients follow from the identity

$$(s - \gamma_k)\bar{G}(s) = \sum_{j=1}^{n} \left( \frac{s - \gamma_k}{s - \gamma_j} \right) C_j$$

On letting $s \to \gamma_k$ all terms except $j = k$ vanish. If the roots are distinct, the limiting coefficient of $C_k$ is 1, which proves (52). The frequency function (50) is simply the expansion of $\bar{G}(j2\pi f)$. The impulse response

(51) follows on transforming the expansion term by term, using the elementary transform (42).

The impulse response (51) was first obtained by Heaviside in the 1890s, long before a rigorous theory of the Laplace transform was developed. It used to be called Heaviside's expansion theorem, and the name would still be appropriate.

*Corollary* The poles $\gamma_k$ are either real or occur in complex conjugate pairs with, for example

$$\gamma_1^* = \gamma_2, \qquad C_1^* = C_2$$

For otherwise $g(t)$ would not be real. If

$$\gamma_1 = \alpha + j\beta, \qquad \gamma_2 = \alpha - j\beta$$
$$C_1 = A + jB, \qquad C_2 = A - jB$$

then the corresponding components of the frequency and impulse responses are

$$\frac{C_1}{s - \gamma_1} + \frac{C_2}{s - \gamma_2} = \frac{2A(s - \alpha) - 2B\beta}{(s - \alpha)^2 + \beta^2} \tag{54}$$

$$C_1 e^{\gamma_1 t} + C_2 e^{\gamma_2 t} = 2e^{\alpha t}(A \cos \beta t - B \sin \beta t) \tag{55}$$

*Addendum to Theorem 10* The case of multiple poles is a little more complicated but is stated here for reference. Suppose that the pole $\gamma_k$ is of multiplicity $m_k$, that is

$$B(s) = \prod_k (s - \gamma_k)^{m_k}$$

Then the expansion in partial fractions is

$$\bar{G}(s) = \sum_k \sum_{r=1}^{m_k} \frac{C_{kr}}{(s - \gamma_k)^r} \tag{56}$$

where

$$C_{kr} = \frac{1}{(m_k - r)!} \left\{ \left(\frac{d}{ds}\right)^{m_k - r} \left[ (s - \gamma_k)^{m_k} \bar{G}(s) \right] \right\}_{s = \gamma_k},$$

$$r = 1, 2, \ldots m_k - 1 \tag{57}$$

$$C_{km_k} = \{ (s - \gamma_k)^{m_k} \bar{G}(s) \}_{s = \gamma_k}$$

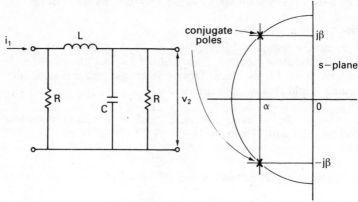

*Figure 2.3.8 Lumped network example*

which reduces to Equation (52) in respect of any poles of multiplicity 1. The transform of (56) is

$$g(t) = \sum_k e^{\gamma_k t} \sum_{r=1}^{m_k} C_{kr} t^{r-1} \tag{58}$$

*Example*  The network of Figure 2.3.8 has for its transfer imped-ance $v_2/i_1$

$$\bar{G}(s) = \frac{R}{1 + (1 + sCR)(1 + sL/R)}$$

which having a second-degree denominator is of the form (54) with $A = 0$. According to the values of the circuit elements, $\beta^2$ may be

(i) positive: in which case the poles are a conjugate pair as in Figure 2.3.8(b) and $g(t)$ is an exponentially-decaying sinusoid
(ii) negative: in which case the poles are real and distinct and $g(t)$ is the sum of two decaying exponentials
(iii) zero: in which case the poles are coincident and $g(t)$ is the product of a decaying exponential and a first-degree polynomial.

EXERCISE  In the network of Figure 2.3.8, find the parameters $\alpha$, $\beta$ and $B$ as functions of the element values. Calculate the impulse response in each of the three regimes listed above, and show that the regime is determined by the value of the parameter $R(C/L)^{1/2}$.

## 2.4 PERIODIC FUNCTIONS AND FOURIER SERIES

### Periodic and sampled functions

*Definition 1*: a function $h(t)$ is periodic, with period $T$, if for all $t$

$$h(t+T)=h(t) \tag{1}$$

Clearly a periodic function repeats indefinitely; any value assumed at the epoch $t=x$ recurs at $t=x+nT$ for all integral $n$.

*Definition 2*: a repetition is the sum of an infinite series of similar terms located at uniformly spaced epochs,

$$\text{rep}_T\, g(t) \equiv \sum_{m=-\infty}^{\infty} g(t-mT) \tag{2}$$

A repetition defines a periodic function uniquely. Also, a periodic function can be expressed as a repetition; an obvious element is a segment of length $T$. However, this is not unique; an infinite set of repetitions are equivalent (Figure 2.4.1(a)).

A repetition can be visualised in two ways. If $g(t)$ is confined to an interval less than $T$, the periodic aspect is obvious (Figure 2.4.1(b)). If $g(t)$ spreads more widely, then the repetitions overlap and the value at any epoch is clearly a summation, equation (2).

*The impulse-repetition.* An important periodic function is the impulse-repetition,

$$\text{rep}_T\, \delta(t) = \sum_{m=-\infty}^{\infty} \delta(t-mT) \tag{3}$$

Any repetition can be expressed as a convolution of an element with an impulse-repetition (Figure 2.4.1(d))

$$\text{rep}_T\, g(t) = g(t)* \text{rep}_T\, \delta(t) \tag{4}$$

For proof, express each repetition as a summation and apply the shift theorem 2.2.5 term by term.

We shall also use the operation of multiplication by an impulse-repetition. Multiplication by a single impulse picks out a spot value of a function, and represents it as the moment of an impulse,

$$h(t)\delta(t-\tau)=h(\tau)\delta(t-\tau) \tag{5}*$$

---

* Do not confuse this with convolution or sifting; there is no integration in this equation.

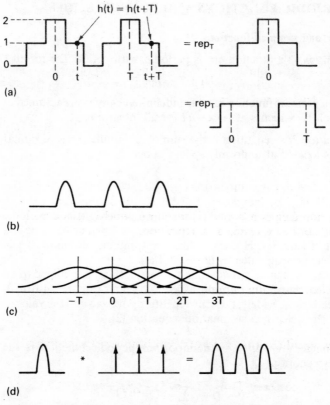

*Figure 2.4.1 Repetitions. (a) Repitions equivalent to periodic functions; (b) Discrete repetitions; (c) Overlapping repetitions; (d) Repetition as convolution*

Multiplication by an impulse-repetition picks out a set of spot values, and represents each as the moment of an impulse:

$$h(t)\,\mathrm{rep}_T\delta(t) = \sum_{m=-\infty}^{\infty} h(mT)\delta(t-mT) \qquad (6)$$

*Definition 3*: a spot value of a function, selected by multiplication with an impulse, is called a sample. The train of impulses representing a set of uniformly spaced samples (equation 6) is called a sampled function.

Any set of impulses $\sum_m a_m \delta(t - mT)$ can be considered as samples from a function $h(t)$ such that $h(mT) = a_m$; the function so defined is not unique.

*Theorem 1*: the Fourier transform of a periodic function of period $T$ is a sampled function of interval $T^{-1}$. The Fourier transform of a sampled function of interval $T$ is a periodic function of period $T^{-1}$.

*Proof* Let $H(f)$ be the transform of a periodic function $h(t)$. Transforming Equation (1),

$$H(f)(1 - e^{j2\pi fT}) = 0$$

Thus $H(f)$ is zero unless the bracketed factor is zero. The latter is zero only at $f = m/T$ for integer $m$. Thus $H(f)$ can be non-zero only at uniform sampling points $f = m/T$, which proves the first part.

Now let $g(t)$ be a sampled function: then

$$g(t) = \sum_m g(mT)\delta(t - mT)$$

Substituting this in the Fourier integral:

$$G(f) = \sum_m g(mT)e^{-j2\pi fmT}$$

It is easily seen that $G(f + 1/T) = G(f)$ which proves the theorem.

EXAMPLE   A sinusoid

$$\cos(2\pi mt/T) \Rightarrow \tfrac{1}{2}\delta(f - m/T) + \tfrac{1}{2}\delta(f + m/T)$$

is periodic with period $T$, and its spectrum is zero at all frequencies which are not multiples of $1/T$. It is also zero at some multiples of $1/T$, but this is not debarred by the definition.

*Theorem 2*: The Fourier transform of an impulse-repetition is an impulse-repetition:

$$\text{rep}_T \delta(t) \Rightarrow T^{-1} \text{rep}_{1/T} \delta(f) \qquad (7)$$

*Proof* Consider an impulse-repetition of unit period. By the first part of Theorem 1, its Fourier transform is a sampled function of unit interval. But the impulse-repetition is also a sampled function, so by the second part of the theorem its Fourier transform is a periodic function of unit period. The only function with both these properties is an impulse-repetition, so

$$\text{rep}_1 \delta(t) \Rightarrow k \, \text{rep}_1 \delta(f)$$

for some constant $k$. The Fourier transform being reciprocal for even functions, $k = 1$. Applying the similarity theorem 2.3.2 we obtain Equation (7)*.

### Fourier series

*Theorem 3*: if $g(t) \Rightarrow G(f)$, the Fourier transform of a repetition is

$$\text{rep}_T g(t) \Rightarrow G(f)T^{-1} \text{rep}_{1/T} \delta(f) \tag{8}$$

*Proof*  From Equation (4)

$$\text{rep}_T g(t) = g(t) * \text{rep}_T \delta(t)$$

The right-hand side, being a convolution, transforms into a product (Theorem 2.3.6); the transform of $\text{rep}_T \delta(t)$ we have just derived in Theorem 2. The result follows immediately.

*Examples*    (i) A square wave of period $T$ which takes the value 1 for a fraction $k$ of each period, and is otherwise zero:

$$\text{rep}_T \text{rect}(t/kT) \Rightarrow k \, \text{sinc}(fkT)\text{rep}_{1/T} \delta(f) \tag{9}$$

$$= k \sum_{m=-\infty}^{\infty} \text{sinc}(mk)\delta(f - m/T)$$

This is illustrated in Figure 2.4.2.

(ii) In the first example the repeated pulses are distinct; we can equally well deal with overlapping waveforms, such as

$$\text{rep}_T U(t)e^{-\lambda t} \Rightarrow (\lambda + j2\pi f)^{-1} T^{-1} \text{rep}_{1/T} \delta(f) \tag{10}$$

Theorem 3 has a simple physical interpretation. Given a pulse waveform $g(t)$ we can imagine a network having this as its impulse response. Driven with repeated impulses, the network generates the repetitive waveform. The driving wave has a spectrum consisting of impulses at frequencies $m/T$, and the network modifies their magnitudes in accordance with its frequency response $G(f)$.

*Theorem 4* (Fourier series): let $h(t)$ be a periodic waveform of period $T = 1/F$. Then it may be represented by the series

$$h(t) = \sum_{m=-\infty}^{\infty} c_m e^{j2\pi mFt} \tag{11}$$

---

\* The application of similarity is not entirely simple. It requires the relationship $\delta(t/T) = T\delta(t)$, which can be proved by use of the sequence definition 2.2.2.

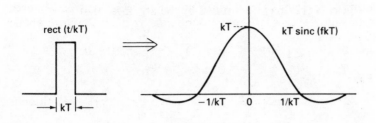

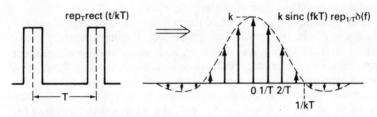

*Figure 2.4.2 Square waves*

whose coefficients are

$$c_m = T^{-1} \int_{-\frac{1}{2}T}^{\frac{1}{2}T} h(t)e^{-j2mFt}dt \tag{12}$$

*First proof* The waveform is the repetition of a segment of length *T*,

$$h(t) = \text{rep}_T \{ h(t) \, \text{rect} \, (t/T) \}$$

whence by Theorem 3 its spectrum is

$$h(t) \Rightarrow T^{-1} \sum_{m=-\infty}^{\infty} \int_{-\frac{1}{2}T}^{\frac{1}{2}T} h(t)e^{-j2\pi mFt}dt\delta(f-mF)$$

Transforming the spectral impulses into sinusoids gives the desired result.

*Second proof* A more conventional approach to Fourier series runs as follows. Assuming that a series of the form (11) exists, the coefficients (12) may be justified by the argument that

$$\int\limits_{-\frac{1}{2}T}^{\frac{1}{2}T} h(t)e^{-j2\pi mFt}dt = \sum_{n=-\infty}^{\infty} c_n \int\limits_{-\frac{1}{2}T}^{\frac{1}{2}T} e^{j2\pi(n-m)Ft}dt$$

$$= Tc_n, \qquad n=m$$

$$= 0, \qquad n \neq m$$

Alternatively, a similar argument may be couched in terms of sines and cosines rather than complex sinusoids.

This argument shows that, if the series exists and represents the function, the coefficients stated are correct. It does not really prove either (i) that the series 'exists' in the usual analytical sense of existence, i.e. convergence; in fact convergence in the neighbourhood of discontinuities is not simple, and series representing impulsive functions do not converge in any normal sense of the word (ii) that the series represents the function; for instance, while a sum of terms each with period $T$ must itself have a period $T$, it is not obvious (without further proof) that the periodicity of the sum implies periodicity $T$ for each and every term. This conventional proof can be made rigorous, but at the expense of much mathematical complexity and some restriction on the class of admissible functions*.

EXAMPLE    A square wave which takes the value 1 for a fraction $k$ of each period: from (12)

$$c_m = T^{-1} \int\limits_{-\frac{1}{2}kT}^{\frac{1}{2}kT} e^{-j2\pi mFt}dt = k\,\text{sinc}(mk)$$

and so from (11)

$$h(t) = k \sum_{m=-\infty}^{\infty} \text{sinc}(mk)e^{j2\pi mFt}$$

which is equivalent to the spectrum (9).

EXERCISE    Find a series for $h(t)$ in Figure 2.4.1 (a) by means of Theorem 4. Then find the spectrum of the same function by means of

---

* Fejér's theory of summation, which is covered by our Theorem 7 below, justifies Fourier series for functions with discontinuities. Impulses, which are enormously useful in communication theory, are not justified by any form of summation.

Theorem 3, taking in turn each of the two elements for repetition shown in the figure. Show that the three results are equivalent.

## Power of a periodic waveform

The instantaneous power of a periodic signal, normalised as the rate of dissipation in a unit resistance, is the square of the instantaneous amplitude. If the amplitude is bounded, its square is integrable over one period; averaging gives the mean power

$$P = T^{-1} \int_{-\frac{1}{2}T}^{\frac{1}{2}T} \{h(t)\}^2 dt \tag{13}$$

The average over any long duration $D$ converges to this value as $D \to \infty$, so we can call $P$ the mean power without ambiguity. The mean power is the sum of the power in the various frequency components:

*Theorem 5* (Parseval's theorem): let a real periodic waveform $h(t)$ have a Fourier series as in Theorem 4. Then

$$T^{-1} \int_{-\frac{1}{2}T}^{\frac{1}{2}T} \{h(t)\}^2 dt = \sum_{m=-\infty}^{\infty} |c_m|^2 \tag{14}$$

An integral over any complete period is equivalent.

*Proof*   The square of $h(t)$ is the double series

$$\{h(t)\}^2 = \sum_{m=-\infty}^{\infty} \sum_{n=-\infty}^{\infty} c_m c_n e^{j2\pi(m+n)Ft}$$

On averaging over a period $T = F^{-1}$, the exponential factor averages to zero unless $m + n = 0$ in which case it unity. Therefore

$$T^{-1} \int_{-\frac{1}{2}T}^{T} \{h(t)\}^2 dt = \sum_{m=-\infty}^{\infty} c_m c_{-m}$$

However, if $h(t)$ is real then $c_m$ and $c_{-m}$ are complex conjugates, by the same reasoning as in the non-periodic case (equation 2.3.40). Then $c_m c_{-m} = |c_m|^2$, which proves the theorem.

EXERCISE   Verify Equation (14) for the waveforms (i) $\sin \alpha t$ (ii) $1 + \cos \alpha t$ (iii) a periodic square wave which takes the value $+1$ for half of each cycle and $-1$ for the other half (iv) the waveform $h(t)$ of Figure

2.4.1(a). Use the last waveform to illustrate the fact that in Theorem 5 (unlike Theorems 3 and 4) the segment $h(t) \operatorname{rect}(t/T)$ cannot be replaced by an arbitrary element whose repetition is equivalent to $h(t)$.

## Truncation and convergence of series

If a Fourier series is to be used for computation, we need to know how rapidly it converges and what is the effect of discarding the remainder after some finite number of terms. Theorem 3 shows that the asymptotic behaviour of the series depends directly upon that of the transform $G(f)$ of an element $g(t)$. The general problem of asymptotic estimation is treated in section 2.8; however, we may anticipate some of its results by quoting established examples. If $g(t)$ contains an impulse, $G(f) = O(1)$ and hence the series does not converge: if $g(t)$ has a discontinuity, $G(f) = O(f^{-1})$ so the series may be convergent but not absolutely convergent: if $g(t)$ is continuous, $G(f) = o(f^{-1})$ and so the series should converge absolutely. The nature of the error due to truncation emerges from the following theorem.

*Theorem 6* (truncation): let a periodic waveform $h(t)$ be represented by a Fourier series (11). Then a truncated series of $2N+1$ terms represents the function

$$h_N(t) \equiv \sum_{m=-N}^{N} c_m e^{j2\pi mFt} = h(t) * \left(\frac{2N+1}{T}\right) \operatorname{sinc}\left\{\frac{(2N+1)t}{T}\right\}$$

$$= h(t) \operatorname{rect}(t/T) * \frac{\sin\left\{(2N+1)\pi t/T\right\}}{\sin(\pi t/T)} \qquad (15)$$

which is an approximation to $h(t)$.

*Proof* The true spectrum is

$$H(f) = \sum_{m=-\infty}^{\infty} c_m \delta(f - mF)$$

The spectrum of the approximation is

$$H_N(f) = H(f) \operatorname{rect}\left\{\frac{f}{(2N+1)F}\right\}$$

(Figure 2.4.3). Using the convolution theorem 2.3.6 and the transform $\operatorname{rect} f \rightleftharpoons \operatorname{sinc} t$ the first part of the theorem follows.

For the second part, consider a network with impulse response $h(t) \operatorname{rect}(t/T)$; this when driven with $\operatorname{rep}_T \delta(t)$ would generate $h(t)$. The

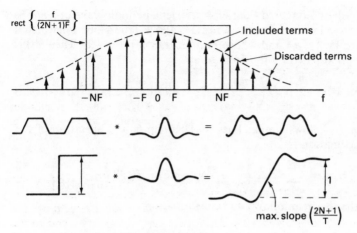

*Figure 2.4.3 Truncation of Fourier series*

approximation $h_N(t)$ is a band-limited version of $h(t)$, as is clear from the first part; this is generated if the network be driven by a suitably band-limited version of $\mathrm{rep}_T \delta(t)$, namely

$$\sum_{m=-N}^{N} e^{j2\pi mFt} = \frac{\sin\{\pi Ft(2N+1)\}}{\sin(\pi Ft)} \tag{16}$$

Then the second part follows from the convolution theorem*.

Some properties of the approximation are readily deduced from Theorem 6. If the original contains an impulse or a short pulse of unit moment, the peak amplitude of the approximation is $(2N+1)T^{-1}$. If it contains a unit discontinuity, or a rapid transition of unit extent, the greatest rate of change of the approximation is $(2N+1)T^{-1}$ and hence its rise time is of the order $T(2N+1)^{-1}$. The waveform $h_N(t)$ is oscillatory in the neighbourhood of a discontinuity; it takes the form of the integral of the sinc function (Figure 2.4.3) which has a substantial overshoot: about 18%. Increasing $N$ does not reduce this overshoot, but merely shortens the time scale; in the limit, therefore, the series does not converge in the neighbourhood of a discontinuity.

EXERCISE  Differentiate Theorem 6 using Equation (2.3.33), and hence prove the statement above about the slope and rise time of $h_N(t)$.

A modification of the Fourier series may improve convergence.

---

* The second part could of course be stated more formally and less picturesquely; it would be a good exercise to do so.

*Theorem 7* (tapered Fourier series): let a periodic waveform $h(t)$ be represented by a Fourier series (11). Let $\Psi(f)$ be a function which is zero for $|f| \geq 1$ and whose Fourier transform is $\psi(t)$. Then $h(t)$ is approximated by the finite series

$$h_N(t) \equiv \sum_{m=-N}^{N} c_m \Psi\left(\frac{m}{N+1}\right) e^{j2\pi mFt} = h(t) * \left(\frac{N+1}{T}\right) \psi\left\{\frac{(N+1)t}{T}\right\} \quad (17)$$

*Proof* follows similar lines to Theorem 6. The spectrum of the approximation is

$$H_N(f) = \sum_{m=-N}^{N} c_m \Psi\left(\frac{m}{N+1}\right) \delta(f-mF) = H(f)\Psi\left\{\frac{f}{(N+1)F}\right\}$$

and the theorem follows on transformation.

EXAMPLES    (i) Theorem 6 is a special case in which

$$\Psi(f) = \text{rect}\left\{\frac{(N+1)f}{(2N+1)}\right\}$$

Why did we not take rect $(\tfrac{1}{2}f)$?
(ii) (ii) Another special case is the triangular taper

$$\Psi(f) = (1-|f|)\,\text{rect}(\tfrac{1}{2}f) \Leftarrow \text{sinc}^2 t$$

which gives

$$\begin{aligned}
h_N(t) &= \sum_{m=-N}^{N}\left\{1 - \frac{|m|}{N+1}\right\} c_m e^{j2\pi mFt} \\
&= h(t) * \left(\frac{N+1}{T}\right) \text{sinc}^2\left\{\frac{(N+1)t}{T}\right\} \quad (18) \\
&= h(t)\,\text{rect}(t/T) * \frac{\sin^2\{(N+1)\pi t/T\}}{\sin^2(\pi t/T)}
\end{aligned}$$

This is known in the mathematical literature as Fejér's summation. On this interpretation the Fourier series for a bounded $h(t)$ converges to the value $\tfrac{1}{2}h(t+0) + \tfrac{1}{2}h(t-0)$; that is, to $h(t)$ where it is continuous, and to the mean value at a discontinuity.

*Finite repetition of waveforms*    A waveform may consist of a finite set of $N$ similar elements, each of form $g(t)$:

$$g(t) * \sum_{m=0}^{N-1} \delta\{t - (m - \tfrac{1}{2}N + \tfrac{1}{2})T\} \quad (19)$$

The set of impulses has been chosen to be symmetrical about the time origin. The spectrum of the finite repetition is

$$G(f)e^{i\pi f(N-1)} \sum_{m=0}^{N-1} e^{-j2\pi fmT} = G(f)\frac{\sin(\pi f NT)}{\sin(\pi f T)} \tag{20}$$

There are obvious similarities to the theory of truncated Fourier series (compare Equation 16). In the limit as $N\to\infty$ this expression approaches a sampling of $T^{-1}G(f)$, in conformity with Theorem 3.

EXERCISE   Derive another expression for the spectrum of a finite repetition by writing the finite set of impulses as an impulse-repetition multiplied by a rectangle function. Show that your result is consistent with (20).

*Summation of series by transformation*   A repetition can be expressed as a summation both in the frequency and in the time domain. It often happens that one summation is analytically simpler than the other, or converges more rapidly; the equivalence can then be used as a technique for summing series.

*Theorem 8* (Poisson's summation): if $g(t)\Rightarrow G(f)$, then

$$\sum_{m=-\infty}^{\infty} g(mT) = T^{-1} \sum_{n=-\infty}^{\infty} G(n/T) \tag{21}$$

*Proof*   Theorem 3, in terms of summations, says that

$$\sum_{m=-\infty}^{\infty} g(t-mT) \Rightarrow T^{-1} \sum_{n=-\infty}^{\infty} G(n/T)\delta(f-n/T)$$

Transforming the right-hand side,

$$\sum_{m=-\infty}^{\infty} g(t-mT) = T^{-1} \sum_{n=-\infty}^{\infty} e^{j2\pi nt/T} G(n/T) \tag{22}$$

and putting $t=0$ gives the theorem as stated.

The more general result (22) is sometimes useful, as we shall see in Section 2.5. So is the similar equation

$$\sum_{n=-\infty}^{\infty} e^{-j2\pi nfT} g(nT) = T^{-1} \sum_{m=-\infty}^{\infty} G(f-m/T) \tag{23}$$

EXAMPLES   (i) If $g(t)$ is non-zero only over a finite interval, $G(n/T)$ may be summed directly; for instance

$$2 \operatorname{rect}(2t) \Rightarrow \operatorname{sinc}(\tfrac{1}{2}f)$$

whence by Theorem 8

$$2 \operatorname{rect}(0) = \sum_{n=-\infty}^{\infty} \operatorname{sinc}(\tfrac{1}{2}n) = 1 + 2 \sum_{n=1}^{\infty} \frac{\sin \tfrac{1}{2}n\pi}{\tfrac{1}{2}n\pi}$$

A little rearrangement gives the well-known numerical series

$$1 - \tfrac{1}{3} + \tfrac{1}{5} - \tfrac{1}{7} \ldots = \frac{\pi}{4}$$

(ii) If $g(t)$ and $G(f)$ are nowhere zero, both sides of Equation (21) are infinite series, but one may be more easily summed; for instance

$$\pi e^{-2\pi|t|} \Rightarrow \frac{1}{1+f^2}$$

whence by Theorem 8

$$\pi + 2\pi \sum_{m=1}^{\infty} e^{-2\pi m} = 1 + 2 \sum_{n=1}^{\infty} \frac{1}{1+n^2} \tag{24}$$

The left-hand side is a geometric progression and is easily summed; it follows that

$$\sum_{n=1}^{\infty} \frac{1}{1+n^2} = \frac{\pi-1}{2} + \frac{\pi}{e^{2\pi}-1}$$

The two series in (24) illustrate a common feature of this transformation: that on the right converges very slowly, that on the left very rapidly. In fact, the first two terms of the latter give the sum to 5 significant figures. Thus, such methods may be useful numerically even if neither series has a simple closed-form summation.

EXERCISE   Use the transform (2.3.27) to prove that

$$\sum_{n=1}^{\infty} \frac{1}{(2n-1)^2} = \frac{\pi^2}{8}$$

## Bessel functions

Let us consider a sinusoid whose argument is itself sinusoidal, for instance

$$g(z, \theta) = e^{jz \sin \theta} \tag{25}$$

Clearly this is periodic in $\theta$, for any given value of $z$, but is not a sinusoid; its exact shape will depend on the value of $z$. So it can be expanded in Fourier series whose coefficients are functions of $z$, thus:

$$g(z,\theta) = \sum_{n=-\infty}^{\infty} J_n(z)e^{jn\theta} \tag{26}$$

The coefficients are, from Equation (12)

$$J_n(z) = \frac{1}{2\pi} \int_{-\pi}^{\pi} e^{j(z\sin\theta - n\theta)}d\theta$$

$$= \frac{1}{\pi} \int_{0}^{\pi} \cos(z\sin\theta - n\theta)d\theta \tag{27}$$

We shall encounter these expressions in several contexts, and they are well-known in mathematical physics.

*Definition 4*: the Bessel function* of the first kind and order $n$ is denoted by $J_n(z)$ and defined by Equation (27).

This is not the only, nor perhaps the most common, definition of Bessel functions; but it is justified both historically and by our present context. The properties given in an extensive literature[†] can be derived from this definition. For example, we can develop a power series in $z$, starting from the exponential series

$$e^x = \sum_{r=0}^{\infty} \frac{x^r}{r!}$$

For $g(z,\theta)$ is the product of two such series:

$$e^{jz\sin\theta} = (e^{\frac{1}{2}ze^{j\theta}})(e^{-\frac{1}{2}ze^{-j\theta}})$$

$$= \sum_{q=0}^{\infty} \frac{1}{q!}(\tfrac{1}{2}z)^q e^{jq\theta} \sum_{r=0}^{\infty} \frac{(-1)^r}{r!}(\tfrac{1}{2}z)^r e^{-jr\theta}$$

Collecting terms for which $q - r = n$ shows that

$$J_n(z) = \sum_{r=0}^{\infty} \frac{(-1)^r(\tfrac{1}{2}z)^{2r+n}}{r!(r+n)!} \tag{28}$$

---

* Named after the astronomer F. W. Bessel (1784–1846) who, while investigating planetary motions, developed analytical methods which have since been applied to the study of complex periodicities in other fields.

† The classic work is by Watson; there are useful shorter books by Tranter and by Sneddon, among others. For tables and formulae see the handbooks by Jahnke and Emde, or Abramowitz and Stegun.

for non-negative $n$, and that

$$J_{-n}(z) = (-1)^n J_n(z) \qquad (29)$$

Since (25) is periodic in $z$, it is plausible that Bessel functions are oscillatory, and this is also indicated by the alternation of signs in the power series (28). However, none of them is strictly periodic. For large arguments $(z \gg n)$ they resemble decaying oscillations, and asymptotically[*]

$$J_n(z) \approx \left(\frac{2}{\pi z}\right)^{1/2} \cos(z - \tfrac{1}{2}n\pi - \tfrac{1}{4}\pi) \qquad (30)$$

the error being of order $z^{-2}$.

*Frequency modulation* Information may be conveyed within a bandpass channel by impressing it as modulation on a carrier wave: we have already referred to amplitude modulation (Equation 2.3.23 and Figure 2.3.4). Another important technique is frequency modulation. To express mathematically the idea of a varying frequency, we note that in sinusoidal functions such as $e^{j2\pi Ft}$ or $\cos 2\pi Ft$ the argument has a rate of change $2\pi F$. Consistently, we define the instantaneous frequency of a signal in terms of the rate of change of phase. A waveform

$$\cos 2\pi\{Ft + \phi(t)\} \qquad (31a)$$

has the instantaneous phase

$$2\pi\{Ft + \phi(t)\} \qquad (31b)$$

and the instantaneous frequency

$$\frac{1}{2\pi}\frac{d}{dt} 2\pi\{Ft + \phi(t)\} = F + \phi'(t) \qquad (31c)$$

Let a baseband signal $h(t)$ be normalised so that $|h(t)| \leqslant 1$, with the equality attained at peaks. To convey this by frequency modulation,

$$\phi'(t) = f_d h(t) \qquad (32a)$$

$$\phi(t) = f_d \int_0^t h(x)dx \qquad (32b)$$

where $f_d$ is a parameter defining the peak frequency deviation.

[*] Tranter, p. 50: Watson, p. 99.

Let the baseband signal be a sinusoid $\cos 2\pi f_m t$. Then

$$\phi(t) = \frac{1}{2\pi} \frac{f_d}{f_m} \sin 2\pi f_m t$$

and the modulated wave is, in exponential form

$$g(t) = e^{j(2\pi F t + \beta \sin 2\pi f_m t)} \tag{33}$$

where $\beta = f_d/f_m$ is a parameter known as the modulation index.

The frequency spectrum of this f.m. wave follows readily from equations (25–26): there are discrete components at frequencies $F \pm n f_m$ whose amplitudes depend on Bessel functions of argument $\beta$, and

$$g(t) = \sum_{n=-\infty}^{\infty} J_n(\beta) e^{j2\pi(F + nf_m)t} \tag{34}$$

The real forms can be deduced from this expression. The bandwidth occupied extends indefinitely, but examination of many examples shows that most of the power is concentrated into a band of $\pm(f_d + f_m)$: this is *Carson's rule*. Frequency modulation is a non-linear process, so the spectrum of a wave with arbitrary modulation cannot be found by superposition: in practice, Carson's rule still applies if $f_m$ be interpreted as the maximum baseband frequency.

## 2.5 UNIFORM DISCRETE SIGNALS

### Distortionless channels for discrete signals

A communication system may employ signals which comprise a sequence of discrete elements, such as pulses. To convey information, the elements must be able to assume different values, which may in general be represented by diversity of amplitude, phase, frequency, epoch, duration or other characteristic. We shall focus attention on a particular class of discrete signals:

*Definition 1*: a signal is a uniform discrete signal if (i) it is comprised of discrete elements (ii) the elements are of equal duration, and (iii) elements representing different values differ in amplitude but are otherwise similar.

Such a signal may be expressed analytically as

$$\sum_{m=-\infty}^{\infty} a_m g(t - mT) \tag{1}$$

where $g(t)$ is the waveform of an element, $T$ is the elementary period, and the sequence of coefficients $a_m$ are values attributed to successive elements. The signalling rate in bauds is the number of elements per second, namely $1/T$.

EXAMPLES   (i) A periodic waveform satisfies the definition, but only in a degenerate sense: all $a_m$ being alike, it conveys no information.
(ii) An isochronous digital signal is a good example: here the $a_m$ have only a limited set of values, such as $\pm 1$ for a binary signal.
(iii) A sampled function, in the sense of Definition 2.4.3, is a good example: here the values $a_m$ may be drawn from a continuum, but the element waveform $g(t)$ is an impulse. We shall, in the sequel, enlarge on the topic of sampled signals, and allow samples to be represented by other pulse waveforms.

A uniform discrete signal can be expressed as the convolution of an element with a train of impulses:

$$g(t)* \sum_{m=-\infty}^{\infty} a_m\delta(t-mT) \tag{2}$$

For proof, apply Theorem 2.2.5 term by term. The spectrum of the signal is

$$G(f) \sum_{m=-\infty}^{\infty} a_m e^{-j2\pi fmT} \tag{3}$$

and since the oscillatory terms are $O(1)$ as $f \to \infty$, the asymptotic behaviour of the spectrum is determined by that of the element spectrum $G(f)$.

An element of short duration necessarily has a spectrum of wide extent, and it may be impossible to achieve or even approximate a distortionless channel in the sense of Definition 2.3.5. However, this is unnecessary, because information may be conveyed by discrete signals without preserving every detail of the waveform. This is obvious in the case of digital signals but is true even if the values are unrestricted.

Let the form of the transmitted element be $g(t) \Rightarrow G(f)$, and let the frequency response of the channel* be $H(f)/G(f)$ so that a received element has the form $H(f) \Leftarrow h(t)$. Then the received signal is

$$\sum_{m=-\infty}^{\infty} a_m h(t-mT) = h(t)* \sum_{m=-\infty}^{\infty} a_m\delta(t-mT) \tag{4}$$

The element $h(t)$ is not in itself significant; it is a vehicle for

* It is assumed that $G(f)$ is non-zero at all frequencies where $H(f)$ is non-zero; this is not a serious limitation.

conveyance of the sequence $a_m$, and we will consider the channel as distortionless if the latter is preserved.

*Definition 2*: a channel is distortionless, with respect to uniform discrete signals of a given rate, if the sequence of element values $a_m$ is recoverable by uniform sampling of the received signal.

For example, the waveforms in Figure 2.5.1a are equivalent, in that the same sequence of values is recoverable from either by sampling. If a transmission channel converts one of them into the other, it is distortionless to uniform discrete signals of rate $1/T$. However, the waveforms in Figure 2.5.1b are not equivalent; no set of uniform samples from one is identical with uniform samples from the other. We shall usually adopt the convention that equivalent signals are shown in alignment, as Figure 2.5.1(a); propagation delays being discounted for convenience.

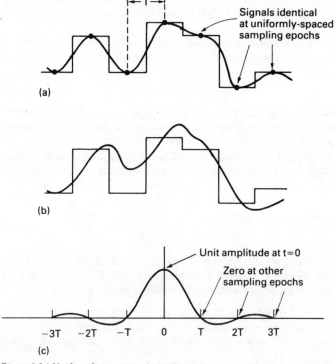

*Figure 2.5.1 Uniform discrete signals. (a) Equivalent signals; (b) Non-equivalent signals; (c) Signal element with zero distortion*

If a channel is distortionless, in the sense of Definition 2, it must be so in respect of each and every sequence $a_m$. In particular, we can consider an isolated unit element surrounded by zero elements; $a_o = 1$, and all other $a_m = 0$. The output waveform $h(t)$ must satisfy the conditions

$$h(0) = 1$$
$$h(mT) = 0, \qquad m \neq 0 \tag{5}$$

as shown in Figure 2.5.1(c). From this reasoning we can derive a general condition for distortionless channels.

*Theorem 1*: a channel with frequency response $H(f)/G(f)$ is distortionless to uniform discrete signals of rate $1/T$ and of element spectrum $G(f)$ if and only if

$$T^{-1} \operatorname{rep}_{1/T} H(f) = 1 \tag{6}$$

A frequency function $H(f)$ satisfying (6) is distortionless if the elements are impulses, and will be called simply a distortionless channel.

*Proof* The channel is distortionless to uniform discrete signals if and only if it is distortionless to a single element. The latter condition implies that

$$h(t) \operatorname{rep}_T \delta(t) = \delta(t) \tag{7}$$

which is equivalent to (5). On Fourier transformation

$$H(f) * T^{-1} \operatorname{rep}_{1/T} \delta(f) = 1 \tag{8}$$

which by Equation (2.4.4) is equivalent to the theorem as stated.

The class of frequency characteristics admitted is very wide.

EXAMPLES (i) A rectangular filter of lowpass bandwidth $1/2T$ is distortionless to rate $1/T$. The Fourier transform gives

$$T \operatorname{rect}(fT) \Leftarrow \operatorname{sinc}(t/T)$$

which satisfies the time-domain condition (5). The frequency-domain repetition (Figure 2.5.2a) satisfies Theorem 1. This filter has the lowest bandwidth compatible with distortionless signalling at the rate $1/T$.

*Definition 3*: the Nyquist* bandwidth is the minimum bandwidth capable of conveying undistorted uniform discrete signals; for a rate of $R$ bauds, it is $\frac{1}{2}R$ Hz. The Nyquist rate is the maximum rate

---

* After H. Nyquist, who established in 1928 the necessary rectangular bandwidth and the principle of vestigial symmetry.

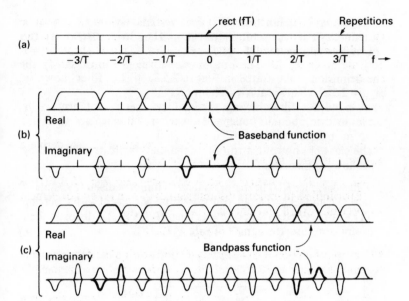

*Figure 2.5.2 Frequency characteristics for uniform discrete signals*

of signalling possible without distortion; for a channel of bandwidth $B$ Hz, it is $2B$ bauds.

(ii) If the transmitted elements are rectangular pulses of duration $kT$ ($k \leqslant 1$) the rectangular filter can be modified to

$$\frac{\text{rect}\,(fT)}{k\,\text{sinc}(kfT)}$$

The denominator, $G(f)$ of Theorem 1, is the element spectrum; its first zero occurs beyond the cutoff of the rectangular filter, so the frequency response is bounded.

(iii) A rectangular bandpass filter of bandwidth $1/T$ and centre frequency $F$

$$\tfrac{1}{2}T\,\text{rect}(f-F) + \tfrac{1}{2}T\,\text{rect}(f+F) \Leftarrow \text{sinc}(t/T)\cos(2\pi fT)$$

This is of adequate bandwidth for double-sideband amplitude modulation, but it must be noted that the present treatment does not imply modulation.

(iv) A low-pass filter with vestigial symmetry about the cutoff frequency $1/2T$.

*Definition 4*: a function $H(f)$ has vestigial symmetry about a frequency $F$ if over a certain transitional bandwidth $H(F + x)$ is the complex conjugate of $1 - H(F - x)$.

The definition is illustrated in Figure 2.5.3a–b. The filter shown in Figure 2.5.2b clearly satisfies Theorem 1.

(v) A bandpass filter having vestigial symmetry, not necessarily similar in form, about its upper and lower cutoff frequencies which are adjacent multiples of $1/2T$ (Figure 2.5.2(c)).

The class of known distortionless channels is greatly enlarged by the following theorem.

*Theorem 2*: let $H(f)$ be distortionless to uniform discrete signals of rate $1/T$, and let $\psi(t)$ be an arbitrary pulse waveform with spectrum $\Psi(f)$, normalised so that $\psi(0) = 1$. Then $H(f)*\Psi(f)$ is distortionless to uniform discrete signals of rate $1/T$.

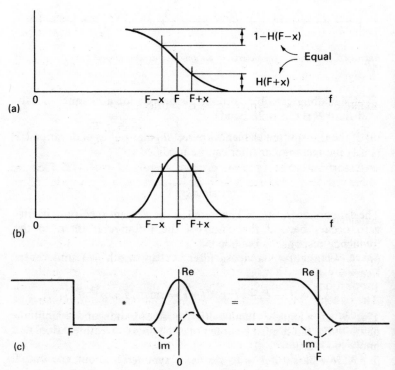

*Figure 2.5.3 Vestigial symmetry. (a) Real part; (b) Imaginary part; (c) Convolution*

*Proof* The impulse response of $H(f)*\Psi(f)$ is the product $h(t)\Psi(t)$. Among the zeros of this function are all the zeros of $h(t)$, so it satisfies the time-domain condition (5) if only its value at the origin is unity. The latter is ensured by the normalisation $\psi(0)=1$.

EXAMPLES (i) A transition with vestigial symmetry can be expressed as a convolution (Figure 2.5.3(c)).
(ii) The previous examplary distortionless channels are confined to finite frequency intervals and so are not realizable exactly. We now construct one which is $O(f^{-2})$ at infinity.

$$\mathrm{sinc}(t/T)e^{-|t|/kT} \Rightarrow T\,\mathrm{rect}\,(fT)* \frac{2kT}{1+(2\pi fkT)^2}$$

$$= \frac{T}{\pi}\{\tan^{-1}(2\pi kTf+\pi k)-\tan^{-1}(2\pi kTf-\pi k)\}$$

$$\approx 1/2kT(\pi f)^2 \qquad \text{as } f\to\infty$$

In fact a distortionless channel with any specified asymptotic behaviour, such as $o(f^{-k})$, Gaussian, etc., could be constructed by choosing $\Psi(f)$ with the right asymptote and combining it with a known distortionless $H(f)$ such as a rectangular filter or one with vestigial symmetry.

EXERCISE Show by three different methods that

$$\tfrac{1}{2}T[1+\cos(\pi fT)\}\,\mathrm{rect}\,(\tfrac{1}{2}fT) \Leftarrow \frac{\mathrm{sinc}(2t/T)}{1-(2t/T)^2} \tag{9}$$

is distortionless to uniform discrete signals of rate $1/T$. Plot the waveform and compare it with the response of a rectangular filter.

## Sampled signals

In many communication systems, a signal is represented by samples taken at regular intervals. At each sampling epoch a switch is closed momentarily so that a very short pulse is generated, of amplitude proportional to the signal amplitude at that epoch (Figure 2.5.4(a)). The switch is, of course, usually an electronic switch or modulator. A sufficiently short pulse is adequately represented by an impulse of the same moment, and so a train of sample pulses can be considered as a sampled function in the sense of Definition 2.4.3.

The samples may be conveyed as short pulses through a channel used in time-division multiplex, or encoded digitally for transmission

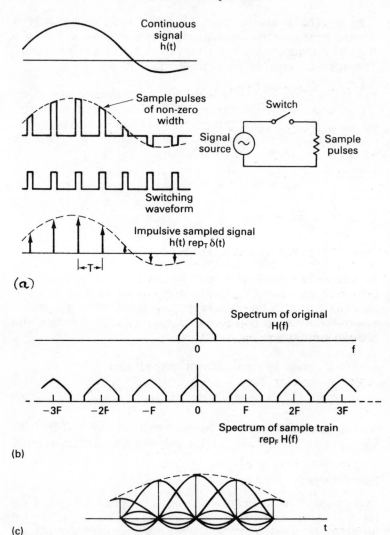

*Figure 2.5.4 Sampled signals*

or processing. In either case, a signal will eventually be recovered which is similar to or in some way derived from the original continuous waveform. To achieve this, some linear operation on the samples is necessary; this is shown as 'Filter 2' in Figure 2.5.5. We shall see that some preliminary filtering ('Filter 1') is usual, so Figure

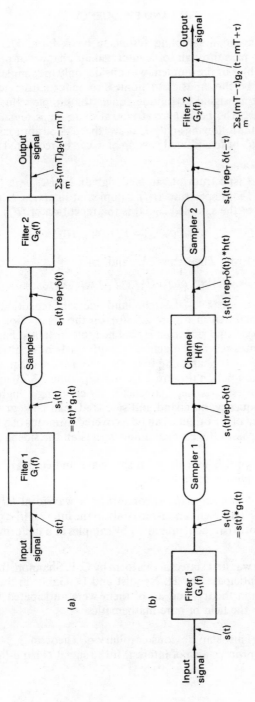

Figure 2.5.5 Sampled systems. (Note: for definitions of $s_r(t)$ see Equation 2.5.18)

2.55(a) is a minimal sampling system in block form. The train of samples may pass through some intermediate channel or process, as Figure 2.5.5(b). For the moment we consider only the simpler system.

If Filter 2 be chosen as distortionless to uniform discrete signals, then the output signal amplitude equals the sample value at each sample epoch. The behaviour at intermediate times remains to be established; the following analysis shows that a good approximateion to the original, or to a filtered version of it, can be recovered from the samples.

*Theorem 3* (spectrum of sampled signal): let $h(t)$ be a bounded waveform, with spectrum $H(f)$, sampled at intervals $T$. Then the spectrum of the sampled signal is the repetition of $H(f)$:

$$h(t) \operatorname{rep}_T \delta(t) \Rightarrow T^{-1} \operatorname{rep}_{1/T} H(f) \tag{10}$$

*Proof* From Theorems 2.3.6 and 2.4.2,

$$h(t) \operatorname{rep}_T \delta(t) \Rightarrow H(f) * T^{-1} \operatorname{rep}_{1/T} \delta(f)$$

and from Equation (2.4.4) the right hand side is the repetition of $H(f)$.

This is illustrated in Figure 2.5.4(b), on the assumption that the original or baseband spectrum is confined to a restricted bandwidth. The spectrum is repeated indefinitely, with sidebands centred about all harmonics of the sampling frequency $F = 1/T$; it is equivalent to amplitude modulation (Figure 2.3.4 and Equation 2.3.23) applied to an infinite series of carrier frequencies. By choosing a high enough sampling frequency, baseband and sidebands can be kept separate. Then a replica of the original can be recovered by means of a low-pass filter which passes the baseband and rejects all the sidebands.

EXERCISE   Apply Theorem 3 to a sine wave and compare with the theory of amplitude modulation.

*Theorem 4* (the sampling theorem): let a waveform $h(t)$ have a spectrum $H(f)$ which is non-zero only in the interval $|f| < \frac{1}{2}F$. Then the waveform can be represented by samples at a uniform spacing of $T = 1/F$.

The theorem was first stated in this form by C. E. Shannon, though he was partly anticipated by H. Nyquist and D. Gabor in the field of communication theory, and all of them were anticipated by E. T. Whittaker in the field of pure mathematics.

*Proof* (i) This is an obvious corollary of Theorem 3.
(ii) A direct proof is also of interest. If the signal is band-limited as

stated, then as a tautology

$$H(f) = \{H(f)^* \operatorname{rep}_F \delta(f)\} \operatorname{rect}(f/F)$$

and on Fourier transformation

$$h(t) = \{h(t) \operatorname{rep}_T \delta(t)\} * \operatorname{sinc}(t/T)$$

$$= \sum_{r=-\infty}^{\infty} h(rT)\operatorname{sinc}\left(\frac{t-rT}{T}\right) \tag{11}$$

The latter version defines a time-domain procedure for recovering the continuous signal. The right hand side of (11) is a set of sinc-shaped pulses, each with its amplitude and epoch defined by one sample (Figure 2.5.4(c)), and having zeros at the other sampling epochs. By Theorem 1, the sum assumes the value of the sampled signal at each sample point. Additional information from Theorem 4 is, that the interpolation between samples is accurate.

Recovery of the original waveform is possible only because we know something about it; namely that its spectrum is confined to the interval $|f| < \frac{1}{2}F$. Without this restriction, the sample train is open to an infinity of interpretations:

*Theorem 5* (ambiguity): the signals $h_1(t) \Rightarrow H_1(f)$ and $h_2(t) \Rightarrow H_2(f)$ are equivalent under sampling at intervals $T$ if and only if

$$\operatorname{rep}_{1/T} H_1(f) = \operatorname{rep}_{1/T} H_2(f) \tag{12}$$

*Proof* The condition is that

$$H_1(f)^* \operatorname{rep}_F \delta(f) = H_2(f)^* \operatorname{rep}_F \delta(f)$$

and on Fourier transformation

$$h_1(t) \operatorname{rep}_T \delta(t) = h_2(t) \operatorname{rep}_T \delta(t)$$

i.e. the sequences of samples are identical.


EXAMPLE   Let $h_1(t)$ be a baseband signal and $h_2(t)$ a product of modulation,

$$h_2(t) = h_1(t)e^{j2\pi mFt}$$

$$H_2(f) = H_1(f - mF)$$

for some integer $m$. It is obvious from Figure 2.5.4(b) that shifting the repetitions by $mF$ leaves them unchanged.

The roles of the filters in Figure 2.5.5(a) now become apparent. The operation of sampling introduces a frequency ambiguity. Filter 1 confines input signals to a specified frequency interval: filter 2 recovers signals in a specified frequency interval, usually the same one. If the input is not confined to an interval of width $\frac{1}{2}F$, then by Theorem 3 the recovered signal is the superposition of components translated from all frequency intervals; this can be represented as a folding of the spectrum (Figure 2.5.6).

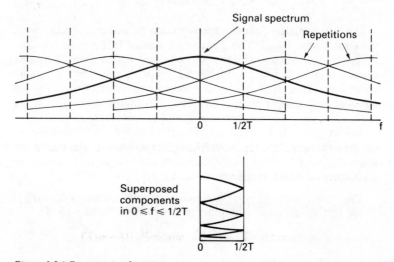

*Figure 2.5.6 Frequency ambiguity*

EXERCISES (i) Let $\Omega = 2\pi/T$, and consider the waveforms (a) $\cos\frac{1}{3}\Omega t$ (b) $\cos\frac{5}{3}\Omega t$ (c) $\frac{1}{2}\cos\frac{2}{3}\Omega t + \frac{1}{2}\cos\frac{4}{3}\Omega t$. Show that they all yield identical samples at epochs $t = mT$.

(ii) Prove that a signal can be recovered from samples at intervals $T$ if it is band-limited to $\frac{1}{2}mF < |f| < \frac{1}{2}(m+1)F$ for any integer $m$. Show by means of a counter-example that band-limiting to an arbitrary interval of width $\frac{1}{2}F$ is not sufficient.

*Samples of non-zero duration* Practical signals have elements of non-zero width. There are two mechanisms which must be distinguished: (i) the sampling switch or modulator may be actuated by carrier pulses of non-trivial duration (ii) samples of negligible duration may be prolonged by pulse-shaping circuits. The difference is illustrated in Figure 2.5.7, rectangular pulses being chosen as a simple example.

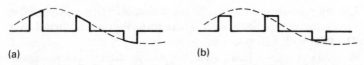

*Figure 2.5.7 Samples of non-zero duration*

*Theorem 6*: let $h(t)$ be a bounded waveform, with spectrum $H(f)$, sampled at intervals $T$ by multiplication with a pulse of waveform $g(t)$ and spectrum $G(f)$. Then the spectrum of the sample train is

$$T^{-1} \sum_{m=-\infty}^{\infty} G(m/T)H(f-m/T) \tag{13}$$

*Proof* The sample train is

$$h(t)\{g(t)* \text{rep}_T \delta(t)\} \Rightarrow H(f)*\{G(f)T^{-1} \text{rep}_{1/T} \delta(f)\}$$

and on writing out the repetition the right hand side is identical with (13).

Theorem 3 is clearly a special case with $G(f)=1$.

EXAMPLE   Sampling with rectangular pulses (Figure 2.5.7(a)) gives

$$h(t) \text{rep}_T \text{rect}(t/kT) \Rightarrow k \sum_{m=-\infty}^{\infty} \text{sinc}(mk)H(f-m/T) \tag{14}$$

EXERCISE   The term $m=0$ in Equation (14) is just $kH(f)$. Generalize this result to show that if the signal is band-limited to $|f|<\frac{1}{2}F$ the recovered baseband is undistorted whatever form of pulse be used.

*Theorem 7*: let $h(t)$ be a bounded waveform, with spectrum $H(f)$, sampled at intervals $T$: and let each sample be represented by a pulse of waveform $g(t)$ and amplitude proportional to the sample value. Then the spectrum of the sample train is

$$T^{-1}G(f) \sum_{m=-\infty}^{\infty} H(f-m/T) \tag{15}$$

*Proof* The sample train is

$$\{h(t)\text{rep}_T \delta(t)\}*g(t) \Rightarrow \{H(f)*T^{-1} \text{rep}_{1/T} \delta(f)\} G(f)$$

and on writing out the repetition the right hand side is identical with (15).

The summation is, of course, the repetition of $H(f)$; it is displayed in this way for comparison with Theorem 6. Again Theorem 3 is a special case with $G(f) = 1$.

EXAMPLE    Rectangular pulses centred on the sample epochs (shown in Figure 2.5.7(b) with a delay of $\frac{1}{2}kT$) give

$$\{h(t)\, \text{rep}_T\, \delta(t)\} * \text{rect}(t/kT)$$

$$\Rightarrow k \, \text{sinc}(kTf) \sum_{m=-\infty}^{\infty} H(f - m/T) \qquad (16)$$

The term $m = 0$ is now $k \, \text{sinc}(kTf)H(f)$. For narrow pulses $k$ is small, the 'sinc' is almost unity, and the baseband component suffers negligible frequency distortion. As $k$ increases, the higher frequency components are attenuated. This is commonly known as 'aperture distortion' since a similar factor arises if images are scanned by a finite non-zero aperture; compare the 'running mean' of Equation (2.2.27).

EXERCISE    Show that with the widest possible non-overlapping pulses the attenuation-frequency distortion is not worse than a factor of $2/\pi$.

## Pulse sequence functions

The transfer characteristics of a minimal sampled system, Figure 2.5.5(a), are clear once the frequency-domain properties of a sampler have been established. We have still to determine the characteristics of the more complex system, Figure 2.5.5(b), in which the samples are subject to a further linear operation. This model serves equally well for two physical situations: (i) the 'channel' consists of a linear network of frequency response $H(f)$ and impulse response $h(t)$, whose output is resampled (ii) sample values are subjected to numerical operations such as weighted addition. We shall visualise the channel initially as a linear network, and revert later to the numerical interpretation.

A series of samples can be considered as having an envelope, a continuous function from which the samples are drawn: the channel, by acting on the samples, modifies the envelope. According to Theorem 5, any set of samples is compatible with an infinity of continuous functions. However, if we make the plausible stipulation that the time origin of the sampling train should not affect the envelope, then the latter is uniquely defined.

*Definition 5*: let a waveform $s(t)$ be sampled at epochs $mT + \theta$, and let a second train of samples at epochs $mT + \theta + \tau$ be constructed by a linear operation on the first train. The envelope $s_\tau(t)$ is a waveform which interpolates between the spot values of the second train, and is independent of the parameter $\theta$.

The output of the channel $H(f)$ in Figure 2.5.5(b) is (ignoring $G_1$ for the time being)

$$\{s(t) \operatorname{rep}_T \delta(t)\} * h(t) = \sum_{m=-\infty}^{\infty} s(mT)h(t - mT)$$

A sample of the output at the epoch $t = nT + \tau$ is also a sample of the envelope $s_\tau(t)$

$$s_\tau(nT + \tau) = \sum_{m=-\infty}^{\infty} s(mT)h(nT - mT + \tau)$$

$$= \sum_{r=-\infty}^{\infty} s(nT - rT)h(rT + \tau) \tag{17}$$

the second version differing only in the index of summation. If the envelope does not vary with choice of sampling epoch, we could replace $nT$ throughout by $nT + \theta$. This implies that, for all $t$

$$s_\tau(t + \tau) = \sum_{r=-\infty}^{\infty} s(t - rT)h(rT + \tau) \tag{18}$$

Having defined the envelope, we can define an operation upon it.

*Definition 6*: let a sampled signal of envelope $s(t) \Rightarrow S(f)$ be subject to a linear operation (such as passage through a network defined by $h(t) \Rightarrow H(f)$, and resampling with delay $\tau$) which generates a sampled signal of envelope $s_\tau(t) \Rightarrow S_\tau(f)$. Then the pulse sequence function of the linear operation is

$$\mathcal{H}(f, \tau) = S_\tau(f)/S(f) \tag{19}$$

For a given resampling delay $\tau$, this is a frequency response operating on the envelope of the sampled signal.

*Theorem 8*: the pulse sequence function of a linear network of impulse response $h(t)$ and frequency response $H(f)$ is

$$\mathcal{H}(f, \tau) = \sum_{r=-\infty}^{\infty} e^{-j2\pi f(rT + \tau)} h(rT + \tau) \tag{20}$$

$$= T^{-1} \sum_{m=-\infty}^{\infty} e^{-j2\pi mF\tau} H(f - mF) \tag{21}$$

*Proof* Taking the Fourier transform of (18),

$$e^{j2\pi f\tau}S_\tau(f) = \sum_{r=-\infty}^{\infty} e^{-j2\pi frT}S(f)h(rT+\tau)$$

Substitution of this equation in (19) gives the series (20). Applying the transformation (2.4.23) to this series gives the series (21); the appropriate substitution is

$$g(t) = h(t+\tau) \Rightarrow e^{j2\pi f\tau}H(f)$$

*Corollary* If a channel is distortionless to uniform discrete signals, it has a constant pulse sequence function

$$\mathcal{H}(f,0) = 1 \qquad (22)$$

For proof, substitute Equation (5) in (20), or Equation (6) in (21).

The two expressions for the pulse sequence function exhibit clearly its two aspects. Equation (20) follows from the dependence of response at any one sample epoch on events at other epochs. Equation (21) follows from the frequency ambiguity of sampling; frequency response in any of the intervals $(n-\frac{1}{2})F < f < (n+\frac{1}{2})F$ makes an equivalent contribution to the envelope of the output samples. Note that $\mathcal{H}(f,\tau)$ is periodic both in $f$ and in $\tau$.

EXAMPLE   If the impulse response is a rectangular pulse

$$h(t) = \text{rect}(t/kT), \qquad k \leqslant 1$$

then

$$\mathcal{H}(f,\tau)\,\text{rect}(\tau/T) = e^{-j2\pi f\tau}\,\text{rect}(\tau/kT)$$

That is, the response is a delay if resampling occurs within the pulse period, and zero otherwise.

EXERCISES   (i) If $H(f)$ is a rectangular filter $\text{rect}(f/kF)$ show that

$$\mathcal{H}(f,\tau)\,\text{rect}(f/F) = \text{rect}(f/kF)$$

and find the bandwidth for which the filter is distortionless to uniform discrete signals of rate $F$.

(ii) Compare two channels comprising respectively (a) a sampler followed by a filter of frequency response $H(f)e^{j2\pi\tau}$ (b) a filter of frequency response $\mathcal{H}(f,\tau)e^{j2\pi f\tau}$: and show that, if driven by the same signal, their outputs are equivalent under sampling. Hint: first prove that for any functions $A$, $B$

$$\text{rep}\{A \text{ rep } B\} = \text{rep}\{B \text{ rep } A\} \tag{23}$$

and then use Theorem 5.

EXAMPLE    A simple $CR$ network such as Figure 2.2.4 has an exponential impulse response

$$h(t) = U(t)e^{-\lambda t}$$

The factor $U(t)$ leads to a truncation of the series (20) on the negative side, since $h(rT + \tau) = 0$ for $r < -\tau/T$. Consequently

$$\mathcal{H}(f, \tau) = \sum_{r=-[\tau/T]}^{\infty} e^{-(\lambda + j2\pi f)(rT + \tau)}$$

$$= \frac{e^{-(\lambda + j2\pi f)T\{\tau/T\}}}{1 - e^{-(\lambda + j2\pi f)T}} \tag{24}*$$

Since $h(t)$ has a discontinuity, there are also discontinuities in $\mathcal{H}(f, \tau)$ considered as a function of $\tau$. Resampling immediately after or before the initial sampling gives

$$\mathcal{H}(f, 0+) = \sum_{r=0}^{\infty} e^{-j2\pi frT} h(rT) = \frac{1}{1 - e^{-(\lambda + j2\pi f)T}} \tag{25}$$

$$\mathcal{H}(f, 0-) = \sum_{r=1}^{\infty} e^{-j2\pi frT} h(rT) = \frac{e^{-(\lambda + j2\pi f)T}}{1 - e^{-(\lambda + j2\pi f)T}} \tag{26}$$

The difference between these expressions is just $h(0+)$, because the first includes the effect of the sample at $\tau = 0$ and the second does not.

If the CR network be driven by a sinusoidally-modulated train of impulses, the resulting waveform is of the type shown by solid lines in Figure 2.5.8. There is a jump as each impulse is applied, proportional to the magnitude of the impulse. The broken lines show the envelopes of the input train, the output values after each jump and the output values before each jump.

Given some target $\mathcal{H}(f, \tau)$, we can find a network which realises it, by deducing $h(t)$ or $H(f)$ and using conventional methods of design.

---

* The notation $[x]$ here signifies the integral part of $x$. The notation $\{x\}$ signifies the fractional part of $x$, that is, $x - [x]$.

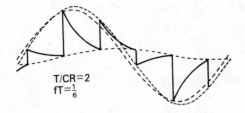

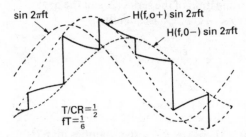

*Figure 2.5.8 Response of CR method to sinusoidally modulated pulses*

*Theorem 9* (inversion of pulse sequence function): let a channel of impulse response $h(t)$ have a pulse sequence function $\mathcal{H}(f,\tau)$ defined for $|f| < \frac{1}{2}F$. Then

$$h(rT+\tau) = F^{-1} \int\limits_{-\frac{1}{2}F}^{\frac{1}{2}F} \mathcal{H}(f,\tau) e^{j2\pi f(rT+\tau)} df \qquad (27)$$

*Proof*   $\mathcal{H}(f,\tau)$ is periodic in $f$, with period $F = 1/T$. For given $\tau$ it can be expanded in Fourier series

$$e^{j2\pi f\tau} \mathcal{H}(f,\tau) = \sum_{n=-\infty}^{\infty} c_n e^{j2\pi fnT}$$

where

$$c_n = F^{-1} \int\limits_{-\frac{1}{2}F}^{\frac{1}{2}F} e^{j2\pi f\tau} \mathcal{H}(f,t) e^{-j2\pi fnT} df$$

But we have a series of this form, namely Equation (20). Equating coefficients term by term proves the theorem.

EXAMPLE   Taking the pulse sequence function of equation (24),

$$h(rT+\tau)=F^{-1}\int_{-\frac{1}{2}F}^{\frac{1}{2}F}\sum_{n=-[\tau/T]}^{\infty}e^{-\lambda(nT+\tau)}e^{j2\pi f(rT-nT)}df$$

$$=e^{-\lambda(rT+\tau)}\qquad r\geqslant-[\tau/T]$$

$$=0\qquad r<-[\tau/T]$$

The interval for which $h(t)$ is zero is given by

$$\frac{t}{T}<r+\frac{\tau}{T}\leqslant\left\{\frac{\tau}{T}\right\}$$

The lowest value of the right hand side being zero, we conclude that

$$h(t)=U(t)e^{-\lambda t}$$

Note that $h(t)$ is specified for all $t$ only if $\mathcal{H}(f,\tau)$ is defined for a full period of $\tau$. Frequently, the pulse sequence function is defined only for some specific $\tau$, such as $0+$. In this case, $h(t)$ is specified only at sample epochs; hence, by Theorem 5, $H(f)$ is not uniquely specified at any frequency. The relationship between $h(t)$ and $\mathcal{H}(f,0+)$ is however very useful in the treatment of digital and discrete systems, as we shall see later.

## 2.6  CORRELATION AND POWER SPECTRUM

### Time and ensemble averages

Many physical effects and observations depend not on the precise waveform of a signal but upon some property averaged or integrated over a period of time.

*Definition 1*: (time average): the average or mean of any quantity $x(t)$ over a continuous time interval $t_1<t<t_2$ is

$$\bar{x}=\frac{1}{t_2-t_1}\int_{t_1}^{t_2}x(t)dt\qquad(1)$$

The average over an infinite time interval, if it exists, may be found by a limiting process. The average of a set of discrete values $\{x_i\}$ $(i=1,2,3,\dots n)$ is

$$\bar{x}=\frac{1}{n}\sum_{i=1}^{n}x_i\qquad(2)$$

The concepts embodied in these equations coalesce if the discrete values are (or are regarded as) samples from a continuous function, say $x_i = x(iT)$, averaged over $n$ sampling periods: then

$$\bar{x} = \frac{1}{nT} \int_{\frac{1}{2}T}^{(n+\frac{1}{2})T} x(t)\{T \operatorname{rep}_T \delta(t)\} dt \qquad (3)$$

the expression $T \operatorname{rep}_T \delta(t)$ being a sampling train of unit average value. In evaluating (1) it is necessary to avoid impulses on the extremes of the interval; we have done so in (3).

The most important average or integrated properties are all related to energy and power. They are:

(i) Energy, which by Theorem 2.3.9 is the square of the signal integrated over either time or frequency

(ii) Spectral distribution of energy

(iii) Power, which is the time derivative of energy. By Theorem 2.4.5, periodic waveforms (which have infinite energy by reason of infinite duration) have a definable mean power which may be summed over time or frequency

(iv) Spectral distribution of power

(v) Autocorrelation, which is the average product of mutually displaced signal samples $h(t)h(t + \tau)$.

Energy spectrum, power spectrum and autocorrelation are defined and discussed initially as properties of a single signal, averaged or integrated over an interval of time. However, this is not the only type of average we shall need. A signal conveying novel information is not precisely specified in advance. It is selected as required from a repertoire of possible signals, so the properties of the repertoire are significant. We consider an ensemble of signals; that is to say, a set of signals drawn from the repertoire in defined proportions or according to defined rules, and representative of the signals to be expected in a working system. Properties such as energy, power, and autocorrelation may be averaged over the ensemble.

*Definition 2* (ensemble average): let $x_i(t)$ represent the $i$th member of a finite ensemble whose $n$ members are equiprobable. Then the expectation, or ensemble average, is

$$E(x) = \langle x_i(t) \rangle = \frac{1}{n} \sum_{i=1}^{n} x_i(t) \qquad (4)$$

(Both terms and both notations are common usage.) The average over an infinite ensemble may be found by a limiting process.

Equivalently, if the members of the infinite ensemble are distinguished by a parameter $\theta$ (continuous and equiprobable over some interval $\theta_1 < \theta < \theta_2$) we write them as $x(t, \theta)$ and define the expectation as

$$E(x) = \frac{1}{\theta_2 - \theta_1} \int_{\theta_1}^{\theta_2} x(t, \theta) d\theta \tag{5}$$

EXAMPLE  The mean power of a sinusoid $h(t) = A \cos(2\pi Ft + \theta)$ can be found by time-averaging (Figure 2.6.1(a)); from equation (2.3.41) it is $\frac{1}{2}A^2$, independent of $\theta$.

To find an ensemble average, we must define an ensemble. Let this consist of sine waves with fixed amplitude and frequency, but different phases (Figure 2.6.1(b). This is a realistic ensemble; phase modulation is a common means of conveying information. The average is then

$$\langle h^2 \rangle = \frac{1}{2\pi} \int_0^{2\pi} \{A \cos(2\pi Ft + \theta)\}^2 d\theta = \frac{1}{2}A^2 \tag{6}$$

This example illustrates two important properties shared by many (though not all) of the signals with which we shall be concerned:

(i) The ensemble average is independent of time
(ii) The ensemble average and time average are equal.

Statistical theory will be developed more formally in Chapter 4 (Vol. 2). Meanwhile, the concepts here outlined enable us to define several 'average' properties of signals.

## Energy spectrum of a signal element

An elementary signal such as a pulse can be integrated, so time averaging is inappropriate. We establish its properties integrated over time, starting from the spectrum which is itself a time integral (Equation 2.3.22).

*Definition 3*: let a signal have a real absolutely integrable waveform $g(t) \Rightarrow G(f)$. Its energy spectrum is $|G(f)|^2$.

The energy spectrum is a frequency function characteristic of a signal, but compared with the spectrum $G(f)$ it has two significant differences. Being the square of $G(f)$, it has the dimensions of energy rather than voltage or current. Being an absolute value, it is unaffected by the

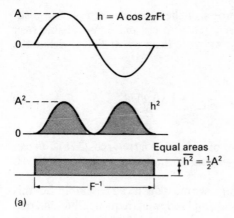

(a)

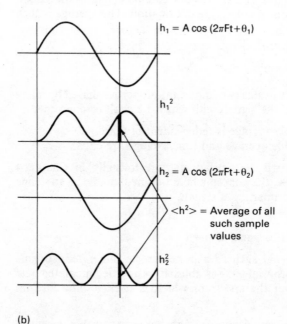

(b)

*Figure 2.6.1 Average power of a sine wave. (a) Time average; (b) Ensemble average*

phase of the spectral component. Thus it does not define a signal uniquely; this, of course, is normally true of practical measurements of power or energy.

*Theorem 1*: the Fourier transform of the energy spectrum is

$$|G(f)|^2 \Leftarrow \int\limits_{-\infty}^{\infty} g(x)g(x+\tau)dx \qquad (7)$$

*Proof* Since $g(t)$ is real, the real and imaginary parts of $G(f)$ are even and odd respectively (see Equation 2.3.40). Consequently,

$$|G(f)|^2 = G(f)G(-f)$$

Transforming the right-hand side,

$$G(f)G(-f) \Leftarrow g(t)*g(-t)$$

and the convolution can be written in the form (7).

The integrand in (7) is the product of two functions relatively displaced by $\tau$ (Figure 2.6.2). The time variable, being of the nature of a delay, has been denoted by $\tau$ to avoid confusion with real time $t$. The integral is an important characterisation of the signal.

*Definition 4*: the finite autocorrelation function of an absolutely integrable function $g(t)$ is

$$\mathscr{R}_g(\tau) = \int\limits_{-\infty}^{\infty} g(t)g(t+\tau)dt \qquad (8)$$

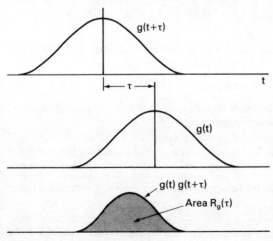

*Figure 2.6.2 Autocorrelation of a pulse*

Autocorrelation is a measure of the mutual similarity of the distant parts of a waveform: the greater its value, the closer the similarity between samples separated by an interval $\tau$. Clearly it is a real, even, function. Its value at the origin $\tau = 0$ is the total energy, Equation (2.3.38): it vanishes, not necessarily monotonically, as $\tau \to \infty$. It is unaffected by shift of the time origin, just as the energy spectrum is unaffected by phase shift.

EXAMPLE   The autocorrelation of rect $t$ is the triangle

$$\{1 - |t|\} \, \text{rect}(\tfrac{1}{2}t)$$

This is easily derived by either (i) carrying out the convolution graphically, or (ii) transforming rect $t \Rightarrow \text{sinc} f$, squaring, and transforming back again.

EXERCISE   Show that the half-cosine pulse $\cos(\pi t)$ rect $t$ has the autocorrelation function and energy spectrum

$$\left\{ \frac{\sin \pi |\tau|}{2\pi} + \frac{(1 - |\tau|)}{2} \cos \pi\tau \right\} \text{rect}(\tfrac{1}{2}\tau) \Rightarrow \left\{ \frac{2 \cos \pi f}{\pi(4f^2 - 1)} \right\}^2 \tag{9}$$

If the waveform contains impulses, so does its autocorrelation function. The autocorrelation of $\delta(t)$ is $\delta(\tau)$, and its energy spectrum is a unit constant. This shows that the energy spectrum can exist even though the total energy be infinite by reason of infinite amplitude. If it is infinite by reason of infinite repetition, however, the spectrum contains impulses, and the energy spectrum is undefined.*

EXERCISE   Show that the impulse-pair $\delta(t - k) + \delta(t - k - 1)$ has the autocorrelation function and energy spectrum

$$2\delta(\tau) + \delta(\tau + 1) + \delta(\tau - 1) \Rightarrow (2 \cos \pi f)^2 \tag{10}$$

independent of $k$. Compare with Figure 2.3.6 and the related account of second-order distortion products.

The autocorrelation of a finite train of impulses is a simple generalisation of the last exercise. It is useful in finding the autocorrelation of any waveform which can be resolved into similar elements.

*Theorem 2*: let the waveform $h(t)$ comprise a finite series of similar

---

* The convolution of two impulses is an impulse: see Equation (2.2.14). The square of an impulse is undefined, because the square of a sequence as used in Definition 2.2.2 does not converge to a limit.

elements,

$$h(t) = \sum_{m=1}^{n} a_m g(t - t_m)$$

Then its autocorrelation is

$$\mathcal{R}_h(\tau) = \mathcal{R}_g(\tau) * \mathcal{R}_a(\tau) \tag{11}$$

where $\mathcal{R}_g(\tau)$ is the autocorrelation of the element $g(t)$, and

$$\mathcal{R}_a(\tau) = \sum_{m=1}^{n} \sum_{k=1}^{n} a_m a_k \delta(\tau - t_m + t_k) \tag{12}$$

is the autocorrelation of an impulse train

$$\sum_{m=1}^{n} a_m \delta(t - t_m)$$

*Proof* By definition

$$\mathcal{R}_h(\tau) = h(t) * h(-t)$$

$$= \left\{ g(t) * \sum_{m=1}^{n} a_m \delta(t - t_m) \right\} * \left\{ g(-t) * \sum_{m=1}^{n} a_m \delta(t + t_m) \right\}$$

where we have, as usual, represented the shifted elements by means of Equation (2.2.32). The convolutions may be performed in any order (by the Corollary to Theorem 2.3.6; compare also Figure 2.3.6b) so the factors can be paired thus:

$$g(t) * g(-t) = \mathcal{R}_g(\tau)$$

$$\left\{ \sum_{m=1}^{n} a_m \delta(t - t_m) \right\} * \left\{ \sum_{m=1}^{n} a_m \delta(t + t_m) \right\} = \mathcal{R}_a(\tau)$$

proving the theorem.

The autocorrelation of the impulses is a series of impulses, so the autocorrelation of the signal is a series of terms each similar to the autocorrelation of the element. The energy spectrum follows readily as

$$|H(f)|^2 = |G(f)|^2 \sum_{m=1}^{n} \sum_{k=1}^{n} a_m a_k e^{-j2\pi f(t_m - t_k)} \tag{13}$$

*Corollary* If $h(t)$ is a block* of $n$ elements from a uniform discrete

---

* There are many words commonly used to denote a finite series of elements (block, word, character, sequence...) of which 'block' is perhaps the least ambiguous.

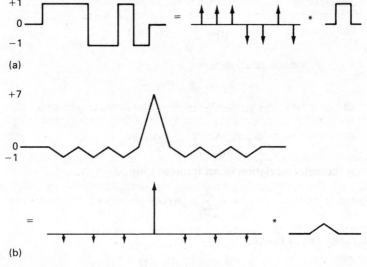

(a)

(b)

*Figure 2.6.3 Autocorrelation of a block. (a) The waveform; (b) The autocorrelation*

signal, with coefficients $\{a_m\}$ and period $T$, then its autocorrelation $\mathcal{R}_h(\tau)$ is a block of $2n-1$ uniform elements $\mathcal{R}_g(\tau)$ with period $T$ and coefficients $\{c_k\}$ given by

$$c_k = \sum_m a_m a_{m+k} \tag{14}$$

*Example*   The block of isochronous rectangular pulses in Figure 2.6.3(a) has element values $\{+ + + - - + -\}$, using $\pm$ for brevity to mean $\pm 1$. Its autocorrelation is a series of triangles with element values $\{-1,0,-1,0,-1,0,7,0,-1,0,-1,0,-1\}$. The peak at the origin is particularly sharp, and is not approached in magnitude by any subsidiary peaks; the sequence was devised to have this property, which is useful in the synchronizing of digital systems.[†]

### Energy spectrum of an ensemble

Given an ensemble of signal elements $\{g_i(t)\}$ whose Fourier transforms are $\{G_i(f)\}$ and autocorrelation functions $\{\mathcal{R}_{gi}(\tau)\}$ respectively, we can define the energy spectrum and autocorrelation of the ensemble.

† Barker (1)

*Definition 5*: The energy spectrum of the ensemble $\{g_i(t)\}$ is the ensemble average $\langle |G_i(f)|^2 \rangle$. The finite autocorrelation function is the ensemble average

$$\langle \mathscr{R}_{gi}(\tau) \rangle = \int_{-\infty}^{\infty} \langle g_i(t)g_i(t+\tau) \rangle \, dt$$

the two forms being equivalent because the operations of time integration and ensemble averaging, both being linear summations, may be taken in either order.

Clearly the functions so defined are related by the Fourier transform, since corresponding members of the averaged ensembles are so related. For convenience of notation, we shall often drop the suffix $i$ unless it is needed to identify a particular member of the ensemble.

EXAMPLES  (i)  An ensemble of similar elements $a_i g(t)$, such as might be used in a uniform discrete signal (Definition 2.5.1), has the properties

Energy spectrum $\qquad = |G(f)|^2 \langle a^2 \rangle$ \hfill (15)

Autocorrelation function $= \mathscr{R}_g(\tau) \langle a^2 \rangle$ \hfill (16)

If $a$ is uniformly distributed over the range $-1$ to $+1$, then by Equation (5)

$$\langle a^2 \rangle = \tfrac{1}{2} \int_{-1}^{+1} a^2 \, da = \tfrac{1}{3}$$

If $a$ has the binary values $\pm 1$, then $\langle a^2 \rangle = 1$.

(ii) A four-phase digital signal might use the elements

$$g_i(t) = \cos(2\pi nt + \theta_i)\operatorname{rect} t \Rightarrow \tfrac{1}{2}e^{j\theta_i}\operatorname{sinc}(f-n)$$
$$+ \tfrac{1}{2}e^{-j\theta_i}\operatorname{sinc}(f+n)$$

where $\theta_i$ ($i = 1, 2, 3, 4$) are phases uniformly spaced at intervals $\tfrac{1}{2}\pi$. The energy spectrum of one element is

$$G_i(f)G_i(-f) = \tfrac{1}{4}\operatorname{sinc}^2(f-n) + \tfrac{1}{4}\operatorname{sinc}^2(f+n)$$
$$+ \tfrac{1}{2}\cos 2\theta_i \operatorname{sinc}(f-n)\operatorname{sinc}(f+n)$$

and the energy spectrum of the ensemble is

$$\langle G(f)G(-f) \rangle = \tfrac{1}{4}\operatorname{sinc}^2(f-n) + \tfrac{1}{4}\operatorname{sinc}^2(f+n) \qquad (17)$$

the ensemble average $\langle \cos 2\theta \rangle$ being zero.

*Blocks of uniform discrete elements*   A block of isochronous elements, such as a telegraph character signal made up of 5 bits, may be a member of an ensemble; in this case the ensemble of character signals.

EXAMPLE   The 8 possible blocks of 3 binary elements (here rectangular pulses of amplitude $\pm 1$) are shown in Figure 2.6.4 together with their autocorrelations. If the blocks are equiprobable, the ensemble autocorrelation is similar to that of the elementary pulse. This result is generalised in Theorem 3 below.

*Theorem 3*: let $h(t)$ be a block of $n$ uniform discrete elements with coefficients $\{a_m\}$. Then the autocorrelation of the ensemble $\{h(t)\}$ is

$$\mathcal{R}_h(\tau) = \mathcal{R}_g(\tau) * \mathcal{R}_a(\tau) \qquad (18)$$

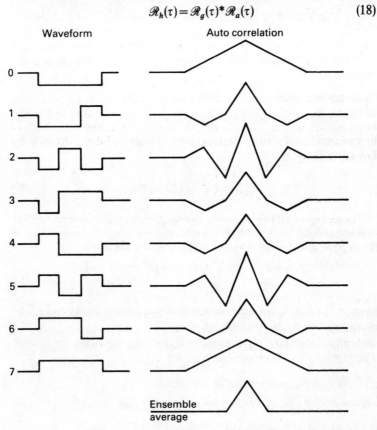

*Figure 2.6.4 Ensemble of binary characters*

where $\mathcal{R}_g(\tau)$ is the autocorrelation of the element $g(t)$, and

$$\mathcal{R}_a(\tau) = \sum_{k=-n+1}^{n-1} \sum_{m=1}^{n} \langle a_m a_{m+k} \rangle \delta(\tau - kT) \tag{19}$$

*Proof* By Theorem 2, any member of the ensemble has an autocorrelation function of the form

$$\mathcal{R}_g(\tau)^* \sum_k c_k \delta(\tau - kT)$$

with $c_k$ given by (14). The desired autocorrelation is the ensemble average of such functions. The processes of convolution, summation of series, and ensemble averaging all being linear summations, we may take them in any order; taking the average first leads to the result stated.

*Corollary* If for some $k \neq 0$ and some $m$

$$\langle a_m a_{m+k} \rangle = 0$$

then the $m$th and $(m+k)$th elements are said to be uncorrelated; knowing the value of one such element does not enable us to infer anything about the other. If this is true for all $m$ and all $k \neq 0$, the block is said to consist of uncorrelated elements. The autocorrelation of such a block is

$$\mathcal{R}_h(\tau) = \left\{ \sum_{m=1}^{n} \langle a_m^2 \rangle \right\} \mathcal{R}_g(\tau) \tag{20}$$

Theorem 3 is a fairly obvious deduction from Theorem 2 and the definition of an ensemble average. Nevertheless it is a useful tool for finding the autocorrelation of an ensemble, especially if some or all of the elements are uncorrelated.

EXAMPLE   Consider a binary element with values $\pm 1$. The ensemble of blocks of $n$ elements has $2^n$ members. If all blocks are equiprobable, then all pairs of elements are uncorrelated, since in forming $\langle a_m a_{m+k} \rangle$ with any designated $a_m$ the values $a_{m+k} = \pm 1$ occur equiprobably. Thus for blocks of uncorrelated binary elements

$$\mathcal{R}_h(\tau) = n \mathcal{R}_g(\tau) \tag{21}$$

Figure 2.6.4 shows the particular case with rectangular elements with $n = 3$.

It might be thought that this simplification occurs only if all blocks are equiprobable and all elements independent, but such is not the case, as the following instance demonstrates.

EXERCISE    A block of $n$ binary elements with values $\pm 1$ has the constraint that the number of elements with value $+1$ must be even. (In data communication practice this is called 'even parity'.) Show that the ensemble has $2^{n-1}$ members, and that its autocorrelation is given by Equation (21) if $n \geqslant 3$.

### Power spectrum of a single signal

Power is the rate of dissipation of energy. A signal of infinite duration may not have a finite energy, but it may nevertheless have a definable mean power.

A signal of finite duration $T$ has an energy spectrum which accords with Definition 3 and Theorem 1. If a finite total energy $E$ be dissipated in time $T$ the mean power is the mean rate of dissipation, $E/T$. If the energy in a given spectral interval of width $df$ is $E(f)df$, then the mean power in this spectral interval is $T^{-1}E(f)df$. These quantities are time averages in the sense of Definition 1: but since the quantity averaged (power) is the derivative of that given (energy) no integration is needed.

Now consider a signal $h(t)$ which is defined over an infinite interval. Conceptually we can select a segment of finite duration $T$ and treat it as a finite signal:

$$h(t)\,\mathrm{rect}(t/T) \Rightarrow H(f)*T\,\mathrm{sinc}\,fT \tag{22}$$

If $T$ is large compared with the periodic time of dominant spectral components, then $\mathrm{sinc}\,fT$ has a relatively narrow peak, and the convolution approximates $H(f)$. Under certain conditions, limiting properties are approached as $T \rightarrow \infty$ and these can be attributed to the original signal $h(t)$.

*Definition 6*: let a signal have a real waveform $h(t) \Rightarrow H(f)$ defined for all $t$. Its power spectrum is

$$\mathscr{P}(f) = \lim_{T\to\infty} T^{-1}|H(f)*T\,\mathrm{sinc}\,fT|^2 \tag{23}$$

if the limit exists and is non-zero. Otherwise it is undefined.

EXAMPLE    Consider the cosine wave

$$2\cos 2\pi\alpha t \Rightarrow \delta(f-\alpha) + \delta(f+\alpha)$$

The power spectrum is, from Definition 6,

$$\text{Limit}_{T\to\infty} T\{\text{sinc}(f-\alpha)T + \text{sinc}(f+\alpha)T\}^2$$

The product contains two squared terms which in the limit becomes impulses

$$\text{Limit}_{T\to\infty} T\{\text{sinc}^2(f-\alpha)T + \text{sinc}^2(f+\alpha)T\} = \delta(f-\alpha) + \delta(f+\alpha) \tag{24}$$

There is also a cross-product

$$T\,\text{sinc}(f-\alpha)T.\,\text{sinc}(f+\alpha)T$$

which is $O(T^{-1})$ except at $f = \pm\alpha$ where it is $O(1)$. This in the limit contributes impulses of zero moment, coincident with the impulses of unit moment. While these are not strictly zero, they are null functions which contribute nothing to an integral, so have zero Fourier transforms and zero energy. Consequently, the power spectrum is given by (24). The total power is the integral of the power spectrum, namely 2; which is consistent with Theorem 2.4.5 and with the well-known mean square value of a sine wave.

*Theorem 4*: let $h(t) \Rightarrow H(f)$ have a power spectrum according to Definition 6. Then the Fourier transform of the power spectrum is

$$\text{Limit}_{T\to\infty} T^{-1}|H(f)*T\,\text{sinc}\,fT|^2$$

$$\Leftarrow \text{Limit}_{T\to\infty} T^{-1} \int_{-\frac{1}{2}T}^{\frac{1}{2}T} h(x)h(x+\tau)dx \tag{25}$$

*Proof* This is similar to Theorem 1. Fourier transformation of the left-hand side gives

$$\text{Limit}_{T\to\infty} T^{-1}\{h(t)\,\text{rect}(t/T)\}*\{h(-t)\,\text{rect}(t/T)\}$$

$$= \text{Limit}_{T\to\infty} T^{-1} \int_{-\frac{1}{2}T-\tau U(-\tau)}^{\frac{1}{2}T-\tau U(\tau)} h(x)h(x+\tau)dx \tag{26}$$

For any given $\tau$, (25) and (26) are equivalent in the limit.

*Definition 7*: the autocorrelation function of a function $h(t)$ which is not absolutely integrable is

$$\mathscr{R}_h(\tau) = \underset{T \to \infty}{\text{Limit}} \; T^{-1} \int_{-\frac{1}{2}T}^{\frac{1}{2}T} h(x)h(x+\tau)dx \qquad (27)$$

if the limit exists and is non-zero. Otherwise it is undefined.

The autocorrelation function is a measure of the mutual similarity of samples of $h(t)$ separated by an interval $\tau$. It is a real, even function, unaffected by shift of time origin. Its value at the origin is the total mean power

$$P = \underset{T \to \infty}{\text{Limit}} \; T^{-1} \int_{-\frac{1}{2}T}^{\frac{1}{2}T} [h(t)]^2 dt \qquad (28)$$

It is the Fourier transform of the power spectrum, by Theorem 4.

The definition (27) with limits of integration $\pm\frac{1}{2}T$ is the conventional one, and is valid in the limit. It could be taken, wrongly, to imply an approximation to $\mathscr{R}(\tau)$ before passage to the limit, for any $\tau$; whereas a truncated function of length $T$ provides no information whatsoever about correlation over a length $\tau > T$. The expression (26) is less misleading in this respect.

EXAMPLE    The cosine wave $2\cos 2\pi\alpha t$ has the autocorrelation

$$\mathscr{R}(\tau) = 2\cos 2\pi\alpha\tau \qquad (29)$$

This follows either from evaluation of (27) or Fourier transformation of (24).

EXERCISE    (i) Show that the phase-shifted wave $2\cos(2\pi\alpha t + \theta)$ also has the autocorrelation (29).
(ii) Derive this result from expressions (26) and (27) and show that they are equivalent in the limit.

*Theorem 5*: let

$$h(t) = c_0 + \sum_{n=1}^{\infty} \{c_n e^{j2\pi\alpha_n t} + c_n {}^* e^{-j2\pi\alpha_n t}\} \qquad (30)^*$$

be a real waveform consisting of periodic components, not

---

* The notation $x^*$ signifies the complex conjugate of $x$.

necessarily commensurable in frequency, and either finite or denumerably infinite in number. Then its power spectrum exists and is

$$c_0^2 \delta(f) + \sum_{n=1}^{\infty} |c_n|^2 \{\delta(f - \alpha_n) + \delta(f + \alpha_n)\}$$

$$\Leftarrow c_0^2 + 2 \sum_{n=1}^{\infty} |c_n|^2 \cos 2\pi\alpha_n\tau \tag{31}$$

*Proof* The power spectrum is, from Definition 6, the limit as $T \to \infty$ of

$$T\{c_0 \operatorname{sinc} fT + \sum_n c_n \operatorname{sinc}(f - \alpha_n)T + c_n^* \operatorname{sinc}(f + \alpha_n)T\} \times$$

$$\times \{c_0 \operatorname{sinc} fT + \sum_n c_n^* \operatorname{sinc}(f - \alpha_n)T + c_n \operatorname{sinc}(f + \alpha_n)T\}$$

$$= Tc_0^2 \operatorname{sinc}^2 fT + T\sum_n c_n c_n^* \{\operatorname{sinc}^2(f - \alpha_n)T + \operatorname{sinc}^2(f + \alpha_n)T\}$$

$$+ \text{crossproducts of form } \operatorname{sinc}(f \pm \alpha_n)T \operatorname{sinc}(f \pm \alpha_m)$$

$$\text{and } \operatorname{sinc} fT \operatorname{sinc}(f \pm \alpha_n)T$$

As in the derivation of Equation (24), the terms of form $T \operatorname{sinc}^2(f - \alpha_n)T$ become impulses in the limit, while the crossproducts contribute at most null functions. This proves the left-hand side of (31): the right-hand side is a simple Fourier transform.

We shall refer to such signals briefly as 'line-spectrum signals'.

*Corollary* The mean power of a line-spectrum signal is

$$P = \underset{T \to \infty}{\text{Limit }} T^{-1} \int_{-\frac{1}{2}T}^{\frac{1}{2}T} \{h(t)\}^2 dt = 2 \sum_{n=1}^{\infty} |c_n|^2 + c_0^2 \tag{32}$$

This includes Theorem 2.4.5 as a special case.

EXAMPLES (i) A sampled line-spectrum signal, and a carrier amplitude-modulated by a line-spectrum signal, are also line-spectrum signals (see exercises below).
(ii) A carrier which is frequency-modulated by a line-spectrum signal;

for instance

$$\cos(2\pi\beta t + k \sin 2\pi\alpha t) \Rightarrow J_0(k)\delta(f \pm \beta)$$

$$+ \sum_{n \neq 0} J_n(k)\delta\{f \pm (\beta + n\alpha)\} \tag{33}$$

The coefficients $J_n(k)$ are Bessel functions of the first kind according to Definition 2.4.4.

(iii) Any waveform generated by means of a recursive relationship:

$$h(t) = \sum_n a_n h(t - \tau_n) \tag{34}$$

For Fourier transformation of (34) gives

$$H(f)\left\{1 - \sum_n a_n e^{-j2\pi f \tau_n}\right\} = 0 \tag{35}$$

and $H(f)$ can be non-zero only at the zeros of the bracketed factor (which are denumerably infinite in number). Compare Theorem 2.4.1. The recursive technique is often used to generate pseudo-random waveforms.

EXERCISES   (i) Show that the amplitude-modulated wave

$$(1 + k \cos 2\pi\alpha t)2 \cos 2\pi\beta t$$

has the power spectrum and autocorrelation

$$\delta(f \pm \beta) + \tfrac{1}{4}k^2\delta(f \pm \beta \pm \alpha) \Leftarrow (1 + \tfrac{1}{2}k^2 \cos 2\pi\alpha\tau)2 \cos 2\pi\beta\tau \tag{36}$$

(ii) Show that the sampled sinusoid

$$2 \cos 2\pi\alpha t \, \text{rep}_{1/\beta} \, \delta(t)$$

has the power spectrum and autocorrelation

$$\beta^2 \, \text{rep}_\beta \, \delta(f \pm \alpha) \Leftarrow 2\beta^2 \cos 2\pi\alpha\tau \, \text{rep}_{1/\beta} \, \delta(\tau) \tag{37}$$

(iii) In the foregoing examples, consider the special case $\alpha = \beta$ and show that the results quoted are invalid. Find some other particular frequencies for which one or the other result is invalid; try to state a general rule. Show that Theorem 5 remains valid in all cases.

Formally, we have defined the power spectrum, the autocorrelation function, and also the mean power

$$\int_{-\infty}^{\infty} \mathscr{P}(f)df = \mathscr{R}(0) \tag{38}$$

for any signal which satisfies the condition in Definitions 6 and 7, that the time average has a limiting value as $T \rightarrow \infty$. This condition clearly is satisfied for a line-spectrum signal, but its general implications for a single determinate signal are not so clear. The concept is most fruitful in a statistical context, so we procede to consider an ensemble of signals.

### Power spectrum of an ensemble

Given an ensemble of signals $\{g_i(t)\}$ with power spectra $\{\mathscr{P}_i(f)\}$ and correlation functions $\{\mathscr{R}_i(\tau)\}$ respectively, we can define the power spectrum and autocorrelation of the ensemble.

*Definition 8*: The power spectrum of the ensemble $h_i(t)$ is the ensemble average

$$\mathscr{P}(f) = \langle \mathscr{P}_i(f) \rangle$$

and the autocorrelation function is the ensemble average

$$\mathscr{R}(\tau) = \langle \mathscr{R}_i(\tau) \rangle = \underset{T \rightarrow \infty}{\text{Limit}}\, T^{-1} \int_{-\frac{1}{2}T}^{\frac{1}{2}T} \langle h_i(t)h_i(t+\tau) \rangle dt$$

The two forms of $\mathscr{R}(\tau)$ are equivalent because the operations of time integration and ensemble averaging, both being linear summations, may be taken in either order (subject to convergence requirements which will normally be satisfied in a physical context).

The most significant feature of Definition 8 is the second form for the autocorrelation function. By taking an ensemble average before the limiting operation, we admit a large and important class of signals for which the limit exists and is obvious.

EXAMPLE (i) Consider a uniform discrete signal of uncorrelated elements, like the blocks defined in the corollary to Theorem 3 and its ensuing example but of infinite extent. This is

$$h(t) = \sum_{m=-\infty}^{\infty} a_m g(t - mT)$$

where $g(t)$ is an element waveform. The only correlation is within elements, and this is invariant, so

$$\mathscr{R}_h(\tau) = T^{-1}\mathscr{R}_g(\tau) \tag{39}$$

where $\mathscr{R}_g(\tau)$ is the finite autocorrelation of an element. We can average Equation (21) over a period $nT$; the expression is independent of the period and so is valid in the limit. The power spectrum is

$$\mathscr{P}_h(f) = T^{-1}|G(f)|^2 \tag{40}$$

namely the energy spectrum of an element, averaged over period $T$. (ii) The autocorrelation, hence the spectrum, is also found readily if the correlation extends over a finite block of elements or diminishes exponentially with increasing $\tau$. The latter case is best treated in the context of random process theory, and is deferred until section 4.6.

EXERCISE Find the autocorrelation and power spectrum of an uncorrelated digital signal using phase-shift keying. (Hint: see Equation 17).)

## 2.7 SYMMETRY AND PARTITIONING OF SIGNALS AND SPECTRA

Paradoxically, the fluent user of Fourier transform theory may but rarely evaluate an integral or sum a series. He will be thoroughly familiar with certain general relationships and asymptotic properties which he can apply in two ways: to gain some idea of the behaviour of a time or frequency function without evaluating it exactly, and to simplify the derivation of exact equations when these are essential. Many of the theorems in previous sections can be used for such purposes; for instance, those concerning similarity, shifting, differentiation, integration, convolution, sampling, repetition. In this section and the next, we derive some further properties of this kind.

### Symmetry

*Definition 1*: a function $g(x)$ is *even* if $g(x) = g(-x)$. It is *odd* if $g(x) = -g(-x)$. It is *hermitean* if $g(x) = g^*(-x)$; that is, its real part is even and its imaginary part odd. A function which is neither odd nor even may be expressed as the sum of even and odd parts, respectively

$$a(x) = \tfrac{1}{2}g(x) + \tfrac{1}{2}g(-x)\ldots \text{even}$$
$$b(x) = \tfrac{1}{2}g(x) - \tfrac{1}{2}g(-x)\ldots \text{odd}$$

EXAMPLES   (i) Rect $x$, sinc $x$, cos $x$, $x^4$, $e^{-x^2}$ are even functions.
(ii) Sin $x$, sgn $x$, $x^{-1}$, $x^3$ are odd functions.
(iii) Many familiar complex functions are hermitean, for instance $(1+jx)^{-1}$ and $e^{jx}$. These and another example are drawn in Figure 2.7.1.

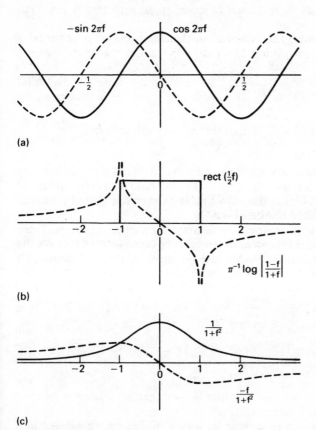

(a)

(b)

(c)

*Figure 2.7.1 Hilbert transform*

(iv) $U(x)$ is the sum of the even function $\frac{1}{2}$ and the odd function $\frac{1}{2}\operatorname{sgn} x$; $e^x$ is the sum of the even function $\cosh x$ and the odd function $\sinh x$.

Fourier series and integrals have many symmetry properties, most of which are subsumed under the following theorem.

*Theorem 1*: Pairs of functions related by the direct or inverse Fourier transform have the following relationships between their symmetries (if any):

$$\text{Real even} \Leftrightarrow \text{Real even}$$
$$\text{Imaginary even} \Leftrightarrow \text{Imaginary even}$$
$$\text{Real odd} \Leftrightarrow \text{Imaginary odd}$$

That is to say, a real even function transforms into a real even function, and so on.

*Proof* follows readily from the hermitean nature of the factor $e^{\pm j2\pi ft}$ in the integrand of the Fourier integrals. Consider for example a real even function $g(t) \Rightarrow G(f)$:

$$G(f) = \int_{-\infty}^{\infty} g(t)\cos 2\pi ft\, dt - j\int_{-\infty}^{\infty} g(t)\sin 2\pi ft\, dt$$

The second integral vanishes because the integrand is an odd function of $t$. The first is non-zero, because the integrand is an even function of $t$; and even, because the integrand is an even function of $f$. Similar arguments apply to other cases.

An arbitrary function can be separated into terms of the types listed in Theorem 1; the theorem then applies to each term individually. By Theorem 2.4.3, similar relationships apply to the coefficients of a Fourier series.

EXERCISES(i) Transform some of the even, odd and hermitean functions quoted as examples after Definition 1, and check their symmetries.

(ii) Show that the transform of a real function is hermitean. This fact has been used in Theorems 2.3.9 and 2.4.5.

(iii) Show that the convolution of two even functions is even: the convolution of two odd functions is even: the convolution of one even with one odd function is odd.

(iv) Show that an even periodic waveform can be represented as a series of cosines, and an odd periodic waveform as a series of sines.

## Single-sided functions

*Definition 2*: a function $g(x)$ is single-sided if it is zero for all $x < 0$ and non-zero for some part of the interval $x > 0$. Equivalently, its even and odd parts $a(x)$, $b(x)$ satisfy the equation

$$a(x) = b(x)\operatorname{sgn} x \qquad (1)$$

The Fourier transforms of single-sided functions have distinctive properties which follow readily from the symmetry relationship (1).

*Causal systems*   Consider a time function $g(t)$ which is the impulse response of a realizable network or filter. It must obey the causal relationship: that is, the response cannot begin before the stimulus is applied. Consequently, $g(t)$ is single-sided. The frequency response of a causal system must therefore satisfy the following theorem.

*Theorem 2*: let $g(t)$ be a causal impulse response or other single-sided real integrable function. Then the real and imaginary parts of its Fourier transform $G(f) = A(f) + jB(f)$ satisfy the equations

$$A(f) = B(f)*(\pi f)^{-1} \qquad (2)$$

$$B(f) = -A(f)*(\pi f)^{-1} \qquad (3)$$

*Proof*   By Theorem 1, the even and odd parts of $g(t)$ transform respectively into the real and imaginary parts of $G(f)$; that is,

$$a(t) \Rightarrow A(f), \qquad b(t) \Rightarrow jB(f)$$

But for a single-sided function

$$a(t) = b(t)\operatorname{sgn} t, \qquad b(t) = a(t)\operatorname{sgn} t$$

On Fourier transformation the first of these equations yields

$$A(f) = jB(f)*(j\pi f)^{-1}$$

which is Equation (2). Similarly, the second equation leads to (3).

EXAMPLES   (i) A cosine real part is associated with a sine imaginary part (Figure 2.7.1(a)). This is easily derived by transforming the time function $\delta(t - 1)$.
(ii) The rectangular real part $A(f) = \operatorname{rect}(\tfrac{1}{2}f)$ is associated with the imaginary part

$$B(f) = \pi^{-1} \log \left| \frac{1-f}{1+f} \right| \qquad (4)$$

shown in Figure 2.7.1(b). This is most easily derived by carrying out the convolution (3).

EXERCISES   (i) Find the Fourier transform of the real and imaginary parts of $(1+jf)^{-1}$, which are drawn in Figure 2.7.1(c). Show that they are even and odd, respectively; and that they satisfy equation (1).
(ii) Show that the real part $\delta(f)$ is associated with the imaginary part $-1/\pi f$ by (a) evaulating (3) directly, (b) taking a limiting case of (4), (c) considering the Fourier transform of $U(t)$.
(iii) If $A(f)+jB(f)$ is the frequency response of a causal network show that

$$B(f)=-\frac{2f}{\pi}\int_0^\infty \frac{A(x)dx}{f^2-x^2} \tag{6}$$

$$A(f)=\frac{2}{\pi}\int_0^\infty \frac{xB(x)dx}{f^2-x^2} \tag{7}$$

The relationship (3) is known as the Hilbert transform.

*Definition 3*: The Hilbert transform of a real function $g(x)$ is

$$\hat{g}(x)=\frac{1}{\pi}\int_{-\infty}^\infty \frac{g(y)dy}{y-x}=-g(x)*(\pi x)^{-1} \tag{8}$$

The inverse transform is

$$g(x)=\frac{-1}{\pi}\int_{-\infty}^\infty \frac{\hat{g}(y)dy}{y-x}=\hat{g}(x)*(\pi x)^{-1} \tag{9}$$

The inversion would, of course, have the status of a theorem but for the fact that we have proved it incidentally as part of Theorem 2. In the usual mathematical approach, the convergence of integrals such as (8) and (9) has to be justified; this too we have done incidentally, by proving at an early stage the validity of Fourier transforms of functions such as sgn $t$.

We have frequently cited ideal signal waveforms which are real and even, and so have real even Fourier transforms. It is clear that such a signal cannot be the impulse response of a causal system. However, it may be related to a causal waveform in one of two ways. Firstly, a delayed version may be causal: for example, rect $t$ is not causal but rect $(t - \frac{1}{2})$ is. Secondly, a single-sided version of the signal is causal; and its Fourier transform is related to that of the even version.

*Theorem 3*: Let $g(t) \Rightarrow G(f)$ be a real even waveform. Then the corresponding single-sided waveform has the Fourier transform

$$g(t)U(t) \Rightarrow \tfrac{1}{2}G(f) + \tfrac{1}{2}j\hat{G}(f) \tag{10}$$

where $\hat{G}(f)$ is the Hilbert transform of $G(f)$.

*Proof* The single-sided waveform may be written

$$\tfrac{1}{2}g(t) + \tfrac{1}{2}g(t)\operatorname{sgn} t \Rightarrow \tfrac{1}{2}G(f) + \tfrac{1}{2}G(f)*(j\pi f)^{-1}$$

which is equivalent to (10).

Thus many results derived from ideal even functions yield similar results valid for some causal system. Moreover, the impulse response of a causal system may be calculated from the real part of its frequency response, without reference to the associated imaginary part.

EXAMPLE   A causal network whose frequency function has the real part rect $f$ has the impulse response $2U(t)\operatorname{sinc} t$.

EXERCISE   Show that the impulse response of a causal network may also be calculated from the imaginary part, without reference to the real part of the frequency response.

*The analytic signal*   We can also take Hilbert transforms in the time domain, and define a waveform $\hat{g}(t)$ related to a given $g(t)$ by Equation (8).

*Theorem 4*: let $g(t) \Rightarrow G(f)$ be a real waveform with zero d.c. component. Then its Hilbert transform has the spectrum

$$\hat{g}(t) \Rightarrow jG(f)\operatorname{sgn} f \tag{11}$$

*Proof* The waveform $\hat{g}(t)$ may be written

$$g(t)*j(-j\pi t)^{-1} \Rightarrow G(f)j\operatorname{sgn} f$$

which is identical with (11).

Thus the Hilbert transform has components of the same amplitudes and frequencies as the original waveform but in phase quadrature. The stipulation that there be zero d.c. component is made to avoid ambiguity, the Hilbert transform of any constant being zero.

*Corollary* The positive and negative frequency components of a spectrum have the transforms

$$G(f)U(f) \Leftarrow \tfrac{1}{2}g(t) - \tfrac{1}{2}j\hat{g}(t) \equiv g_+(t) \tag{12}$$

$$G(f)U(-f) \Leftarrow \tfrac{1}{2}g(t) + \tfrac{1}{2}j\hat{g}(t) \equiv g_-(t) \tag{13}$$

EXAMPLE   For the sinusoid $g(t) = \cos 2\pi F t$,

$$\hat{g}(t) = -\sin 2\pi F t, \qquad g_+(t) = \tfrac{1}{2}e^{j2\pi F t}, \qquad g_-(t) = \tfrac{1}{2}e^{-j2\pi F t}$$

*Definition 4*: Let $g(t)$ be a real waveform with zero d.c. component. The corresponding analytic signal is

$$g(t) - j\hat{g}(t)$$

It is common to use the complex exponential form of a sinusoid for signal analysis; the analytic signal is a generalisation of this practice, useful in modulation theory. Clearly, from (12), it has a single-sided spectrum.

EXERCISES   (i) Show that the waveforms $g(t)$ and $\hat{g}(t)$ have the same autocorrelation function.
(ii) In the examples of Figure 2.7.1 the Hilbert transform of an even function is odd, and vice versa. Prove that this is a general rule.

Expressing the analytic signal in polar coordinates, we obtain an envelope and a phase, analogous to the amplitude and argument of a sinusoid but defined for an arbitrary signal.

*Definition 5*: Let $g(t)$ be a real waveform with zero d.c. component, and $\hat{g}(t)$ its Hilbert transform. Then the *envelope* of the signal is

$$r(t) = \{[g(t)]^2 + [\hat{g}(t)]^2\}^{1/2} \tag{14}$$

and the *phase* is

$$\theta(t) = -\tan^{-1}\frac{\hat{g}(t)}{g(t)} \tag{15}$$

It follows immediately that

$$g(t) = r(t)\cos\theta(t), \qquad \hat{g}(t) = -r(t)\sin\theta(t) \tag{16}$$

$$g_+(t) = \tfrac{1}{2}r(t)e^{j\theta(t)}, \qquad g_-(t) = \tfrac{1}{2}r(t)e^{-j\theta(t)} \tag{17}$$

Note that without some such device we cannot unambiguously assign an amplitude envelope to a modulated carrier; the first of Equations (16) if taken alone is compatible with an infinity of pairs $(r, \theta)$.

EXAMPLE   Consider an amplitude-modulated signal

$$g(t) = s(t)\cos(2\pi\alpha t + \phi)$$

where $s(t) \Rightarrow S(f)$ is strictly band-limited to $|f| < \alpha$. Then the positive frequency content comprises only the shifted baseband $\frac{1}{2}e^{i\phi}S(f - \alpha)$ whose Fourier transform is

$$g_+(t) = \frac{1}{2}s(t)e^{j(2\pi\alpha t + \phi)} \tag{18}$$

whence

$$\hat{g}(t) = -s(t)\sin(2\pi\alpha t + \phi)$$

$$r(t) = s(t), \qquad \theta(t) = 2\pi\alpha t + \phi$$

This signal is double-sideband, in that its spectrum extends both above and below the carrier frequency as in Figure 2.3.3. From the single-sided property of the analytic signal, we can define a modulated wave having only an upper sideband, for instance

$$g(t) = s(t)\cos 2\pi\alpha t + \hat{s}(t)\sin 2\pi\alpha t \tag{19}$$

This has a positive component

$$g_+(t) = \frac{1}{2}[s(t) - j\hat{s}(t)]e^{j2\pi\alpha t}$$

Writing $r_s(t)$, $\theta_s(t)$ for the envelope and phase of $s(t)$, the envelope and phase of the single-sideband wave are

$$r(t) = r_s(t), \qquad \theta(t) = 2\pi\alpha t + \theta_s(t)$$

EXERCISE   Prove that (19) has an upper sideband only. Find an expression for a signal with lower sideband only. (Hint: consider the baseband analytic signal translated in frequency by modulation on a complex carrier $e^{j2\pi\alpha t}$.) Examine the waveforms and spectra of modulated waves comprising upper, lower or double sidebands in the special case of sinusoidal modulation.

## Quadrature components

In formulating the analytic signal we have used components in phase quadrature and constrained by a definite relationship. It is often useful in modulation theory to partition an arbitrary signal into quadrature components, expressing it in the form

$$g(t) = g_1(t)\cos 2\pi\alpha t + g_2(t)\sin 2\pi\alpha t \tag{20}$$

for some carrier frequency $\alpha$. In general the components $g_1(t)$, $g_2(t)$

may be quite independent, though they will often occupy the same frequency band and have similar statistical properties. How may such components be extracted from a given composite signal $g(t)$?

There is one obvious pair of components

$$g_1(t) = g(t)\cos 2\pi\alpha t$$

$$g_2(t) = g(t)\sin 2\pi\alpha t \tag{21}$$

which satisfy Equation (20) for arbitrary $g(t)$ and $\alpha$. However, if we think of $g(t) \Rightarrow G(f)$ as a narrow-band signal centred on frequency $\alpha$, it seems plausible that $g_1(t)$ and $g_2(t)$ should be confined to a low-frequency region: which expressions (21) manifestly are not. A more useful formulation is given in the following theorem.

*Theorem 5*: Let

$$g(t) = g_1(t)\cos 2\pi\alpha t + g_2(t)\sin 2\pi\alpha t \tag{22}$$

be a band-limited signal confined to the frequency region $||f| - \alpha| < \beta < \alpha$. Let $H(f) \Leftarrow h(t)$ be a low-pass filter whose response is zero outside the band $|f| < \beta$. Then

$$g_1(t)*h(t) = 2[g(t)\cos 2\pi\alpha t]*h(t) \tag{23}$$

$$g_2(t)*h(t) = 2[g(t)\sin 2\pi\alpha t]*h(t) \tag{24}$$

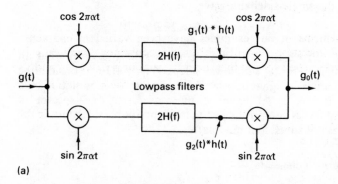

(a)

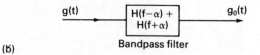

(b)

*Figure 2.7.2 Quadrature components*

*Proof*   Substituting (22) in the right hand side of (23) gives

$$h(t)^*\{g_1(t)[1+\cos 4\pi\alpha t] + g_2(t)\sin 4\pi\alpha t\} = h(t)^*g_1(t)$$

the terms in $\cos 4\pi\alpha t$, $\sin 4\pi\alpha t$ being filtered out by $H(f)$. Similarly Equation (24) gives

$$h(t)^*\{g_1(t)\sin 4\pi\alpha t + g_2(t)[1 - \cos 4\pi\alpha t]\} = h(t)^*g_2(t)$$

*Corollary (1)*   Let $H(f) = \text{rect}(f/2\beta)$. Then equations (23), (24) give simply $g_1(t)$, $g_2(t)$.

*Corollary (2)*   Lowpass and symmetrical bandpass filtering operations are interchangeable, if the signals are band-limited as prescribed in the theorem. For we can generate the filtered quadrature components according to Equations (23), (24) and re-modulate on to quadrature carriers, as in Figure 2.7.2; the output $g_0(t)$ is identical with the output of the bandpass filter shown.

EXERCISE   Why does Corollary (2) fail (a) if the signal is not band-limited (b) if the bandpass filter is not symmetrical (c) if either branch of the circuit in Figure 2.7.2(a) be omitted?

## 2.8 ASYMPTOTIC PROPERTIES OF SIGNALS AND SPECTRA

The waveforms in our examples have been varied in character, including impulses, discontinuities and continuous functions of several types. Their spectra have been correspondingly varied and, in particular, have exhibited asymptotic behaviour related to the smoothness of the waveforms, insofar as we can judge the latter intuitively. Some examples are displayed in Table 2.8.1 and Figure 2.8.1. They suggest a definition of smoothness, and a theorem concerning asymptotes.

*Definition 1*: if a function and its first $n-1$ derivatives are continuous but the $n$th derivative is discontinuous, the function has smoothness of order $n$ ($n \geqslant 1$). If a function and its first $m$ integrals are discontinuous but the $(m+1)$th integral is continuous, the function has smoothness of order $-m$ ($m \geqslant 0$).

It is assumed that appropriate derivatives and integrals are Fourier-transformable, and that the number of points of discontinuity is finite or denumerably infinite.

**Table 2.8.1** ASYMPTOTIC BEHAVIOUR OF SPECTRA

| Waveform property | Waveform | Spectrum | Spectrum asymptote |
|---|---|---|---|
| Impulsive | $\delta(t)$ | $1$ | $O(1)$ |
| Discontinuous | sgn $t$ | $(j\pi f)^{-1}$ | $O(f^{-1})$ |
| | rect $t$ | sinc $f$ | |
| Continuous but with discontinuous derivative | $\{1-|t|\}\,\text{rect}(\tfrac{1}{2}t)$ | $\text{sinc}^2 f$ | $O(f^{-2})$ |
| | $\cos(\pi t)\,\text{rect}(t)$ | $\dfrac{2\cos(\pi f)}{\pi(1-4f^2)}$ | |
| Continuous waveform and first derivative, second derivative discontinuous | $\tfrac{1}{2}(1+\cos \pi t)\,\text{rect}(\tfrac{1}{2}t)$ | $\dfrac{\text{sinc } 2f}{1-4f^2}$ | $O(f^{-3})$ |
| All derivatives continuous | $e^{-\pi t}$ | $e^{-\pi f^2}$ | $o(f^{-n})$ for all $n$ |

*Theorem 1*: let $g(t)$ be a real function with smoothness of order $n$. Then the asymptotic behaviour of its Fourier transform is

$$G(f) = O(f^{-n-1})$$

*Proof* Suppose the theorem to be true for some specific $n$, and consider any function $g(t) \Rightarrow G(f)$ with smoothness of order $n+1$. Its derivative

$$g'(t) \Rightarrow j2\pi f G(f)$$

has smoothness of order $n$, so by hypothesis its spectrum is $O(f^{-n-1})$; thus $G(f) = O(f^{-n-2})$, and the theorem is true for order $n+1$. Now consider a function with smoothness of order $n-1$. The convolution

$$g(t) * \text{rect } t \Rightarrow G(f)\,\text{sinc} f$$

has smoothness of order $n$, so by hypothesis its spectrum is $O(f^{-n-1})$: thus $G(f) = O(f^{-n})$, and the theorem is true for order $n-1$. But the theorem is obviously true for $n = 0$, since a function with smoothness of order zero can be represented as a sum of terms of the form $\text{sgn } t \Rightarrow (j\pi f)^{-1}$ together with a function of greater smoothness. By induction, it is true for all $n$.

*Corollary* if $G(f)$ has smoothness of order $n$, then $g(t) = O(t^{-n-1})$.

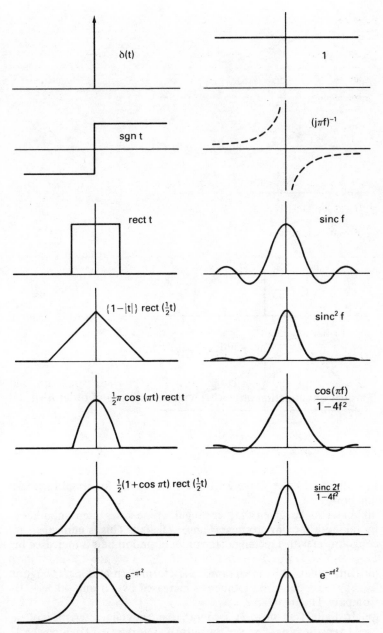

*Figure 2.8.1 Fourier transforms of Table 2.8.1*

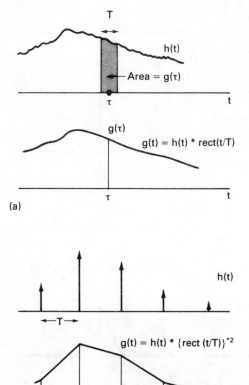

(a)

(b)

*Figure 2.8.2 Moving averages*

EXAMPLES    (i) See Table 2.8.1 and Figure 2.8.1 for several specific functions.

(ii)  A statistician given a rather irregular time series often smoothes it by taking a moving average (Figure 2.8.2(a)). This is equivalent to convolution with a rectangle; the order of smoothness is increased by 1.

(iii)  Interpolation between samples is a form of smoothing. In Figure 2.8.2(b) the order of smoothness is increased by 2 (from $-1$ to $+1$). Compare Theorem 2.5.7.

(iv)  In digital transmission, a smooth frequency characteristic is often used to ensure rapid decay of the pulse waveforms; see Theorem 2.5.2.

EXERCISE    A frequency-shift-keyed data signal might take the form of a uniform discrete signal with elements

$$\cos\left(\frac{4\pi t}{T}+\phi_1\right)\text{rect}\left(\frac{t}{T}\right),\qquad \cos\left(\frac{6\pi t}{T}+\phi_2\right)\text{rect}\left(\frac{t}{T}\right)$$

signifying (binary) 0 and 1 respectively. Draw the element waveforms for various values of the phases $\phi_1,\phi_2$. Find values of $\phi_1,\phi_2$ for which the spectrum of an arbitrary message vanishes asymptotically as $f^{-1}$, $f^{-2}$ and $f^{-3}$ respectively.

This quantification of smoothness, though significant in the present context, is perhaps not entirely in accord with intuition. For example, the choice of averaging period affects the general appearance of a moving average, but not the order of smoothness as defined. It is possible to smooth a signal to arbitrary order while still approximating the original waveform closely, using a filter with a suitable asymptote. Similarly, a change of asymptote is compatible with preservation of useful properties such as the ability to convey uniform discrete signals (Theorem 2.5.2). Nevertheless the concept of smoothness is often intuitively useful; moreover, in the sequel we shall develop it into a theory of asymptotic estimation.

*Non-integral powers*    The asymptotic powers in Theorem 1 and the examples are all integers; but we know that non-integer powers can occur. Consider the Bessel function $J_0()$ defined by Equation (2.4.27). The substitution $\sin\theta=f$, $z=2\pi t$ in this equation gives

$$J_0(2\pi t)=\frac{1}{\pi}\int_{-1}^{+1} e^{j2\pi ft}\frac{df}{(1-f^2)^{1/2}}$$

which is equivalent to the Fourier transform

$$J_0(2\pi t)\Rightarrow\frac{\text{rect}\,(\tfrac{1}{2}f)}{\pi(1-f^2)^{1/2}} \tag{1}$$

Application of Theorem 2.7.3 gives

$$U(t)J_0(2\pi t)\Rightarrow\frac{1}{2\pi(1-f^2)^{1/2}} \tag{2}$$

the right hand side being an analytic function whose real part is confined to the interval $|f|<1$ and is similar to the frequency function in (1). This is one of the standard transforms*

* Campbell and Foster, (1), no. 5/5.2

$$U(t)J_n(2\pi t) \Rightarrow \frac{1}{2\pi(1-f^2)^{1/2}[(1-f^2)^{1/2}+jf]^n} \tag{3}$$

which are useful in the theory of image-terminated lines and filters. We note from Equation (2.4.30) that asymptotically $J_n(2\pi t) = O(t^{-1/2})$, which is intermediate between the transforms of a discontinuity and an impulse. The functional $(1-f^2)^{-1/2}$ clearly diverges at $f = \pm 1$, but is not impulsive.

As a prelude to the general study of fractional powers we define a well-known standard function.

*Definition 2*: the *gamma function* is defined by

$$\Gamma(\alpha) = \int\limits_0^\infty x^{\alpha-1}e^{-x}dx \tag{4}$$

This function occurs in many areas of applied mathematics, including probability (see Section 4.2); its properties and numerical values are given in reference books. The only properties we shall use here are easily established, as follows:

(i) $\Gamma(1) = 1$ (an elementary integral)
(ii) $\Gamma(\tfrac{1}{2}) = \pi^{1/2}$ (with change of variable, the integrand becomes the Gaussian probability density of Equation 4.2.26)
(iii) $\Gamma(\alpha+1) = \alpha\Gamma(\alpha)$ (integrate by parts)
(iv) $\Gamma(n+1) = n!$ for positive integer $n$ (from i and iii)
(v) $\Gamma(\alpha)$ exists for all real $\alpha$ except non-positive integers (the defining integral clearly converges for $\alpha > 0$, which by property iii extends the definition to negative non-integers; the integral diverges for non-positive integers)

The defining integral is reminiscent of the Laplace transform, Definition 2.3.7; it is this which serves our immediate purpose of investigating the transforms of fractional powers. For, under the Laplace transform

$$t^{\alpha-1} \overset{\mathscr{L}}{\Rightarrow} \Gamma(\alpha)s^{-\alpha} \tag{5}$$

which follows immediately on substituting $x = st$ in the integral (4). The relationship between exponents of $t$ and $s$, which is crucial to our present argument, depends not on any esoteric properties of the gamma function but simply on the scaling of the variables. A further change of variable takes the Laplace into the Fourier transform. Some care is needed in dealing with noninteger powers of complex quantities, so we write

$$s = j2\pi f = 2\pi |f| e^{j\frac{1}{2}\pi \operatorname{sgn} f}$$

which gives the Fourier transform

$$U(t)t^{\alpha-1} \Rightarrow \frac{\Gamma(\alpha)e^{-j\frac{1}{2}\pi\alpha\operatorname{sgn} f}}{(2\pi|f|)^{\alpha}} \tag{6}$$

unless $\alpha$ is an integer $\leqslant 1$. It is easy to deduce transforms such as

$$|t|^{-1/2} \Rightarrow |f|^{-1/2} \tag{7}$$

$$|t|^{-1/2}\operatorname{sgn} t \Rightarrow -j|f|^{-1/2}\operatorname{sgn} f \tag{8}$$

by combining terms of the form (6).

In the light of these results, it seems reasonable to extend the definition of smoothness to include non-integer orders:

*Definition 1A*: If a function and its first $n-1$ derivatives are continuous but the $n$th derivative diverges in the vicinity of some point $t_m$ as $|t-t_m|^{-\beta}$ then the function has smoothness of order $n-\beta$.

The transform (6) shows that Theorem 1 remains true under this extended definition.

*Asymptotic estimation*    It is clear from Theorem 1 and from the examples cited that the asymptotic behaviour of the transform is critically dependent on the behaviour of the original function at isolated points which are called *singularities*.

*Definition 3*: A function $g(t)$ is said to have a finite number of singularities $t=t_m$ $(m=1,2,\dots M)$ if in any interval not including one of the $t_m$ it is everywhere differentiable any number of times (in the ordinary sense of differentiation). Associated with each singularity $t_m$ is a singularity function $g_m(t)$ whose only singularity is at $t_m$, chosen so that $g(t)-g_m(t)$ is smoother than $g_m(t)$ over an interval including $t_m$.

By the 'ordinary sense of differentiation' we exclude the sequence definition under which for example $U'(t)=\delta(t)$; thus $g(t)$ is continuous and has continuous derivatives except at the points $t_m$. The purpose of the singularity functions $g_m(t)$ is to approximate the behaviour of $g(t)$ in the vicinity of $t_m$. The repertoire of functions clearly includes $U(t-t_m)$ and $\operatorname{sgn}(t-t_m)$: $\delta(t-t_m)$: $\delta'(t-t_m)$ and other higher-order impulses obtained by differentiation of the defining sequence (2.2.3): $U(t)t^{\alpha}, |t|^{\alpha}, |t|^{\alpha}\operatorname{sgn} t$ for any real $\alpha$ other than the non-positive integers.

There are also other types of singularity, such as $|t|^x \log|t|$, which we have not discussed.* Using these concepts, the fundamental theorem of asymptotic estimation may be stated as follows.

*Theorem 2*: Let $g(t)$ be an absolutely integrable function with a finite number of singularities $t_m$. Let the behaviour at $t_m$ be approximated by a singularity function $g_m(t)$, leaving a remainder $g(t) - g_m(t)$ with smoothness of order $n$ in an interval including $t_m$. Then asymptotically as $f \to \infty$

$$G(f) \approx \sum_{m=1}^{M} G_m(f) + O(f^{-n-1}) \qquad (9)$$

*Proof*  The requirement that $g(t)$ be absolutely integrable eliminates d.c. or periodic terms. The asymptotic components are those of the $G_m(f) \Leftarrow g_m(t)$, and of the transform of the remainder $g(t) - \sum g_m(t)$. This remainder is by definition smooth with order $n$ in the vicinity of each $t_m$, and has no singularities elsewhere; its asymptote is therefore bounded by Theorem 1.

*Corollary*  By reciprocity, the asymptotes of $g(t)$ can be derived from the singularities of $G(f)$.

EXAMPLE   We illustrate the method with an example which can be checked against the exact transform. The frequency function

$$G(f) = \pi^{-1}(1 - f^2)^{-1/2} \, \text{rect}(\tfrac{1}{2}f)$$

has singularities at $f = \pm 1$. In the vicinity of $-1$ it can be expanded in series

$$G(f) = \frac{U(1+f)}{\pi} \left\{ \frac{1}{2^{1/2}(1+f)^{1/2}} + O[(1+f)^{1/2}] \right\}$$

The dominant singularity is

$$G_1(f) = \frac{U(1+f)}{2^{1/2}\pi(1+f)^{1/2}} \Leftarrow g_1(t) = e^{j2\pi t} \left\{ \frac{1 - j \, \text{sgn} \, t}{2^{3/2}\pi|t|^{1/2}} \right\}$$

The singularity at $+1$ similarly gives rise to $G_2(f) = G_1(-f) \Leftarrow g_1(-t)$. It follows that as $t \to \infty$

$$g(t) \approx g_1(t) + g_1(-t) + O(t^{-3/2})$$
$$= \pi^{-1} t^{-1/2} \cos(2\pi t - \tfrac{1}{4}\pi) + O(t^{-3/2}) \qquad (10)$$

---

* Lighthill (1), Chapter 3 gives a thorough treatment of all types of singularity.

From the transform (1), however, we know that $g(t) = J_0(2\pi t)$; and the leading term of its asymptotic expansion, Equation (2.4.30), agrees precisely with the present estimate.

Figure 2.8.3 shows the functions $G(f)$ and $g(t)$ together with their approximations.

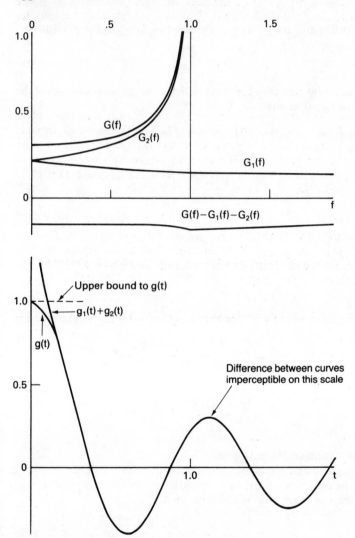

*Figure 2.8.3 Asymptotic estimation example*

*Moments and bounds* Another approximation, complementing the asymptotic expression derived above, is the power series about the origin:

$$G(f) = \sum_{n=0}^{\infty} c_n f^n \tag{11}$$

The coefficients are by Taylor's theorem related to the derivatives

$$c_n = \frac{G^{(n)}(0)}{n!} \tag{12}$$

We shall show that they are also related to the global properties of the original function $g(t)$.

*Theorem 3*: If $G(f) \Leftarrow g(t)$ has a power series (11) then the coefficients are

$$c_n = \frac{(-j2\pi)^n}{n!} \int_{-\infty}^{\infty} t^n g(t) dt \tag{13}$$

*Remark* The integral converges only if $g(t) = o(t^{-n-1})$. This implies, by the converse of Theorem 1, that $G(f)$ has smoothness of order $> n$, which is a necessary condition for the $n$th derivative $G^{(n)}(f)$ to be continuous.

*Proof* (a) Expanding Equation (2.3.5) in power series

$$\sum_{n=0}^{\infty} c_n f^n = \int_{-\infty}^{\infty} g(t) \sum_{n=0}^{\infty} \frac{(-j2\pi f t)^n}{n!} dt$$

$$= \sum_{n=0}^{\infty} \frac{(-j2\pi f)^n}{n!} \int_{-\infty}^{\infty} t^n g(t) dt$$

and equating coefficients gives (13).
(b) For a similar proof in a probabilistic context see Theorem 4.2.4. The integrals in (13) are the moments of the function $g(t)$; compare the moments of a distribution, Definition 4.1.5.

*Corollary* By reciprocity, a power series for $g(t)$ has in its coefficients the moments of $G(f)$.

EXERCISE   Let  $G(f) = \pi^{-1}(1-f^2)^{-1/2}\operatorname{rect}(\tfrac{1}{2}f)$.  Show  that  $g(t) = 1 - \pi^2 t^2 + O(t^4)$. Note that this matches the waveform $g(t) = J_0(2\pi t)$ very closely in the region near the origin where the asymptotic expression (10) diverges.

A somewhat similar theorem enables us to set upper bounds to a transform and its derivatives, with a similar reservation that the original function must exhibit suitable convergence.

*Theorem 4*: Let $g(t) \Rightarrow G(f)$. Then the transform $G(f)$ and its derivatives $G^{(n)}(f)$ are bounded by

$$|G^{(n)}(f)| \leqslant (2\pi)^n \int_{-\infty}^{\infty} |t^n g(t)| dt \qquad (14)$$

*Proof*   By Theorem 2.3.7

$$G^{(n)}(f) \Leftarrow (-j2\pi t)^n g(t)$$

On substitution in the defining integral (2.3.5)

$$|G^{(n)}(f)| = \left| \int_{-\infty}^{\infty} (-j2\pi t)^n g(t) e^{-j2\pi f t} dt \right| \leqslant \int_{-\infty}^{\infty} |(-j2\pi t)^n g(t)| dt$$

which is the inequality (14).

*Corollary (1)*   By reciprocity, $g(t)$ and its derivatives can be bounded in terms of $G(f)$.

*Corollary (2)*   Let $G(f)$ be band-limited to an interval $|f| \leqslant F$. Then

$$|g^{(n)}(t)| \leqslant (2\pi)^n \int_{-F}^{F} |f^n G(f)| df \leqslant (2\pi F)^n \int_{-F}^{F} |G(f)| df$$

That is to say, if $G(f)$ is absolutely integrable (always true in any physical case) the waveform and all its derivatives are bounded.

## 2.9  DISCRETE AND FINITE TRANSFORMS

We have seen in Sections 2.4 and 2.5 that series of discrete quantities may be encountered in the theory of communication signals, via the operations of repetition and sampling which occur naturally in any system employing discrete signals and indeed may arise in others as incidental to modulation or scanning. Much of the theory of discrete communication systems is a hybrid of continuous and discrete methods, of which Section 2.5 gives a fair taste. However, with the increasing use of digital processing both within communication systems, and as a means of simulating or estimating their performance, we need to be equally familiar with techniques of an uncompromisingly discrete nature. Most of the material is implicit in our general theory (which is, by design, equally applicable to continuous or discrete special cases, or to any mixture). It will perhaps be useful to bring it out explicitly. We begin by developing the $z$-transform, which is discrete in one domain and continuous in the other; and later proceed to a transform which is discrete in both domains.

## The $z$-transform

*Definition 1*: Let $\{h_n\}$ be a series of numbers, which may or may not be samples of a continuous function $h(t)$ such that $h_n = h(nT)$. The $z$-transform of $\{h_n\}$ or $h(t)$ is

$$\mathscr{H}(z) = \sum_{n=-\infty}^{\infty} h_n z^{-n} \qquad (1)$$

where $z$ is a variable which may have any real or complex value such that (1) converges either in the classical sense or by the sequence techniques of section 2.2. If $h(t)$ has a discontinuity at $t = nT$ then $h_n = h(nT+)$, the limit of $h(t)$ taken from the right. We shall use the notations

$$\{h_n\} \overset{z}{\Rightarrow} \mathscr{H}(z), \qquad h(t) \overset{:.T}{\Rightarrow} \mathscr{H}(z) \qquad (2)$$

If the $h_n$ are samples, then the $z$-transform is a special case of the pulse-sequence function; for by comparison with Equation (2.5.20) $\mathscr{H}(z) = \mathscr{H}(f, 0+)$ if we identify $z = e^{j2\pi fT}$. Even for quite general sequences $\{h_n\}$ we can write

$$\sum_n h_n \delta(t - nT) \Rightarrow \sum_n h_n e^{-j2\pi fnT} = \mathscr{H}(e^{j2\pi fT}) \qquad (3)$$

so for values of $z$ on the unit circle, any $z$-transform can be interpreted as the Fourier transform of a series of impulses. As such it is necessarily periodic in $f$.

More generally, we can identify $z = e^{sT}$ where $s$ is the Laplace-transform variable of Definition 2.3.7, which reduces to $j2\pi f$ if only real frequencies are in question. Then for all meaningful $z$ the $z$-transform can be interpreted as a Laplace transform of a pulse sequence.

Some authorities define a single-sided $z$-transform, with the lower limit of summation $n=0$. We shall indicate this range, where necessary, by means of the discrete step function.

*Definition 2*: The discrete step function $\{u_n\}$ is defined by

$$u_n = 0, \qquad n < 0 : u_n = 1, \qquad n \geqslant 0 \tag{4}$$

The discrete impulse $\{\delta_n\}$ is defined by

$$\delta_n = 1, \qquad n = 0 : \delta_n = 0, \qquad n \neq 0 \tag{5}$$

Many results both general and specific can be derived either directly from Definition 1 or by use of the Fourier or Laplace transform and the equivalence (3).

EXAMPLES   (i) A few specific $z$-transforms are

$$\{u_n\} \overset{z}{\Rightarrow} \frac{1}{1 - z^{-1}} \tag{6}$$

$$\{\delta_n\} \overset{z}{\Rightarrow} 1 \tag{7}$$

$$\{u_n a^n\} \overset{z}{\Rightarrow} \frac{1}{1 - az^{-1}} \tag{8}$$

$$U(t)e^{-\lambda t} \overset{z,T}{\Rightarrow} \frac{1}{1 - z^{-1}e^{-\lambda T}} \tag{9}$$

the last of which follows either from (8) or from (2.5.25).

(ii) Given any $\{h_n\} \overset{z}{\Rightarrow} \mathscr{H}(z)$ for which the respective series are defined, the following relationships are true:

$$\{h_{n-r}\} \overset{z}{\Rightarrow} z^{-r}\mathscr{H}(z) \tag{10}$$

which is the counterpart of the time-domain shift (2.3.13);

$$\{nh_n\} \overset{z}{\Rightarrow} -z\mathscr{H}'(z) \tag{11}$$

which is the counterpart of frequency-domain differentiation (2.3.32);

$$\{a^n h_n\} \overset{z}{\Rightarrow} \mathscr{H}(a^{-1}z) \tag{12}$$

which (with a little more interpretive effort than for the previous two operations) is the counterpart of the frequency-domain shift (2.3.14);

$$\{h_{-n}\} \overset{z}{\Rightarrow} \mathscr{H}(z^{-1}) \tag{13}$$

which is obvious from Equation (1) and is related to the similarity Theorem (2.3.10).

EXERCISE   (i) Prove that

$$\{u_n e^{-\alpha n} \cos \beta n\} \overset{z}{\Rightarrow} \frac{z(z - e^{-\alpha}\cos \beta)}{z^2 - 2ze^{-\alpha}\cos \beta + e^{-2\alpha}} \tag{14}$$

(ii) Find the inverse transform of

$$\frac{24 - 16z^{-1}}{8 - 10z^{-1} + 3z^{-2}}$$

Hint: resolve into partial fractions.

There is an inversion theorem, analogous to those for the Fourier and Laplace transforms, and like the latter requiring contour integration in the complex plane; this is treated in several standard works.* We shall not go into it here, as our need for inverse $z$-transforms is satisfied by the use of standard results derived in the forward sense, or by Fourier inversion.

Two properties of particular importance call for formal definition and proof.

*Definition 3*: The discrete convolution

$$\{f_n\} = \{g_n\} * \{h_n\}$$

is defined by

$$f_n = \sum_r g_r h_{n-r} = \sum_r g_{n-r} h_r \tag{15}$$

This is equivalent to Definition 2.2.4 if the discrete sequences be

---

* A comprehensive treatment of the $z$-transform is Jury (1). Bracewell, in his book on the Fourier transform, includes sections on related transforms including the $z$-transform. There are several books on digital signal processing relevant to the whole of this section; my personal favourite is Oppenheim and Schafer (1).

interpreted as impulse sequences of the form (3).

*Theorem 1*: If $\{g_n\} \overset{z}{\Rightarrow} \mathcal{G}(z)$ and $\{h_n\} \overset{z}{\Rightarrow} \mathcal{H}(z)$ then

$$\{g_n\}*\{h_n\} \overset{z}{\Rightarrow} \mathcal{G}(z)\mathcal{H}(z) \tag{16}$$

*Proof* (i) Multiply two series of the form (1) and collect terms of like degree.

(ii) The result also follows from Theorem 2.3.6 on using the representation (3) for each sequence.

(iii) The $z$-transform is closely related to the generating function used in probability and combinatorial theory. For a proof in a probabilistic context see Theorem 4.2.1.

EXERCISE    Show that

$$\{a^{|n|}\} = (1-a^2)\{u_n a^n\}*\{u_{-n}a^{-n}\} \overset{z}{\Rightarrow} \frac{1-a^2}{(1-az^{-1})(1-az)} \tag{17}$$

Verify the transform by another method.

The properties of continuous linear systems are naturally expressed in linear differential equations, which by virtue of Theorem 2.3.7 can be converted by the Fourier or Laplace transforms into algebraic equations as an aid to solution. The properties of discrete linear systems are commonly expressed as difference equations, which can be solved in a similar way using the $z$-transform. It is possible to develop a theory of difference equations using the forward and backward differences of numerical analysis as the discrete counterparts of derivatives. In our present context, however, the structure of a discrete processing system often prescribes a form of difference equation which can be solved directly, as follows.

A discrete processing system operates on an input sequence of samples $\{x_n\}$ and generates an output sequence $\{y_n\}$. There may, of course, be several inputs and outputs but we develop the basic theory in terms of the simplest case. If the system is linear and invariant then its structure is fixed and incorporates only the operations of (i) addition of samples present at the same time (ii) multiplication of a sample value by a constant (iii) storage or delay of samples enabling them to be used in a later position. We will indicate these operations in block diagrams on the model of Figure 2.9.1, where (a) shows the

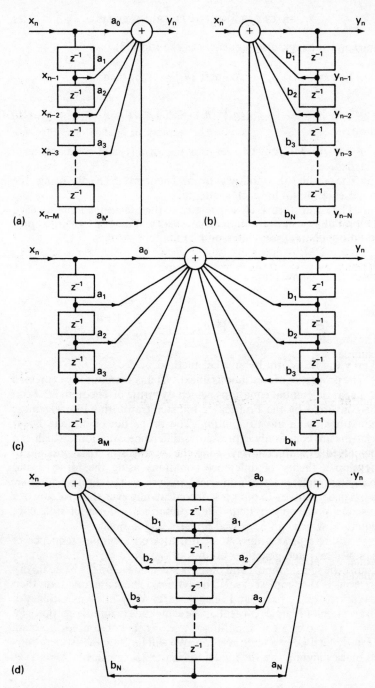

*Figure 2.9.1 Linear discrete processing structures*

mechanism for generating

$$y_n = \sum_{r=0}^{M} a_r x_{n-r} \tag{18}$$

The unit delay is denoted by $z^{-1}$, for reasons which will appear shortly. Let a discrete impulse be applied to such a structure, i.e. $\{x_n\} = \{\delta_n\}$. The output is

$$\begin{aligned} y_n &= a_n, \quad n = 0, 1, 2 \ldots M \\ &= 0, \quad \text{otherwise} \end{aligned} \tag{19}$$

This is known as a finite impulse structure (FIR), since the output due to an impulse vanishes after a finite number of steps.

Figure 2.9.1(b) shows a structure in which the current output $y_n$ depends on past output values $y_{n-r}$: specifically,

$$y_n = x_n + \sum_{r=1}^{N} b_r y_{n-r} \tag{20}$$

The impulse response of this structure continues indefinitely. For example if $N = 1$ we have

$$y_n = x_n + b_1 y_{n-1} \tag{21}$$

and the output corresponding to $\{x_n\} = \{\delta_n\}$ is

$$y_n = u_n b_1^n \tag{22}$$

If $|b_1| < 1$ then the system is stable but has an infinite impulse response (IIR).

Figure 2.9.1(c) shows a more general structure which combines both of the above types and so is clearly IIR. Its governing equation is

$$y_n = \sum_{r=1}^{N} b_r y_{n-r} + \sum_{r=0}^{M} a_r x_{n-r} \tag{23}$$

which we can solve by means of the $z$-transform. Applying the shift rule (10), the transformed equation is

$$\mathscr{Y}(z) = \sum_{r=1}^{N} b_r z^{-r} \mathscr{Y}(z) + \sum_{r=0}^{M} a_r z^{-r} \mathscr{X}(z) \tag{24}$$

This yields a transfer function relating input and output,

$$\mathscr{Y}(z) = \mathscr{X}(z) \mathscr{G}(z) \tag{25}$$

where

$$\mathcal{G}(z) = \frac{\sum_{r=0}^{M} a_r z^{-r}}{1 - \sum_{r=1}^{N} b_r z^{-r}} \equiv \frac{A(z^{-1})}{B(z^{-1})} \tag{26}$$

This transfer function is the product of two functions associated respectively with two structures in tandem; the FIR structure of Figure 2.9.1(a) has the transfer function $A(z^{-1})$, and the IIR structure of Figure 2.9.1(b) has the transfer function $1/B(z^{-1})$. There are many equivalent structures with a transfer function of the form (26), namely a ratio of polynomials in $z^{-1}$ (or $z$). A particularly interesting one is Figure 2.9.1(d), which by inverting the order of the tandem sections reduces the number of delay or storage elements required. Another obvious possibility is to factorise $\mathcal{G}(z)$ and partition the factors among tandem sections each of which may have any of the forms shown.[*]

Equation (26) is reminiscent of the description of linear lumped networks by polynomials in $s$, and indeed we can find the discrete impulse response by a method analogous to Theorem 2.3.10. In the discrete case we cannot assume that $N > M$, as it is not unusual for a long FIR structure to be incorporated.

*Theorem 2*: Let a discrete signal processor have the transfer function

$$\mathcal{G}(z) = \frac{A(z^{-1})}{B(z^{-1})} + \sum_j c_j z^{-j} \tag{27}$$

where $B(\ )$ is a polynomial of higher degree than $A(\ )$. Let $B(\ )$ have distinct roots $\gamma_k$ ($k = 1, 2, \ldots N$). Then the discrete impulse response of the processor is

$$\{g_n\} = \sum_{k=1}^{N} C_k \{u_n \gamma_k^{-n-1}\} + \sum_j c_j \{\delta_{n-j}\} \tag{28}$$

where the coefficients are

$$C_k = \left\{ (\gamma_k - z^{-1}) \frac{A(z^{-1})}{B(z^{-1})} \right\}_{z^{-1} = \gamma_k} \tag{29}$$

*Proof*   The discrete impulse response is, of course, the inverse $z$-

---

[*] For a further discussion of equivalent structures see Oppenheim and Schafer (1), Chapter 4.

transform of $\mathcal{G}(z)$. The inversion depends on the partial fraction expansion

$$\frac{A(z^{-1})}{B(z^{-1})} = \sum_{k=1}^{N} \frac{C_k}{\gamma_k - z^{-1}}$$

with coefficients (29) similar in form to those of Theorem 2.3.10. The inverse $z$-transform of each term follows from (8).

EXAMPLE   In the structure of Figure 2.9.1(d) let $N = M = 2$, with coefficients $a_0 = 4$; $a_1 = -13/4$; $a_2 = 3/8$; $b_1 = -5/4$; $b_2 = 3/8$. Then

$$\mathcal{G}(z) = \frac{32 - 26z^{-1} + 3z^{-2}}{8 - 10z^{-1} + 3z^{-2}} = 1 + \frac{2}{1 - \frac{1}{2}z^{-1}} + \frac{1}{1 - \frac{3}{4}z^{-1}}$$

$$\{g_n\} = \{\delta_n\} + 2\{(\tfrac{1}{2})^n\} + \{(\tfrac{3}{4})^n\}$$

of which the last two terms should be familiar if you worked out the preceding $z$-transform exercise.

The foregoing theory is widely applied to the design of digital filters.

## The discrete Fourier transform

If digital computation is to provide a counterpart to all our usual techniques of signal analysis and processing, we must have a transform which is discrete in both domains. It is natural to ask, whether the Fourier transform is valid if we take uniform samples both of the signal waveform and of the spectrum. Now from Theorem 2.4.1, sampling in one domain implies periodicity in the other; so sampling in both domains implies periodicity in both. Let us consider a waveform segment $h(t)$ of duration $T$, which is non-zero only in the interval $0 \leqslant t < T$ (note that the interval is chosen to include one and only one end-point). Let this be sampled at uniform intervals $T/N$, so that there are exactly $N$ samples in the interval. The sampled segment is

$$h(t)\,\text{rep}_{T/N}\,\delta(t) \Rightarrow \frac{N}{T}\,\text{rep}_{N/T}\,H(f) \tag{30}$$

where $H(f)$ is the spectrum of $h(t)$. Now let the segment be repeated, so as to produce a periodic signal of period $T$. The repeated sample train is

$$\text{rep}_T\{h(t)\,\text{rep}_{T/N}\delta(t)\} \Rightarrow \left\{\frac{N}{T}\,\text{rep}_{N/T}H(f)\right\}\frac{1}{T}\,\text{rep}_{1/T}\delta(f) \tag{31}$$

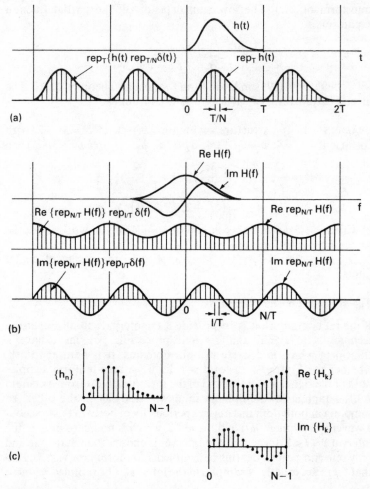

*Figure 2.9.2 Discrete Fourier transform*

The operation is illustrated in Figure 2.9.2 (a) and (b). The spectrum is periodic, with period $N/T$, and each period contains $N$ lines at uniform intervals $1/T$. Each line is a spectral sample, not just of the segment spectrum $H(f)$, but of this plus its repetitions; so we have the usual ambiguity property of sampling (Theorem 2.5.5). If $H(f)$ is concentrated mainly in a sufficiently narrow band, then the effect of the repetitions is small, and the samples are a good approximation in both domains; that is, for a sufficient number of samples $N$, interpolation between the time samples reconstructs a good approximation to $h(t)$, and interpolation between the frequency samples reconstructs a good approximation to $H(f)$.

Since (31) is periodic in both domains, we can represent it by a single period in each. Furthermore, each single period can be represented by a numerical sequence which we denote by $\{h_n\}$ and $\{H_k\}$ in time and frequency respectively:

$$h_n = h(nT/N), \qquad n = 0, 1, 2, \ldots N-1$$

$$H_k = H(k/T), \qquad k = 0, 1, 2, \ldots N-1 \tag{32}$$

illustrated in Figure 2.9.2(c). For a real waveform $h(t)$, the spectrum $H(f)$ may be complex but by Theorem 2.7.1 has Hermitean symmetry; that is, values in symmetrical locations are complex conjugates. It follows that the spectral samples may be complex, but have the symmetry relation

$$H_k^* = H_{N-k} \tag{33}$$

so that in each domain there are essentially $N$ independent magnitudes which specify the discrete signal.

Given a discrete sequence such as $\{h_n\}$ we can define its discrete Fourier transform as follows:

*Definition 4*: Let $\{h_n\}$, $n = 0, 1, 2, \ldots N-1$ be a real discrete sequence. Let the complex quantity $w_N$ be defined by

$$w_N = e^{-j2\pi/N} \tag{34}$$

Then the discrete Fourier transform of $\{h_n\}$ is the discrete sequence $\{H_k\}$, $k = 0, 1, 2, \ldots N-1$ defined by

$$H_k = \sum_{n=0}^{N-1} h_n w_N^{kn} \tag{35}$$

We shall use the notation $\{h_n\} \Rightarrow \{H_k\}$.

Theorem 2.4.4 shows that (35) is the Fourier series coefficient for the sampled periodic waveform (31), in the special case $T = 1$; so in this case the sequence $\{H_k\}$ is identical with that of equation (32). The parameter $T$ is, of course, irrelevant when operating on sequences in a purely numerical fashion, and we shall normally take it as 1 for convenience.

The inversion theorem for the discrete Fourier transform is:

*Theorem 3*: The sequence $\{h_n\}$ and its discrete Fourier transform

$\{H_k\}$ are related by the summation

$$h_n = \frac{1}{N} \sum_{k=0}^{N-1} H_k w_N^{-kn} \tag{36}$$

*Proof* (i) As $h_n$ and $H_k$ of Definition 4 can be identified with the time and frequency-domain samples of (31), we can apply Theorem 2.4.4 to show that (36) is a Fourier series coefficient for the periodic frequency function.

(ii) For a direct proof of the discrete relationship, without reference to the concept of sampling, take the sum on the right hand side of (36) and substitute for $H_k$ from (35). The result is

$$\frac{1}{N} \sum_{k=0}^{N-1} w_N^{-kn} \sum_{m=0}^{N-1} h_m w_N^{km} = \frac{1}{N} \sum_{m=0}^{N-1} h_m \sum_{k=0}^{N-1} w_N^{k(m-n)}$$

But by symmetry the right-hand sum is zero if $(m-n)$ is a non-zero integer; if $m=n$, the sum is $N$. Consequently, the only term remaining is $h_n$, which proves (36). This argument is a discrete counterpart to the second proof of Theorem 2.4.4.

Note that Definition 4 and Theorem 3 can be stated and proved without reference to sampling or periodicity. So it is quite legitimate to apply the discrete Fourier transform to a finite sequence, or to a set of samples from a waveform of short duration, without any implication that the sequence or waveform is repeated. However, there are some properties of the discrete Fourier transform which, though rather subtle if we confine ourselves to the direct approach, are obvious concomitants of periodicity.

EXAMPLE   The sequence

$$\begin{aligned} h_n &= 1, \qquad n = 0, 1, \dots M-1 \\ &= 0, \qquad n = M, M+1, \dots N-1 \end{aligned} \tag{37}$$

is a rectangular pulse of $M$ similar samples. Its transform is

$$H_k = \sum_{n=0}^{N-1} h_n w_N^{kn} = \sum_{n=0}^{M-1} w_N^{kn} = \frac{1 - w_N^{kM}}{1 - w_N^k}$$

Recalling the definition (34), this is

$$H_k = e^{-j\pi k(M-1)/N} \frac{\sin(\pi kM/N)}{\sin(\pi k/N)} \tag{38}$$

EXERCISE   Calculate and plot the foregoing example for $N = 16$,

$M = 1, 2, 4, 8$. Compare your results with (a) the spectrum of a continuous rectangular wave (b) a truncated Fourier series (see Theorem 2.4.6).

*Relationship to the z-transform*  Consider a discrete sequence $\{h_n\}$ of finite length $\leqslant N - 1$. Its z-transform is, by Definition 1

$$\mathscr{H}(z) = \sum_{h=-\infty}^{\infty} h_n z^{-n} = \sum_{n=0}^{N-1} h_n z^{-n}$$

Comparing this with Definition 4, we see that the frequency-domain elements of the discrete Fourier transform may be written as

$$H_k = \mathscr{H}(w_N^{-k}) = \mathscr{H}(e^{j2\pi k/N}) \tag{39}$$

namely the samples of the z-transform at $N$ uniformly-spaced points around the unit circle. We have already seen that the real frequency axis maps periodically on to the unit circle in the z-domain; so this is entirely consistent with periodic sampling in the frequency domain.

EXERCISE  Find the z-transform of the rectangular pulse (37), and check that the results of the previous exercise are consistent with it.

*Cyclic shift and convolution*  Among the most useful operations in continuous Fourier theory are shifting and convolution. They have their discrete counterparts, but with a difference.

*Definition 5*: Let $\{h_n\}$ be a discrete sequence of length $N$. Its *cyclic shift* by $+r$ or $-r$ places is a sequence $\{h_{n\oplus r}\}$ or $\{h_{n\ominus r}\}$ respectively, where the notation implies

$$n \oplus r = n + r \qquad \text{modulo } N$$

$$n \ominus r = n - r \qquad \text{modulo } N$$

This is also known as a circular or periodic shift. The example shown in Figure 2.9.3(a) demonstrates that the linear shift of a periodic sequence induces a cyclic shift within any one period.

When dealing with a finite sequence in the context of the discrete Fourier transform, the cyclic shift is the most natural one, as we shall see.

*Theorem 4*: Let $\{h_n\}$ be a discrete sequence with discrete Fourier transform $\{H_k\}$. Then

$$\{h_{n\oplus r}\} \Rightarrow \{w_N^{-kr} H_k\} \tag{40}$$

$$\{H_{k\oplus r}\} \Leftarrow \{w_N^{nr} h_n\} \tag{41}$$

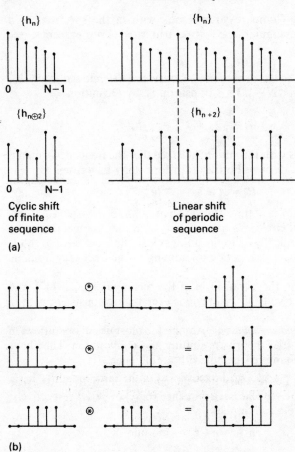

Figure 2.9.3 *Cyclic shift and convolution.* (a) Shift; (b) Convolution

*Proof* (i) Substituting $n \oplus r$ for $n$ in the transform (36) gives

$$\frac{1}{N}\sum_{k=0}^{N-1} H_k w_N^{-k(n \oplus r)}$$

From the definition (34), $w_N$ is the $N$th root of unity and its powers recur periodically. So

$$w_N^{-k(n \oplus r)} = w_N^{-k(n+r)}$$

the difference in the exponents being an integral multiple of $N$. The summation is therefore equal to

$$\frac{1}{N}\sum_{k=0}^{N-1}(w_N^{-kr}H_k)w_N^{-kn}$$

which proves (40). Proof of (41) is similar.

(ii) The result is a corollary of Theorem 2.3.3 if we interpret the cyclic shift as a linear shift of a periodic sequence.

Convolution depends on shifting operations, and so has to be redefined if shifts are interpreted cyclically.

*Definition 6*: Let $\{g_n\}$ and $\{h_n\}$ be discrete sequences of length $N$. Their *cyclic convolution* is a discrete sequence of the same length,

$$\{f_n\}=\{g_n\}\circledast\{h_n\}$$

whose elements are

$$f_n=\sum_{m=0}^{N-1}g_mh_{n\ominus m}=\sum_{m=0}^{N-1}g_{n\ominus m}h_m \tag{42}$$

This differs from the linear discrete convolution, Definition 3, in that all shifts are interpreted cyclically modulo $N$. It is illustrated in Figure 2.9.3(b) by way of examples. A special case worth noting is

$$\{g_n\}\circledast\{\delta_{n-m}\}=\{g_{n\ominus m}\} \tag{43}$$

which is the discrete counterpart of Equation (2.2.32).

*Theorem 5*: Let $\{g_n\}$, $\{h_n\}$ be sequences of the same length $N$, with discrete Fourier transforms $\{G_k\}$, $\{H_k\}$ respectively. Then

$$\{g_n\}\circledast\{h_n\}\Rightarrow\{G_kH_k\} \tag{44}$$

$$\{g_nh_n\}\Rightarrow\frac{1}{N}\{G_k\}\circledast\{H_k\} \tag{45}$$

*Proof* (i) The first convolution may be written as follows, and transformed by means of (40):

$$\sum_{m=0}^{N-1}h_m\{g_{n\ominus m}\}\Rightarrow\sum_{m=0}^{N-1}h_m\{w_N^{km}G_k\}$$

By Equation (36) the right hand side is

$$\frac{1}{N}\sum_{m=0}^{N-1}\sum_{q=0}^{N-1}H_qw_N^{-qm}\{w_N^{km}G_k\}$$

$$=\left\{G_k\sum_{q=0}^{N-1}H_q\frac{1}{N}\sum_{m=0}^{N-1}w_N^{(k-q)m}\right\}$$

By symmetry, the right-hand sum is zero if $(k-q)$ is a non-zero integer; if $k=q$, the sum is $N$. Consequently the only term remaining in the double summation is $H_k$, which proves (44). Proof of (45) is similar.

(ii) The result follows from Theorem 2.3.6 if we consider the convolution of one finite sequence with the periodic repetition of the other.

EXERCISE    Fill in the details of the second proof above. Why do we not consider the convolution of two periodic sequences?

*Accuracy and resolution of discrete processing*    The discrete Fourier transform may be used to simulate a continuous system numerically, or to estimate its performance. It may be used to implement a digital filter whose design has been based on a continuous analogue. In any of these applications, we need to know how closely the discrete system approximates its continuous counterpart.

One major discrepancy arises from sampling ambiguity (Theorem 2.5.5); frequency components separated by a multiple of the sampling rate are indistinguishable. This property is also known as *aliasing*, the implication being that frequency components outside the normal baseband are translated into it.

We can distinguish several types of signal processing, according as the input and output are in time or frequency domains:

(i)  Input time, output frequency; for example, spectral analysis of waveforms. See the block diagram of Figure 2.9.4(a).

(ii)  Input time, output time; for example digital filtering of waveforms. See the block diagram of Figure 2.9.4(b).

(iii)  Input frequency, output time; for example the synthesis of a waveform from spectral parameters. This is similar to (i) with the domains transposed.

(iv)  Input frequency, output frequency; for example, spectral analysis of modulation or demodulation processes incorporating time-domain multiplication. This is similar to (ii) with the domains transposed.

The cases (i) and (ii) shown in Figure 2.9.4 are of common occurrence, both in isolation and as blocks in larger systems; they are also a guide to the transposed cases (iii) and (iv).

The principal feature of case (i) follows from the transform (31). The discrete Fourier transform generates a replicated spectrum, on which any further operation is performed. For example, a narrow-band filter

133

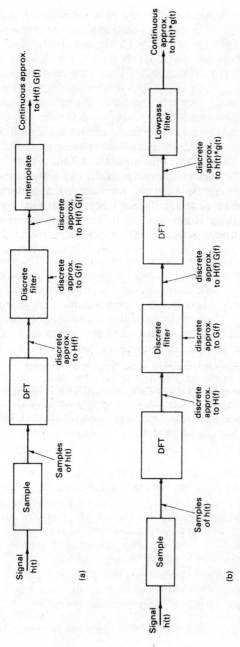

Figure 2.9.4 Signal processing using discrete Fourier transform. (a) Spectral analysis; (b) Filtering

$G(f)$ separates not just a narrow band of the original $H(f)$ but the superposition of a set of narrow bands spaced at intervals $N/T$. Since the spectrum is sampled at intervals $1/T$, spectral detail finer than this cannot be resolved. For any given $N$ there is a compromise between accuracy (which requires large $N/T$) and resolution (which requires small $1/T$).

Clearly the same factor enters into case (ii); but we can add another derived from Theorem 5. The processor generates the cyclic convolution of sample trains drawn from $g(t)$ and $h(t)$. This introduces a time-domain aliasing, which is confined to one period if $g(t)$ and $h(t)$ are themselves so confined; this implies that $T$ must be at least equal to the sum of the effective durations of the two waveforms, for high accuracy. Since the waveforms are sampled at intervals $T/N$, temporal detail finer than this cannot be resolved. If the waveforms decay gradually, as is common in practice, then again there is a compromise between accuracy and resolution.

*Computation of the discrete Fourier transform* The summations (35) and (36) imply that a transform comprises $N$ sums each of $N$ products; one or both factors in each product may be complex. An algorithm directly implementing these summations would call for approximately $N^2$ complex additions and multiplications. The accuracy/resolution compromise noted above is eased as $N$ becomes larger, but the increase in computing cost as $N^2$ is a powerful deterrent. Practical computational algorithms take advantage of the symmetry and periodicity of the factors to reduce the number of operations. There is a family of algorithms, with differences in detail but obvious similarity in principle, which require a number of operations of the order $N \log_2 N$; these are known collectively as the *fast Fourier transform* or FFT.

The significant properties are

(i) The Fourier coefficients $H_k$ have a symmetry relationship (33) which halves the number of magnitudes required to specify them.

(ii) From the definition (34), $w_N$ is an $N$th root of unity and its powers recur periodically. So the $2N^2$ factors $w_N^{\pm kn}$ used in the transform have only $N$ distinct values, including $w_N^0 = 1$. If $N$ is even, then $w_N^{\frac{1}{2}N+m} = -w_N^m$; multiplication by $-1$ being relatively simple, there are only $\frac{1}{2}N-1$ distinct complex factors.

(iii) The several coefficients are not independent; two or more coefficients may have partial sums in common, and by calculating these once for all many operations may be saved.

The last two properties emerge most obviously, and the algorithms are most efficient, if $N$ is a power of 2; the following explanation is confined to this case. The principle is to reduce the calculation by successive dichotomy: each $N$-point transform is represented as the combination of two $\frac{1}{2}N$-point transforms, and so on.

The summatuon (35) can be split into two partial sums, of the even and odd-numbered terms respectively:

$$H_k = \sum_{r=0}^{\frac{1}{2}N-1} h_{2r} w_N^{2kr} + \sum_{r=0}^{\frac{1}{2}N-1} h_{2r+1} w_N^{k(2r+1)} \tag{46}$$

Since $w_N^2 = w_{N/2}$ we can write this as

$$H_k = \sum_{r=0}^{\frac{1}{2}N-1} h_{2r} w_{N/2}^{kr} + w_N^k \sum_{r=0}^{\frac{1}{2}N-1} h_{2r+1} w_{N/2}^{kr} \tag{47}$$

The index $k$ ranges over $0, 1, 2, \ldots N-1$, but there is a relationship between coefficients in the upper and lower halves of the range. For if we substitute $k + \frac{1}{2}N$ for $k$ in Equation (47) and simplify powers of $w_{N/2}$, $w_N$ the result is

$$H_{k+\frac{1}{2}N} = \sum_{r=0}^{\frac{1}{2}N-1} h_{2r} w_{N/2}^{kr} - w_N^k \sum_{r=0}^{\frac{1}{2}N-1} h_{2r+1} w_{N/2}^{kr} \tag{48}$$

Now each of the summations in (47) and (48) is a discrete Fourier transform with $\frac{1}{2}N$ points. Moreover, the same transforms occur in both equations. The dichotomy has reduced the number of complex multiplications required to compute the transform. The procedure is shown in the signal flow graph, Figure 2.9.5(a), which is drawn for $N = 8$. Every node of this diagram is a summing node, which delivers to its output lines the sum of the signals on its input lines. The notation against a line is a multiplying factor, omitted if it is unity.

The dichotomy can be continued, with the $\frac{1}{2}N$-point transforms reduced to a pair of $\frac{1}{4}N$-point transforms, and so on. Figure 2.9.5(b) shows the complete signal flow graph for an 8-point transform. The only complex multiplying factors needed are $w_8$, $w_8^2$ ($= w_4$) and $w_8^3$. Generalisation to $N = 2^M$ should be obvious. There are $M = \log_2 N$ stages of dichotomy, each requiring $N$ additions and less than $N$ multiplications (of which $\frac{1}{2}N$ are just sign changes).

There is also another type of dichotomy. The summation (35) is split into two partial sums, with the index $n$ in the lower and upper halves of the range respectively:

$$H_k = \sum_{n=0}^{\frac{1}{2}N-1} h_n w_N^{kn} + (-1)^k \sum_{n=0}^{\frac{1}{2}N-1} h_{n+\frac{1}{2}N} w_N^{kn} \tag{49}$$

where we have used the fact that $w_N^{N/2} = -1$. Writing the even and odd

136

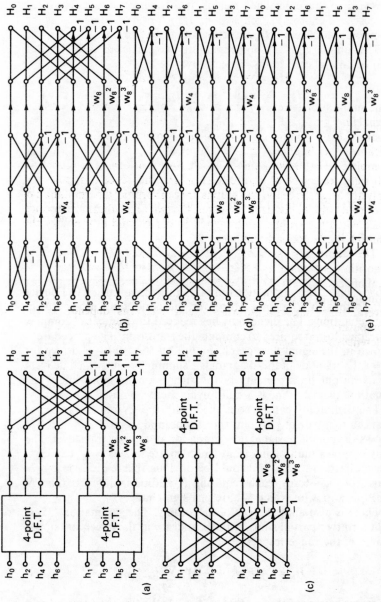

Figure 2.9.5 Fast Fourier transform algorithms

numbered terms separately, and simplifying powers of $w_N^2 = w_{N/2}$, gives

$$H_{2r} = \sum_{n=0}^{\frac{1}{2}N-1} (h_n + h_{n+N/2}) w_{N/2}^{rn} \tag{50}$$

$$H_{2r+1} = \sum_{n=0}^{\frac{1}{2}N-1} w_N^n (h_n - h_{n+N/2}) w_{N/2}^{rn} \tag{51}$$

The summations are $\frac{1}{2}N$-point discrete Fourier transforms, and the signal flow graph is Figure 2.9.5(c). This is dichotomy in frequency, as distinct from Figure 2.9.5(a) which is dichotomy in time. The dichotomy in frequency can be continued; Figure 2.9.5(d) shows the complete signal flow graph for an 8-point transform. The graph is a left/right transpose of Figure 2.9.5(b). The difference of topology is only apparent, since the two graphs are isomorphic; a permutation of the vertices in (b) gives (e). However, the two algorithms are distinct, since when the graphs are arranged to correspond in topology the multiplying factors are different.

The pioneering work of Cooley and Tukey (1) who gave an algorithm equivalent to Figure 2.9.5(e) has been followed by a good deal of development. The time-dichotomy and frequency-dichotomy principles can be generalised to any composite value of $N$. There are several other algorithms, whose relative merits depend on the computing mechanism postulated. For a summary and further references see Oppenheim and Schafer (1975), Chapter 6.

# Chapter 3

# Spatial and spatio-temporal patterns: multi-dimensional analysis

### 3.1 MULTI-DIMENSIONAL FUNCTIONS AND TRANSFORMS

In expounding one-dimensional signal analysis we have taken for granted the familiar properties of a mathematical function. By writing an expression such as $g(t)$ we imply that, given any value of the independent variable $t$, a corresponding value of the dependent variable may be found; and, following the practice of engineers rather than that of mathematicians, we have loosely used the notation $g(t)$ to signify either the dependent variable, or the functional relationship. To deal with patterns in space and in space–time, we must use functions of several variables; for simplicity we start with two dimensions only. The notation $g(x, y)$ implies that there are two independent variables $x$ and $y$: and that, given a pair of values for $x$ and $y$, a corresponding value of the dependent variable is defined. A one-dimensional function may be plotted as a graph; a two-dimensional function requires something more like a relief map (Figure 3.1.1). By an extension which is not difficult to conceive but, alas, virtually impossible to draw convincingly, we can consider functions of three or more variables.

EXERCISES    (i) Sketch a representation similar to Figure 3.1.1 for the following functions, choosing in each case some convenient intervals of $x$ and $y$:

$$\sin x \qquad \sin y \qquad \sin(x+y)$$

$$x \cos y \qquad y \cos x$$

$$(x^2 + y^2)^{1/2} \qquad e^{-(x^2 + y^2)}$$

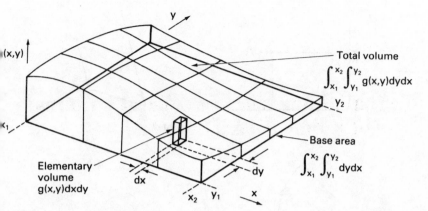

*Figure 3.1.1 Two-dimensional function*

(ii) Evaluate the integrals

$$\int_0^\pi \int_0^1 x \cos y \, dx \, dy \qquad \int_{-\infty}^\infty \int_{-\pi/2}^{\pi/2} \cos x \, e^{-\pi y^2} \, dx \, dy$$

Remarks: (a) The first function in (i) is independent of $y$, but nevertheless can be considered in two dimensions. (b) Some but not all functions of $x$ and $y$ can be expressed as a product of the form $g(x, y) = g_1(x)g_2(y)$: this is called 'separation of variables'. (c) The integrals are easily evaluated because the integrands are separable.

The position of a point in a plane may be defined by a pair of numbers in many ways (Figure 3.1.2), and we often need to transform from one coordinate system to another. General methods are given in textbooks of integral calculus; here we look at two common examples. The general linear transformation Figure 3.1.2(b) relates the variables by linear equations

$$x' = ax + by$$
$$y' = cx + dy \qquad (1)$$

which are easily inverted to yield

$$x = \Delta^{-1}dx' - \Delta^{-1}by'$$
$$y = -\Delta^{-1}cx' + \Delta^{-1}ay' \qquad (2)$$

where $\qquad\qquad \Delta = ad - bc$

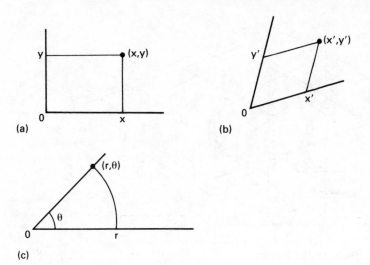

*Figure 3.1.2 Co-ordinate systems in a plane. (a) Rectangular cartesian; (b) Linear (non-rectangular) (c) polar*

To integrate with respect to transformed variables, we must know what element of area is implied by a notation such as $dx'dy'$. Consider the convex region bounded by the lines $x'=0$, $x'=1$, $y'=0$, $y'=1$: this is shown in Figure 3.1.3(a), together with the Cartesian coordinates of its vertices. By the dissection illustrated in Figures 3.1.3(b–d) we see that the area enclosed is

$$x_1 y_2 - x_2 y_1 = \Delta^{-1}$$

By similarity, the element indicated in Figure 3.1.3(e) has the area $\Delta^{-1} dx'dy'$. The volume of a solid such as that in Figure 3.1.1(b) is

$$\int\int h(x', y')\Delta^{-1} dx'dy' \tag{3}$$

where $h(x', y') = g(x, y)$ and the limits of integration are chosen appropriately.

Polar and rectangular coordinates are related by

$$r = (x^2 + y^2)^{1/2}$$
$$\theta = \tan^{-1}(y/x) \tag{4}$$

and inversely

$$x = r\cos\theta$$
$$y = r\sin\theta \tag{5}$$

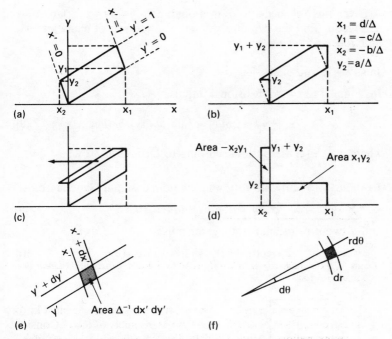

*Figure 3.1.3 Transformation of coordinates*

The area of the element shown in Figure 3.1.3(f) is clearly $(dr)(rd\theta)$ and so the integrals in polar coordinates take the form

$$\int\int f(r, \theta)rdrd\theta \qquad (6)$$

again with suitable limits; the limits of $\theta$ normally fall in the closed interval $(0, 2\pi)$.

EXERCISES   (i) Find the volume of a trapezoidal prism, using an integral of the form (3).
(ii) Find the volume of a circular cone, using an integral of the form (6).
(iii) Prove that

$$\int\limits_{-\infty}^{\infty} e^{-\pi x^2}dx = 1 \qquad (7)$$

Hint: consider the square of this expression as a double integral in Cartesian coordinates, and transform to polar coordinates.

Given these elementary ideas about functions of two variables, we can readily find the two-dimensional counterparts of many familiar functions and operations.

## Impulses in two dimensions

*Definition 1*: a two-dimensional impulse is

$$\delta(x, y) = \delta(x).\delta(y) = \lim_{a,b \to \infty} ag(ax).bh(by) \qquad (8)$$

where $g(x)$, $h(y)$ are pulses according to Definition 2.2.1.*

EXAMPLES    Figure 3.1.4 shows a two-dimensional Gaussian pulse

$$a^2 \phi(ax, ay) = a^2 \phi(ax)\phi(ay) = a^2 e^{-\pi a^2(x^2 + y^2)} \qquad (9)$$

and a two-dimensional rectangular pulse

$$ab \, \text{rect}(ax, by) = ab \, \text{rect}(ax)\text{rect}(by) \qquad (10)$$

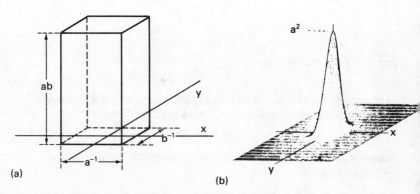

(a)

(b)

*Figure 3.1.4 Two-dimensional pulses. (a) ab rect(ax,by); (b) $a^2 exp[-\pi a^2(x^2 + y^2)]$*

Either of these, on diminishing its breadth and increasing its height, tends to an impulse of unit moment (here to be interpreted as unit volume).

For another physical interpretation, we can think of a function $g(x, y)$ as representing the density of electric charge on a surface. The

---

* This is not the most general definition possible, since we need not be confined to Cartesian coordinates. However, the extension is rarely needed but fairly obvious.

integral $\int\int g(x,y)dxdy$ taken over the surface is the total charge. If $g(x,y)=\delta(x,y)$ then there is a point charge at the origin.

EXERCISE    How would you represent a charge concentrated along a line? Hint: draw sketches of $\delta(x,y)$, $\delta(x)$ and $\delta(y)$ according to the conventions of Figures 3.1.1 and 3.1.4.

*Definition 2*: the convolution of two functions $g(x,y)$ and $h(x,y)$ is defined as

$$g(x,y)*h(x,y) = \int\limits_{-\infty}^{\infty} \int\limits_{-\infty}^{\infty} g(\xi,\eta)h(x-\xi, y-\eta)d\xi d\eta \qquad (11)$$

The formal similarity to Definition 2.2.4 is obvious. For a graphical view of one-dimensional convolution we reverse one function, displace, multiply and integrate. Similarly in two dimensions we give one function a half-turn, displace, multiply and integrate (Figure 3.1.5).

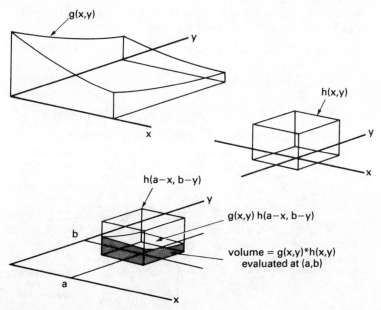

*Figure 3.1.5 Two-dimensional convolution*

*Theorem 1*: a function of two variables may be represented as a superposition of two-dimensional impulses:

$$g(x, y) = \delta(x, y) * g(x, y) \tag{12}$$

*Proof*  is along the lines of Theorems 2.2.1 and 2.2.2.

## Sinusoids in two dimensions

*Definition 3*: a two-dimensional sinusoid is a function of the form

$$e^{j2\pi(ax + by)} = \cos 2\pi(ax + by) + j \sin 2\pi(ax + by) \tag{13}$$

We shall use the word sinusoid to refer generically to the sine, cosine or complex exponential. The analytical convenience of the latter is especially obvious in two dimensions, because it is separable.

The real part of Equation (13), namely $\cos 2\pi(ax + by)$, is depicted in Figure 3.1.6. The diagram shows a corrugated sheet, whose sections along the two axes are $\cos 2\pi ax$ and $\cos 2\pi by$ respectively. The orientation can be defined by drawing a normal to the wavecrests. This line is inclined at an angle $\theta = \tan^{-1}(b/a)$ to the $x$-axis, and the section along it is a cosine wave with a wavelength equal to the pitch of the corrugation, namely $\lambda = (a^2 + b^2)^{-1/2}$.

We may use sinusoids as a means of representing other functions, just as in one-dimensional signal analysis.

*Theorem 2* (Fourier's theorem in two dimensions): A function of

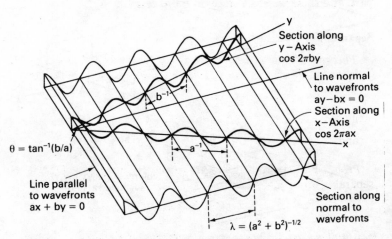

*Figure 3.1.6  Two-dimensional sinusoid $\cos 2\pi(ax + by)$*

two variables $g(x, y)$ may be represented as a superposition of sinusoids:

$$g(x, y) = \int_{-\infty}^{\infty} \int_{-\infty}^{\infty} G(u, v)e^{j2\pi(ux + vy)}dudv \tag{14}$$

The function $G(u, v)$ is given by

$$G(u, v) = \int_{-\infty}^{\infty} \int_{-\infty}^{\infty} g(x, y)e^{-j2\pi(ux + vy)}dxdy \tag{15}$$

*Proof* and conditions for validity are similar to Theorems 1, 4 and 5 of Section 2.3, and will not be elaborated.

*Definition 4*: The function $G(u, v)$ in Theorem 2 is said to be the Fourier transform of $g(x, y)$, and the relationship will be written

$$g(x, y) \Rightarrow G(u, v)$$

$$G(u, v) \Leftarrow g(x, y)$$

We could at this point state and prove many theorems analogous to those of Chapter 2. The similarity is so close that this procedure seems unnecessary. Examples of such results are given in the Appendix, Tables 3–5 and Figure 3.1.9. There are however a number of two-dimensional phenomena which lack any one-dimensional counterpart, and these we shall study in more detail.

## Separability

*Theorem 3* (separability): if $g(x, y) = g_1(x)g_2(y)$ is separable, then so is its transform $G(u, v) = G_1(u)G_2(v)$: and vice versa. Specifically

$$g_1(x)g_2(y) \Rightarrow G_1(u)G_2(v) \tag{16}$$

if $\qquad\qquad g_1(x) \Rightarrow G_1(u)$

and $\qquad\qquad g_2(y) \Rightarrow G_2(v)$

*Proof* Follows immediately on writing the integrand of (15) in the separable form

$$\{g_1(x)e^{-j2\pi ux}\}\{g_2(y)e^{-j2\pi vy}]$$

*Corollary* If a function is independent of one variable, its transform contains an impulse as a factor, for instance

$$g(x, y) = g_1(x) = g_1(x). 1 \Rightarrow G_1(u)\delta(v) \tag{17}$$

EXAMPLES   both of Theorem 3 and its corollary appear in Table 4 of the Appendix and Figure 3.1.9.

*Convolution*   As in one dimension, the convolution theorem

$$g(x, y) * h(x, y) \Rightarrow G(u, v)H(u, v) \tag{18}$$

$$g(x, y)h(x, y) \Rightarrow G(u, v) * H(u, v) \tag{19}$$

is very useful. In two dimensions it has some unfamiliar implications, such as

*Theorem 4*:

$$\{G_1(u)\delta(v)\} * \{G_2(v)\delta(u)\} = G_1(u)G_2(v) \tag{20}$$

*Proof*   follows from Equations (16), (17) and (18).

EXERCISE   Demonstrate Theorem 4 directly by carrying out a graphical convolution. Illustrate with reference to the rectangle

$$\text{rect}(x, y) = \text{rect}(x). \text{rect}(y)$$

$$= \{\text{rect}(x)\delta(y)\} * \{\text{rect}(y)\delta(x)\} \tag{21}$$

## Linear transformations and symmetry

As we have seen in Section 2.7, the symmetry properties of a function affect its Fourier transform profoundly. The one-dimensional symmetries carry over into two dimensions in a simple manner if the variables are separable. Thus if $g_1(x)$ in (16) is even, the function as a whole has even symmetry about the $y$-axis: $G_1(u)$ is even: and the transform as a whole has even symmetry about the $v$-axis. A function such as

$$\text{rect}(x, y) \Rightarrow \text{sinc}(u, v) \equiv \text{sinc}(u)\text{sinc}(v) \tag{22}$$

has a two-fold even symmetry. The further permutations of Theorem 2.7.1 in two dimensions will be fairly obvious.

Yet it is clear that this approach does not yield all the symmetries of a two-dimensional function. Consider the square region defined by $\text{rect}(x, y)$. It has bilateral symmetry about four axes: the $x$ and $y$ axes, and the diagonals. Only the first two of these are obvious from (22). How are the others to be represented, and what counterpart do they have in the Fourier transform $\mathrm{sinc}(u, v)$? We can extend the class of obvious symmetries by using a linear transformation of variables.

*Theorem 5* (linear transformation): let $g(x, y) \Rightarrow G(u, v)$. Then a linear transformation of the variables $x, y$ induces a linear transformation of the variables $u, v$. Specifically:

$$g(ax + by, cx + dy) \Rightarrow \frac{1}{|ad - bc|} G\left(\frac{du - cv}{ad - bc}, \frac{-bu + av}{ad - bc}\right) \tag{23}$$

*Proof*  Define variables $x', y'$ by Equation (1), so that the original function is $g(x', y')$. The exponent appearing in the integrand of the Fourier integral, namely $j2\pi(ux + vy)$, is a linear function of $x'$ and $y'$ and so can be written in the form

$$ux + vy = u'x' + v'y'$$

Equating coefficients on both sides of this identity yields

$$u' = \Delta^{-1}du - \Delta^{-1}cv$$

$$v' = -\Delta^{-1}bu + \Delta^{-1}av$$

where

$$\Delta = ad - bc$$

Thus the variables $u', v'$ are linear functions of $u, v$. On taking the Fourier transform of $g(x^\circ, y')$:

$$g(x', y') \Rightarrow \int\limits_{-\infty}^{\infty} \int\limits_{-\infty}^{\infty} g(x', y') e^{-j2\pi(ux + vy)} dx dy$$

$$= \int\limits_{-\infty}^{\infty} \int\limits_{-\infty}^{\infty} g(x', y') e^{-j2\pi(u'x' + v'y')} dx dy$$

$$= \int\limits_{-\infty}^{\infty} \int\limits_{-\infty}^{\infty} g(x', y') e^{-j2\pi(u'x' + v'y')} \Delta^{-1} dx' dy'$$

the last step being justified by the argument leading to (3). The last expression is just $\Delta^{-1} G(u', v')$, which on making the appropriate substitution proves (23).

EXAMPLES    (i) Scale change is a special case with $b = c = 0$ (Figure 3.1.7(a)). Changes of scale in the two domains are reciprocal.
(ii) Rotation about the origin is a special case with $a = d = \cos\theta$,

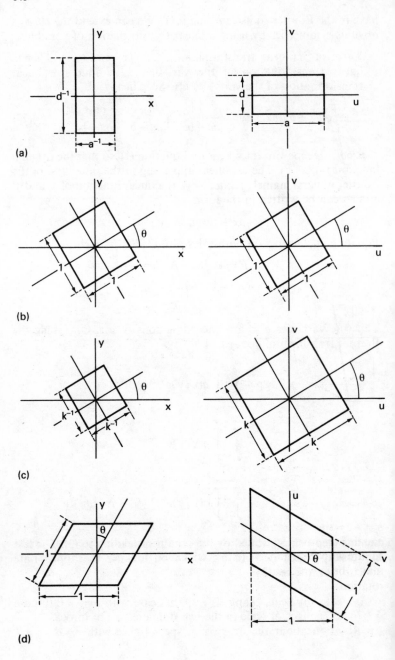

(a)

(b)

(c)

(d)

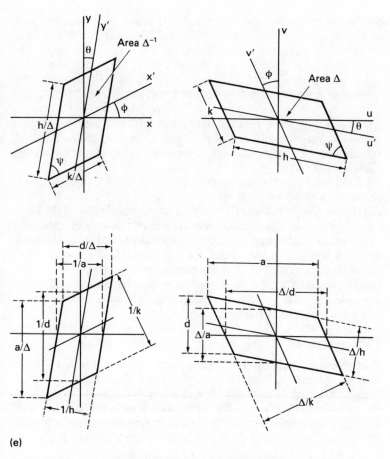

(e)

*Figure 3.1.7 Linear transformations. (a) Scale change; (b) Rotation; (c) Spiral similarity; (d) Shear; (e) The general linear transformation, $\Delta = ad - bc$, $\tan\theta = -b/a$, $h = (a^2 + b^2)^{1/2}$, $\tan\phi = -c/d$, $k = (c^2 + d^2)^{1/2}$, $\sin\psi = \Delta/kh$. Note: The diagrams show co-ordinate axes and the regions defined by rect(x',y') and rect(u',v')*

$b = -c = \sin\theta$ (Figure 3.1.7b). Rotations in the two domains are equal. For example, a function which has the value unity within a square whose diagonals are the coordinate axes, and zero elsewhere, may be written as a rectangle function with a $\frac{1}{4}\pi$ rotation:

$$\text{rect}(\alpha x + \alpha y, -\alpha x + \alpha y) \Rightarrow \text{sinc}(\alpha u + \alpha v, -\alpha u + \alpha v) \qquad (24)$$

where $\alpha = 2^{-1/2}$.

(iii) Spiral similarity, i.e. combined dilatation and rotation, is a special case with $c = -b$, $d = a$ (Figure 3.1.7(c)). The scale factor is $k = (a^2 + b^2)^{1/2}$ and the angle of rotation is $\theta = \tan^{-1}(b/a)$.

(iv) A shear is a special case: if it is parallel to the $x$-axis then $a = 1$, $b = -\tan\theta$, $c = 0$, $d = \sec\theta$ (Figure 3.1.7(d)). Shears in the two domains are equal in angle but orthogonal in direction.

EXERCISES    (i) Show that the right hand side of Equation (24) is an even function both of $u$ and of $v$. Thence show that all the bilateral symmetries of a square have their counterpart in the Fourier transform of rect$(x, y)$.

(ii) Find the Fourier transform of a function which is unity within a rhombus, and zero elsewhere.

(iii) Prove that rotation of a function about the origin of the $(x, y)$ plane leads to an equal rotation of its Fourier transform about the origin of the $(u, v)$ plane. Use a direct method which does not depend on Theorem 5. Hint: consider the Fourier transform of a two-dimensional sinusoid, then use superposition.

(iv) Prove that, if a function has $n$-fold rotational symmetry (like, for example, a regular polygon of $n$ sides) then its Fourier transform also has $n$-fold rotational symmetry.

## Circular symmetry

If a function is unchanged by rotation about an axis, it is said to have circular symmetry. Familiar examples are a disc, ring or cylinder. Such a function is naturally described in polar coordinates; it is independent of $\theta$, and so is effectively a one-dimensional function of $r$. Its Fourier transform also has circular symmetry and is a one-dimensional function of $q = (u^2 + v^2)$, as we procede to prove.

*Theorem 6* (circular symmetry): let a function $g(x, y) = g_r(r)$ have circular symmetry. Then its two-dimensional Fourier transform is

$$G(u, v) \equiv G_q(q) = 2\pi \int_0^\infty g_r(r) J_0(2\pi qr) r\, dr \tag{25}$$

where $J_0(z)$ is the Bessel function of first kind and zero order. The inverse transform is identical, namely

$$g_r(r) = 2\pi \int_0^\infty G_q(q) J_0(2\pi qr) q\, dq \tag{26}$$

*Proof*  By Theorem 5, rotation of $g(x, y)$ induces a corresponding rotation of $G(u, v)$: if the former be unchanged by rotation, so is the latter. Expressing the functions in polar coordinates $r, \theta$ and $q, \phi$ respectively, it is easily shown that

$$ux + vy = qr \cos(\theta - \phi)$$

The Fourier integral (15) therefore becomes

$$\int_0^\infty \int_0^{2\pi} g_r(r) e^{-j2\pi qr \cos(\theta - \phi)} d\theta . r dr$$

which is independent of $\phi$. Making the substitution

$$J_0(z) = \frac{1}{2\pi} \int_0^{2\pi} e^{-jz \cos \theta} d\theta \qquad (27)$$

gives (25) directly. The argument for the inverse transform is similar.

The relationship (25) is often called the Hankel transform of zero order. From our present viewpoint it is best considered as a special case of the Fourier transform. The expression (27) for the Bessel function follows from Equation (2.4.27) which in turn follows from the definition of Bessel functions as coefficients in a Fourier series.

EXAMPLE   We define a function

$$\text{circ}(r) = 1 \qquad r < 1 \atop = 0 \qquad 1 < r \Big\} \qquad (28)^*$$

Its transform is

$$2\pi \int_0^1 r J_0(2\pi qr) dr = q^{-1} J_1(2\pi q) \qquad (29)$$

This equation is easily verified by substituting the series (2.4.28). The function is plotted in Figure 3.1.8 (see also Figure 3.1.9(d)). It has its peak value at $q = 0$, and decays in an oscillatory manner; by (2.4.30) it is $O(q^{-3/2})$ as $q \to \infty$, and the interval between successive zero-crossings approaches 0.5.

---

* Definition 2.2.7, which would prescribe the value $\frac{1}{2}$ at the point of discontinuity, is valid in this case but not for all two-dimensional functions with discontinuities. It is instructive to consider why.

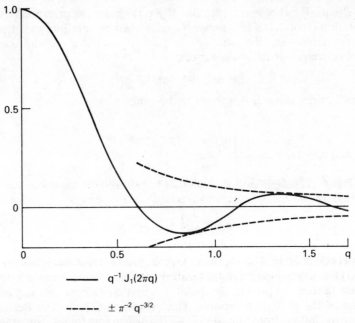

*Figure 3.1.8 Graph of* $q^{-1}J_1(2\pi q)$

**EXERCISE**   (i) Prove that

$$\delta(r-a) \Rightarrow 2\pi a J_0(2\pi aq) \tag{30}$$

and sketch both functions in two dimensions.
(ii) Show that the zero-order Hankel transform of a Gaussian function is another Gaussian function.

*Separability in polar coordinates*   Circular symmetry is a special case of separability in polar coordinates. More generally, if a function can be written as a product

$$g(x, y) = g_r(r)g_\theta(\theta) \tag{31}$$

its Fourier transform can be expressed as a series.

*Theorem 7*: let $g(x, y)$ be separable in polar coordinates. Then its Fourier transform is

$$G(u, v) = \sum_{m=-\infty}^{\infty} (-j)^m c_m e^{jm\phi} \psi_m(q) \tag{32}$$

where

$$c_m = \frac{1}{2\pi} \int_0^{2\pi} g_0(\theta) e^{-jm\theta} d\theta \qquad (33)$$

$$\psi_m(q) = 2\pi \int_0^\infty g_r(r) J_m(2\pi qr) r \, dr \qquad (34)$$

and $q$, $\phi$ are polar coordinates in the $u,v$ plane.

*Proof* The angular component $g_0(\theta)$ is necessarily periodic, with period $2\pi$; so it can be expressed as a Fourier series

$$g_0(\theta) = \sum_{m=-\infty}^{\infty} c_m e^{jm\theta} \qquad (35)$$

By Theorem 2.4.4, the coefficients have the values (33). We can express $g(x, y)$ as a series and transform term by term; it is then enough to show that

$$g_r(r) e^{jm\theta} \Rightarrow (-j)^m e^{jm\phi} 2\pi \int_0^\infty g_r(r) J_m(2\pi qr) r \, dr \qquad (36)$$

Using the substitutions of Theorem 6, the Fourier integral is in the present case

$$\int_0^\infty \int_0^{2\pi} g_r(r) e^{jm\theta} e^{-j2\pi qr \cos(\theta - \phi)} d\theta r \, dr$$

$$= e^{jm(\phi - \pi/2)} \int_0^\infty \int_0^{2\pi} g_r(r) e^{jm(\theta - \phi + \pi/2)} e^{-j2\pi qr \sin(\theta - \phi + \pi/2)} d\theta r \, dr$$

The substitution

$$J_m(z) = \frac{1}{2\pi} \int_0^{2\pi} e^{j(z \sin\theta - m\theta)} d\theta \qquad (37)$$

gives (36) directly and so proves the theorem.

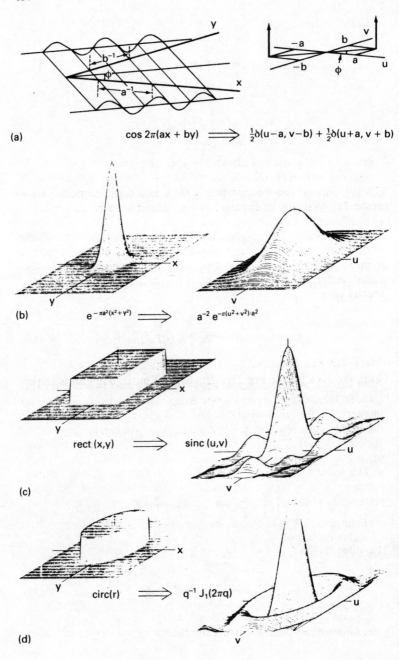

(a)

$$\cos 2\pi(ax + by) \implies \tfrac{1}{2}\delta(u-a, v-b) + \tfrac{1}{2}\delta(u+a, v+b)$$

(b) $\quad e^{-\pi a^2(x^2+y^2)} \implies a^{-2} e^{-\pi(u^2+v^2)/a^2}$

(c) $\quad \mathrm{rect}\,(x,y) \implies \mathrm{sinc}\,(u,v)$

(d) $\quad \mathrm{circ}(r) \implies q^{-1} J_1(2\pi q)$

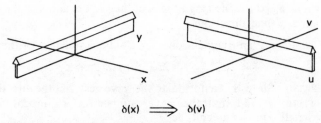

(e)

$$\delta(x) \implies \delta(v)$$

*Figure 3.1.9 Two-dimensional Fourier transforms*

The expression (37) for the Bessel function follows from equation (2.4.27). Again we note that the latter, convenient in form for our present purpose, stems directly from the definition of Bessel functions as coefficients of a Fourier series.

The significant result of this theorem is that sinusoidal components in the angular factor of $g(x, y)$ transform into sinusoidal components in the angular factor of $G(u, v)$; their relative amplitudes depend on the radial factor according to Equation (34).* Circular symmetry is a special case in which only the zero-order term exists; with $n$-fold rotational symmetry, only those terms exist whose orders are multiples of $n$.

## More than two dimensions

After our discussion of signal analysis in one and two dimensions, some features of a generalisation to $n$ dimensions ($n$ being any positive integer) will be fairly obvious. Let $x_1, x_2, \ldots x_n$ be Cartesian coordinates. It is convenient to consider a set of $n$ variables $(x_1, x_2, \ldots x_n)$ as the components of a vector variable $\mathbf{x}$. Similarly a set of $n$ parameters $(a_1, a_2, \ldots a_n)$ can be considered as components of a vector parameter $\mathbf{a}$. The reader is presumed to have some acquaintance with vectors, matrices and related topics; however, we include as definitions statements of the properties most essential to our purpose.

*Definition 5*: The scalar product of two $n$-dimensional vectors is a scalar quantity

$$\mathbf{a} \cdot \mathbf{x} = \sum_{i=1}^{n} a_i x_i = |\mathbf{a}| \, |\mathbf{x}| \cos \phi$$

---

* This relation (the Hankel transform of order $m$) though less familiar is no more complicated than the Fourier transform. Many specific results are available; see for examples the tables of integrals compiled by Gradshteyn and Ryzhik, or Erdelyi.

where $|\mathbf{a}|$, $|\mathbf{x}|$ are the magnitudes of the vectors and $\phi$ is the angle between their directions.

*Definition 6*: an $n$-dimensional sinusoid is a function of the form

$$e^{j2\pi\mathbf{a}\cdot\mathbf{x}} = \cos 2\pi\mathbf{a}\cdot\mathbf{x} + j\sin 2\pi\mathbf{a}\cdot\mathbf{x}$$

EXERCISE   Show that a normal to the wavecrests has the direction of the vector $\mathbf{a}$, and that the wave number (i.e. reciprocal of the wavelength $\lambda$) is its magnitude,

$$\lambda^{-1} = |\mathbf{a}| \equiv \left\{\sum_i a_i^2\right\}^{1/2} \tag{38}$$

(Hint: look at Figure 3.1.6 first.)

*Theorem 8* (Fourier's theorem in $n$ dimensions): a function of $n$ variables $g(\mathbf{x})$ may be represented as a superposition of sinusoids

$$g(\mathbf{x}) = \int G(\mathbf{u})e^{j2\pi\mathbf{u}\cdot\mathbf{x}}d\mathbf{u}$$

where the transform variable $\mathbf{u}$ also has $n$ dimensions, and the integration is performed between infinite limits in all dimensions. The functions $G(\mathbf{u})$ is given by

$$G(\mathbf{u}) = \int g(\mathbf{x})e^{-j2\pi\mathbf{u}\cdot\mathbf{x}}d\mathbf{x}$$

*Definition 7*: the convolution of two $n$-dimensional functions is another $n$-dimensional function

$$g(\mathbf{x})*h(\mathbf{x}) = \int g(\boldsymbol{\xi})h(\mathbf{x}-\boldsymbol{\xi})d\boldsymbol{\xi}$$

where the dummy variable $\boldsymbol{\xi}$ also has $n$ dimensions, and the integration is between infinite limits in all dimensions.

*Theorem 9* (convolution): if $g(\mathbf{x}) \Rightarrow G(\mathbf{u})$ and $h(\mathbf{x}) \Rightarrow H(\mathbf{u})$ then

$$g(\mathbf{x})*h(\mathbf{x}) \Rightarrow G(\mathbf{u})H(\mathbf{u})$$

$$g(\mathbf{x})h(\mathbf{x}) \Rightarrow G(\mathbf{u})*H(\mathbf{u})$$

That is, multiplication transforms into convolution, and vice versa.

*Transformation of variables*   A linear transformation in $n$ dimensions may be written as

$$\begin{bmatrix} x_1' \\ x_2' \\ \vdots \\ x_n' \end{bmatrix} = \begin{bmatrix} a_{11} & a_{12} & \cdots & a_{1n} \\ a_{21} & a_{22} & \cdots & a_{2n} \\ \vdots & \vdots & & \vdots \\ a_{n1} & a_{n2} & \cdots & a_{nn} \end{bmatrix} \begin{bmatrix} x_1 \\ x_2 \\ \vdots \\ x_n \end{bmatrix} \tag{39}$$

or more briefly

$$\mathbf{x}' = \mathbf{A}\mathbf{x} \tag{40}$$

where $\mathbf{A}$ is an $n \times n$ matrix, and the $n$-dimensional vectors $\mathbf{x}$, $\mathbf{x}'$ are considered as column matrices. We require the rule for matrix multiplication, namely

*Definition 8*: Let the matrices $\mathbf{A}$, $\mathbf{B}$, $\mathbf{C}$ be arrays of elements $a, b, c$ respectively. Then $\mathbf{A}\mathbf{B} = \mathbf{C}$ if

$$c_{jk} = \sum_i a_{ji} b_{ik} \tag{41}$$

The first index attached to the element identifies the row, and the second the column. It is implicit that the number of columns in $\mathbf{A}$ equals the number of rows in $\mathbf{B}$.

To paraphrase this definition in words, the element $c_{jk}$ is the scalar product of the $j$th row of $\mathbf{A}$ with the $k$th column of $\mathbf{B}$.

Equations (39), (40) imply an inverse relationship of the form

$$\begin{bmatrix} x_1 \\ x_2 \\ \vdots \\ x_n \end{bmatrix} = \begin{bmatrix} b_{11} & b_{12} & \cdots & b_{1n} \\ b_{21} & b_{22} & \cdots & b_{2n} \\ \vdots & \vdots & & \vdots \\ b_{n1} & b_{n2} & \cdots & b_{nn} \end{bmatrix} \begin{bmatrix} x_1' \\ x_2' \\ \vdots \\ x_n' \end{bmatrix}$$

or more briefly

$$\mathbf{x} = \mathbf{B}\mathbf{x}' \equiv \mathbf{A}^{-1}\mathbf{x}' \tag{42}$$

where $\mathbf{B}$ is the inverse matrix to $\mathbf{A}$.

*Definition 9*: the *inverse* $\mathbf{A}^{-1}$ of a matrix $\mathbf{A}$ is such that

$$\mathbf{A}^{-1}\mathbf{A} = \mathbf{A}\mathbf{A}^{-1} = \mathbf{I}$$

where $\mathbf{I}$ is the unit matrix whose diagonal elements are unity and other elements zero. The *adjoint* adj $\mathbf{A}$ has for its $(i, j)$ element the cofactor $(-1)^{i+j} A_{ji}$, where $A_{ji}$ is the determinant of those elements of $\mathbf{A}$ remaining on deletion of the $j$th row and $i$th column. It may be shown by multiplying out that

$$\mathbf{A} \, \text{adj} \, \mathbf{A} = |A|\mathbf{I} \tag{43}$$

where $|A|$ is the determinant of $\mathbf{A}$. It follows that

$$\mathbf{A}^{-1} = |A|^{-1} \, \text{adj} \, \mathbf{A}$$

so the elements of the inverse matrix are

$$b_{ij} = (-1)^{i+j} \frac{A_{ji}}{|A|}$$

The determinant of the inverse matrix satisfies the equation

$$|B| = |A|^{-1}$$

To integrate with respect to transformed variables, we need to know what element of content (area in 2 dimensions, volume in 3 dimensions, etc.) is implied by a notation such as $dx'_1 dx'_2 \ldots dx'_n$.

*Definition 10*: the Jacobian of a transformation from variables $x_i$ to variables $x'_i$ is the determinant

$$J = \begin{vmatrix} \dfrac{dx_1}{dx'_1} & \dfrac{dx_1}{dx'_2} & \cdots & \dfrac{dx_1}{dx'_n} \\[2mm] \dfrac{dx_2}{dx'_1} & \dfrac{dx_2}{dx'_2} & \cdots & \dfrac{dx_2}{dx'_n} \\[2mm] \vdots & \vdots & & \vdots \\[2mm] \dfrac{dx_n}{dx'_1} & \dfrac{dx_n}{dx'_2} & \cdots & \dfrac{dx_n}{dx'_n} \end{vmatrix}$$

The elements of content in the two coordinate systems are related by

$$dx_1 dx_2 \ldots dx_n = J dx'_1 dx'_2 \ldots dx'_n$$

In a linear transformation, the differential coefficients are constant

$$\frac{dx_i}{dx'_j} = b_{ij}$$

and so

$$J = |B| = |A^{-1}| = |A|^{-1} \tag{44}$$

The simplest proof of the property stated for $J$ would start with the linear case, and then apply the result to infinitesimal elements in curvilinear coordinates. We have already proved the linear property in 2 dimensions (see Figure 3.1.3).

To integrate a function

$$h(x'_1, x'_2 \ldots x'_n) = g(x_1, x_2, \ldots x_n)$$

we can use the relationship

$$\int \ldots \int g(x_1 \ldots x_n)dx_1 \ldots dx_n = \int \ldots \int h(x_1' \ldots x_n')J dx_1' \ldots dx_n' \quad (45)$$

inserting appropriate limits of integration, and substituting for $J$ whichever of the equivalent determinants in (44) is most convenient.

EXERCISES  (i) Use the above integral to find the volume of a 3-dimensional parallelepiped, and compare with the result of a geometrical approach. (Hint: first look at the 2-dimensional treatment in Equations 1 to 3.)

(ii) Consider a transformation from rectangular coordinates $x, y, z$ to cylindrical coordinates $r, \theta, z$ ($r$ and $\theta$ defined by Equations 4). Show that the Jacobian is $r$; use an integral in cylindrical coordinates to find the volume of a right circular cylinder, and compare with the familiar value.

The Fourier transform is an integral to which we can apply the foregoing rules: but first we need one more matrix relationship.

*Definition 11* (reciprocal matrix): the transpose $\mathbf{A}_t$ of a matrix $\mathbf{A}$ is the matrix whose elements are $a_{ji}$; that is, rows and columns of $\mathbf{A}$ are interchanged. The reciprocal matrix $\mathbf{A}^*$ is the transpose of the inverse, or equivalently the inverse of the transpose,

$$\mathbf{A}^* = (\mathbf{A}_t)^{-1} = (\mathbf{A}^{-1})_t$$

The determinant of a matrix is unaffected by transposition, and so

$$|A^*| = |A^{-1}| = |A|^{-1} \quad (46)$$

*Theorem 10* (linear transformation): let $g(\mathbf{x}) \Rightarrow G(\mathbf{u})$. Then a linear transformation $\mathbf{x}' = \mathbf{Ax}$ induces a reciprocal linear transformation of $\mathbf{u}$. Specifically,

$$g(\mathbf{Ax}) \Rightarrow |A^*| G(\mathbf{A}^*\mathbf{u}) \quad (47)$$

*Proof*  Let transformed variables $\mathbf{u}'$ be defined such that

$$\mathbf{u}' \cdot \mathbf{x}' = \mathbf{u} \cdot \mathbf{x} \quad (48)$$

identically. Then the Fourier transform of $g(\mathbf{x}')$ may be written as

$$g(\mathbf{x}') \Rightarrow \int g(\mathbf{x}')e^{-j2\pi\mathbf{u}\cdot\mathbf{x}}d\mathbf{x}$$
$$= \int g(\mathbf{x}')e^{-j2\pi\mathbf{u}'\cdot\mathbf{x}'}d\mathbf{x}$$
$$= \int g(\mathbf{x}')e^{-j2\pi\mathbf{u}'\cdot\mathbf{x}'}J d\mathbf{x}'$$

This is a Fourier integral defining a function $G(\mathbf{u}')$, multiplied by $J$. By Equation (44) the Jacobian $J$ is equal to $|A|^{-1}$ and hence to $|A^*|$.

It remains to find the relationship between $\mathbf{u}'$ and $\mathbf{u}$. On writing out (48) explicitly

$$\sum_i u_i x_i = \sum_j u'_j x'_j = \sum_j u'_j \sum_k a_{jk} x_k$$

Since this is an identity we can equate coefficients of $x_i$, obtaining

$$u_i = \sum_j a_{ji} u'_j$$

which in matrix notation is

$$\mathbf{u} = \mathbf{A}_t \mathbf{u}'$$

Inversion of this equation completes the proof.

EXERCISES    (i) Deduce Theorem 5 from Theorem 10.
(ii) Show that all the symmetries of a cube have their counterpart in the Fourier transform of

$$\text{rect}(x, y, z) \equiv \text{rect}(x)\,\text{rect}(y)\,\text{rect}(z)$$

(iii) Find the effect in the transform domain of a shear parallel to the $x$-axis in 3 dimensions.
(iv) Find a 3-dimensional Fourier transform relationship suitable for use in cylindrical coordinates.
(v) Derive the effect of a scale change in $n$ dimensions (a) from Theorem 10 (b) by separation of variables; and show that your results are consistent.
(vi) Show that

$$|A|\delta(\mathbf{A}\mathbf{x}) = \delta(\mathbf{x}) \tag{49}$$

Hint: take Fourier transforms of both sides.


## 3.2 SAMPLING LATTICES AND NORMAL COORDINATES

As in one dimension, we can define two special classes of function
(i) Periodic or repeated functions
(ii) Sampled functions or series of discrete values
with the property that a function in one class has a transform in the other class (compare Theorem 2.4.1). We can also define impulse-repetitions which are members of both classes. Repetition in several dimensions give rise to a uniform lattice, which we define formally as follows.

*Definition 1*: let $\mathbf{b}_1, \mathbf{b}_2 \dots \mathbf{b}_n$ be linearly independent vectors. Then a uniform lattice in $n$ dimensions is an infinite set of points whose position vectors are

$$r_1\mathbf{b}_1 + r_2\mathbf{b}_2 + \dots r_n\mathbf{b}_n$$

for all integer values of $r_1, r_2 \dots r_n$. The vectors $\mathbf{b}_i$ are the unit vectors of the lattice. The lattice is defined by a matrix $\mathbf{B}$ whose columns are the orthogonal components of the unit vectors; thus $\mathbf{b}_j = (b_{1j}, b_{2j} \dots b_{nj})$ where $b_{ij}$ are matrix elements.

In particular, the unit matrix (see Definition 3.1.9) defines a rectangular lattice of unit spacing. A matrix with non-zero elements off the leading diagonal corresponds to an oblique lattice.

Part of a two-dimensional lattice is shown in Figure 3.2.1(a). The lattice points are the intersections of two families of straight lines. The grid of lines can be taken as defining a coordinate system in which the position vector of the point $(x_1', x_2')$ is $x_1'\mathbf{b}_1 + x_2'\mathbf{b}_2$ (see Figure 3.2.1(b)). The rectangular coordinates of this point are, by a simple substitution

$$x_1 = b_{11}x_1' + b_{12}x_2'$$
$$x_2 = b_{21}x_1' + b_{22}x_2'$$

which can be written in matrix form

$$\mathbf{x} = \mathbf{B}\mathbf{x}' \tag{1}$$

Identifying (1) with Equation (3.1.42) we see that the matrix $\mathbf{B}$ whose columns define the lattice is the inverse transformation matrix of the

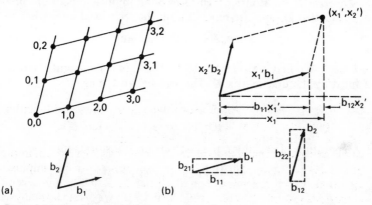

(a)    (b)

*Figure 3.2.1 Two-dimensional lattice*

coordinate system. This is generally true in any number of dimensions.

A repetition in $n$ dimensions is based on a lattice.

*Definition 2*: let **B** be a lattice and $g(\mathbf{x})$ a function, each defined in $n$ dimensions. Then the repetition $\text{rep}_\mathbf{B}\, g(\mathbf{x})$ is the sum of an infinite set of similar terms located respectively around each point of the lattice, i.e.

$$\text{rep}_\mathbf{B} g(\mathbf{x}) = \sum_{\mathbf{x}_B \in \mathbf{B}}^{\infty} g(\mathbf{x} - \mathbf{x}_B) \tag{2}$$

The notation $\mathbf{x}_B \in \mathbf{B}$ implies that the point $\mathbf{x}_B$ is an element of the set constituting the lattice **B**. A repetition suffix in bold type will always imply repetition on a lattice which is defined elsewhere. We may also use suffixes in normal type to denote the lattice parameters, for example

$$\text{rep}_{X,Y} g(x, y) = \sum_{r_1 = -\infty}^{\infty} \sum_{r_2 = -\infty}^{\infty} g(x - r_1 X, y - r_2 Y) \tag{3}$$

consistently with our practice in one dimension (Definition 2.4.2).

As in one dimension, the impulse-repetition is of fundamental importance. Any other repetition can be expressed as a convolution

$$\text{rep}_\mathbf{B}\, g(\mathbf{x}) = g(\mathbf{x}) * \text{rep}_\mathbf{B}\, \delta(\mathbf{x}) \tag{4}$$

(see Figure 3.2.2). Also, an impulse-repetition has for its Fourier transform a reciprocal impulse-repetition; this relationship is central to the theory of periodic and of sampled functions.

*Theorem 1*: the Fourier transform of an impulse-repetition on a lattice **B** is an impulse-repetition on the reciprocal lattice **B\***,

$$\text{rep}_\mathbf{B}\, \delta(\mathbf{x}) \Rightarrow |\mathbf{B}^*| \text{rep}_{\mathbf{B}^*}\, \delta(\mathbf{u}) \tag{5}$$

*Proof* We first consider the special case of a rectangular lattice defined by the unit matrix **U**. This can be written as

$$\text{rep}_\mathbf{U}\, \delta(\mathbf{x}) = \text{rep}_{1,1\ldots1}\, \delta(\mathbf{x})$$
$$= \text{rep}_1\, \delta(x_1) \text{rep}_1\, \delta(x_2) \ldots \text{rep}_1\, \delta(x_n)$$

By separation of variables, the last version transforms into

$$\text{rep}_1\, \delta(u_1) \text{rep}_1\, \delta(u_2) \ldots \text{rep}_1\, \delta(u_n)$$

and so

$$\text{rep}_{1,1\ldots1}\, \delta(\mathbf{x}) \Rightarrow \text{rep}_{1,1\ldots1}\, \delta(\mathbf{u}) \tag{6}$$

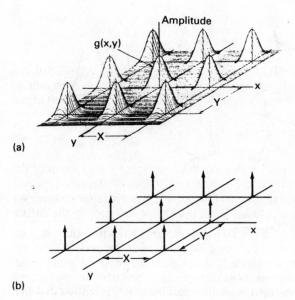

*Figure 3.2.2 Repetition on a lattice.* (a) rep$_{X,Y}$g(x, y); (b) rep$_{X,Y}$δ(x, y)

To deal with the general uniform lattice **B**, we transform to the coordinate system $\mathbf{x}' = \mathbf{B}^{-1}\mathbf{x}$. The impulse-repetition can be written as

$$\mathrm{rep}_{\mathbf{B}}\,\delta(x) = |B|^{-1}\,\mathrm{rep}_{1,1\ldots 1}\,\delta(\mathbf{x}') \tag{7}$$

The unit spacing follows from the definition of the coordinate system, and the factor $|B|^{-1}$ from Equation (3.1.49). The Fourier transform of the right-hand side follows from Equation (6) and Theorem 3.1.10

$$|B|^{-1}\,\mathrm{rep}_{1,1\ldots 1}\,\delta(\mathbf{x}') \Rightarrow \mathrm{rep}_{1,1\ldots 1}\,\delta(\mathbf{u}') \tag{8}$$

where

$$\mathbf{u} = \mathbf{B}^{*}\mathbf{u}' \tag{9}$$

Unit spacing in the transformed coordinates **u**′ corresponds to location on the reciprocal lattice **B\*** (compare Equations 1 and 9). Also, by Equation (3.1.49)

$$\delta(\mathbf{u}') = |B^{*}|\delta(\mathbf{u})$$

Thus the moments and locations of the impulses in (8) are those implied by (5).

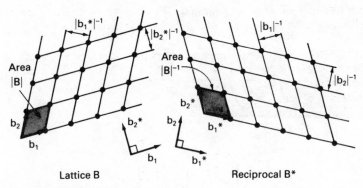

*Figure 3.2.3 Reciprocal lattices*

*The reciprocal lattice.* To assist our understanding and usage of the reciprocal lattice, we derive its geometrical properties. First we recall that the unit vectors $\mathbf{b}_i$ of the original lattice are columns of the matrix $\mathbf{B}$, hence the rows of its transpose $\mathbf{B}_t$. Similarly, the unit vectors $\mathbf{b}_j^*$ of the reciprocal lattice are the columns of $\mathbf{B}^*$. It follows that the scalar product $\mathbf{b}_i \cdot \mathbf{b}_j^*$ is the element in the $i$th row and $j$th column of the product

$$\mathbf{B}_t \mathbf{B}^* = \mathbf{B}_t \mathbf{B}_t^{-1} = \mathbf{U}$$

Consequently,

$$\mathbf{b}_i \cdot \mathbf{b}_i^* = 1 \tag{10}$$

$$\mathbf{b}_i \cdot \mathbf{b}_j^* = 0, \qquad i \neq j \tag{11}$$

Now the scalar product of two non-zero vectors vanishes if and only if they are orthogonal (see Definition 3.1.5). So by Equation (11) $\mathbf{b}_i^*$ is orthogonal to all the $\mathbf{b}_j$ other than $\mathbf{b}_i$; and this defines its direction[†]. The scalar product can be interpreted as the product of the length of either vector with the projection of the other upon it. By Equation (10), the length of each is reciprocal to the projection of the other. These relationships are illustrated, for two dimensions, in Figure 3.2.3.

The content of one cell of the original lattice is $|B|$, and that of the reciprocal cell is $|B^*| = |B|^{-1}$. Thus for two dimensions the areas shaded in Figure 3.2.3 are reciprocal. The impulses on the left of the relationship (5) have unit moment: those on the right, a moment equal to the content of the cell, so that on the average a large region contains

† The sense remains ambiguous, but this makes no difference to the lattice.

a unit density of impulsive moment. This is a generalisation of the well-known relationship for one dimension, Theorem 2.4.2.

EXERCISES   (i) Let $h(x, y)$ be a set of impulses located at all points of a hexagonal lattice with lattice distance $2^{1/2}3^{-1/4}$, and let its Fourier transform be $H(u, v)$. Show that $H(u, v)$ is identical with $h(x, y)$ save for a rotation of $\pi/6$.
(ii) Show that the transformation

$$\begin{bmatrix} x' \\ y' \\ z' \end{bmatrix} = \begin{bmatrix} 1 & 0 & -\alpha \\ 0 & 1 & -\beta \\ 0 & 0 & 1 \end{bmatrix} \begin{bmatrix} x \\ y \\ z \end{bmatrix}$$

represents a shear in three dimensions. Find the lattice vectors of the coordinate system $(x', y', z')$ and of the reciprocal lattice. Sketch a cell of each lattice, and verify the orthogonality which would be expected from Equation (11). Find the Fourier transform of $\mathrm{rect}(x + z, y - z, z)$.

## Sampling on a lattice

A lattice provides the most general uniform frame for sampling in several dimensions. Sampling of a two-dimensional function at points of a rectangular lattice is illustrated in Figure 3.2.4. The Fourier transform of a sampled signal is a repetition.

*Theorem 2*: let $h(\mathbf{x}) \Rightarrow H(\mathbf{u})$ be a bounded function, and let it be sampled at the points of a lattice **B**. Then the Fourier transform of the sampled function is a repetition on a reciprocal lattice **B***

$$h(\mathbf{x})\,\mathrm{rep}_{\mathbf{B}}\,\delta(\mathbf{x}) \Rightarrow |B^*|\,\mathrm{rep}_{\mathbf{B}^*}\,H(\mathbf{u}) \tag{12}$$

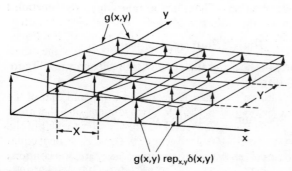

*Figure 3.2.4 Sampling on a lattice*

*Proof* From Theorems 3.1.9 and 3.2.1

$$h(\mathbf{x}) \operatorname{rep}_{\mathbf{B}} \delta(\mathbf{x}) \Rightarrow H(\mathbf{u})*|B^*| \operatorname{rep}_{\mathbf{B}^*} \delta(\mathbf{u})$$

and from Equation (4) the right hand side is identical with that of (12).

*Corollary* A function which is repeated on a lattice has a transform which is non-zero only on the points of a reciprocal lattice,

$$\operatorname{rep}_{\mathbf{B}} g(\mathbf{x}) \Rightarrow |B^*| G(\mathbf{u}) \operatorname{rep}_{\mathbf{B}^*} \delta(\mathbf{u}) \qquad (13)$$

This relationship is simply Theorem 2 with the domains interchanged.

If the spectrum is non-zero only within some finite region $\rho$, then it is possible to choose a sampling frame so that the spectral repetitions do not overlap. The original function can be specified exactly by its samples.

In the domain of $\mathbf{u}$, we choose a lattice $\mathbf{C}$ such that repetitions of $\rho$ centred on each point of $\mathbf{C}$ do not overlap (Figure 3.2.5a); the repetitions may form a space-filling tesselation, or there may be interstices between them. Let the function $\Phi(\mathbf{u}) \Leftarrow \phi(\mathbf{x})$ be the indicator function of $\rho$; that is, it takes the value 1 at points in $\rho$ and 0 elsewhere.[†]

*Theorem 3* (sampling theorem in *n* dimensions): let $h(\mathbf{x})$ have a Fourier transform $H(\mathbf{u})$ which is non-zero only within a finite region $\rho$, and let the lattice $\mathbf{C}$ and function $\phi(\mathbf{x})$ be defined as above. Then

$$h(\mathbf{x}) = |C^*| \{h(\mathbf{x}) \operatorname{rep}_{\mathbf{C}^*} \delta(\mathbf{x})\} * \phi(\mathbf{x}) \qquad (14)$$

*Proof* Under the conditions stated, the Fourier transform may be repeated without overlap. Then, as a tautology, the curtailed repetition equals a single instance of $H(\mathbf{u})$:

$$H(\mathbf{u}) = \{H(\mathbf{u}) * \operatorname{rep}_{\mathbf{C}} \delta(\mathbf{u})\} \Phi(\mathbf{u})$$

Fourier transformation, using the convolution theorem and Theorem 1, gives (14) directly.

EXAMPLES    (i) Spectrum confined to a rectangular region, sampling

---

† For rigour we should also specify that $\Phi(u)$ takes the value $1/r$ at any point where $r$ repetitions meet; for example, $\frac{1}{2}$ on the boundary line between two repetitions on a plane. This emerges naturally if we define a tessellation by 'rect' functions.

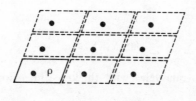

(a)

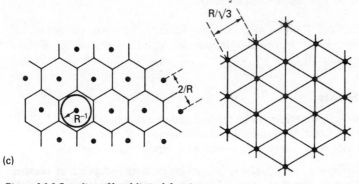

(b)

(c)

*Figure 3.2.5 Sampling of band-limited functions*

on a rectangular lattice (Figure 3.2.5b)

$$\Phi(u,v) = \operatorname{rect}(uX, vY)$$
$$\phi(x,y) = (XY)^{-1}\operatorname{sinc}(x/X, y/Y)$$
$$|C^*| = XY$$

whence

$$h(x, y) = \sum_{m=-\infty}^{\infty} \sum_{n=-\infty}^{\infty} h(mX, nY) \, \text{sinc}\left(\frac{x-mX}{X}, \frac{y-nY}{Y}\right) \quad (15)$$

This has obvious analogies with the one-dimensional expression (2.5.11).

(ii) Spectrum confined to a circular region

$$\Phi(u, v) = \text{circ}(qR)$$

$$\phi(x, y) = (rR)^{-1} J_1(2\pi r/R)$$

Circles do not form a complete tessellation: a lattice could be based on circumscribing squares or hexagons, the latter offering closer packing and hence requiring fewer samples (Figure 3.2.5(c)). The lattice $C$ has a lattice distance $2/R$, the reciprocal lattice $C^*$ a distance $R/\sqrt{3}$, whence $|C^*| = R^2/2\sqrt{3}$. It follows that

$$h(x, y) = \{h(x, y) \, \text{rep}_{C^*} \, \delta(x, y)\} * (2\sqrt{3})^{-1} (r/R)^{-1} J_1(2\pi r/R) \quad (16)$$

Unlike the 'sinc' functions, the interpolating function on the right hand side of the convolution does not vanish at other sampling points: however, it is small at all lattice points except the origin (about 0.046 at the nearest neighbours).

EXERCISE   Find another sampling function for use on the hexagonal lattice. (Hint: represent a hexagonal region as the union of three rhombic cells.)

## Periodicity

A periodic function can be represented as a repetition in an infinity of ways. A function periodic in all dimensions will repeat in every cell of a lattice, and can be considered as a repetition of one cell.

*Definition 3*: let $\mathbf{b}_i$ ($i = 1, 2 \ldots m$) be linearly independent vectors. Then a function $g(\mathbf{x})$ defined in $n \geqslant m$ dimensions has $m$-fold periodicity if for all $\mathbf{x}$

$$g(\mathbf{x}) = g(\mathbf{x} - \mathbf{b}_i) \quad (17)$$

Clearly a periodic function repeats indefinitely, since as a corollary of (17)

$$g(\mathbf{x}) = g(x - \mathbf{x}_B), \qquad \mathbf{x}_B \in \mathbf{B} \quad (18)$$

where $\mathbf{B}$ is the lattice defined by the vectors $\mathbf{b}_i$.

Our definition of periodicity includes constancy: a constant is a function with infinitesimally small period. In one dimension, this special case is trivial. In many dimensions, it may be a complication, since a function can be periodic (with non-zero period) along some axes and constant along others; moreover, these axes need not coincide with the coordinate system (see Figure 3.1.6). However, it does not call for special treatment. Should a function exhibit $m$-fold true periodicity together with constancy along $r$ other axes, we can separate variables and use the following theory in $m$ dimensions. The $r$-fold constancy will, of course, transform into an impulse in $r$ dimensions.

*Theorem 4* (Fourier series in $n$ dimensions): let a function $h(\mathbf{x})$ have $n$-fold periodicity on a lattice **B** with a unit cell $\rho_B$. Then it may be represented by the series of sinusoids

$$h(\mathbf{x}) = \sum_{\mathbf{u}_{B*} \varepsilon \mathbf{B}^*} c(\mathbf{u}_{B*}) e^{j2\pi \mathbf{x} \cdot \mathbf{u}_{B*}} \tag{19}$$

whose coefficients are

$$c(\mathbf{u}_{B*}) = |B^*| \int_{\rho_B} h(\mathbf{x}) e^{-j2\pi \mathbf{x} \cdot \mathbf{u}_{B*}} d\mathbf{x} \tag{20}$$

*Proof*   Consider the restriction of $h(\mathbf{x})$ to the cell $\rho_B$, i.e. a function which is identical with $h(\mathbf{x})$ in $\rho_B$ and zero elsewhere: let this be $h_\rho(\mathbf{x}) \Rightarrow H_\rho(\mathbf{u})$. Since $h(\mathbf{x})$ repeats on the lattice **B**,

$$h(\mathbf{x}) = \mathrm{rep}_\mathbf{B} h_\rho(\mathbf{x})$$

Take the Fourier transform, using Equation (13):

$$\mathrm{rep}_\mathbf{B} h_\rho(\mathbf{x}) \Rightarrow |B^*| H_\rho(\mathbf{u}) \, \mathrm{rep}_{\mathbf{B}*} \delta(\mathbf{u})$$

Now by definition

$$H_\rho(\mathbf{u}) = \int_{\rho_B} h(\mathbf{x}) e^{-j2\pi \mathbf{u} \cdot \mathbf{x}} d\mathbf{x}$$

and so

$$h(\mathbf{x}) \Rightarrow |B^*| \sum_{\mathbf{u}_{B*} \in \mathbf{B}^*} \int_{\rho_B} h(\mathbf{x}) e^{-j2\pi \mathbf{x} \cdot \mathbf{u}_{B*}} d\mathbf{x} \, \delta(\mathbf{u} - \mathbf{u}_{B*})$$

Taking the inverse transform of the right hand side, the impulses yield sinusoids

$$\delta(\mathbf{u}-\mathbf{u}_{B*})\Leftarrow e^{j2\pi\mathbf{x}\cdot\mathbf{u}_{B*}}$$

whose coefficients are given by (20); which proves the theorem.

EXAMPLE   A function

$$h(x,y)=h(x,y+Y)=h(x+X,y)$$

is periodic in two dimensions, along orthogonal axes. The lattice matrix and its reciprocal are

$$\mathbf{B}=\begin{bmatrix} X & 0 \\ 0 & Y \end{bmatrix}, \qquad \mathbf{B}*=\begin{bmatrix} X^{-1} & 0 \\ 0 & Y^{-1} \end{bmatrix}$$

The reciprocal lattice points are $(nX^{-1}, mY^{-1})$ for integral $n,m$. It follows that

$$h(x,y)=\sum_{n=-\infty}^{\infty}\sum_{m=-\infty}^{\infty}c_{nm}e^{j2\pi(nx/X+my/Y)} \qquad (21)$$

where

$$c_{nm}=\frac{1}{XY}\int_{-\frac{1}{2}X}^{\frac{1}{2}X}\int_{-\frac{1}{2}Y}^{\frac{1}{2}Y}h(x,y)e^{-j2\pi(nx/X+my/Y)}dydx \qquad (22)$$

Note that the limits $\pm\frac{1}{2}X$, $\pm\frac{1}{2}Y$ are not unique; any intervals of length $X, Y$ respectively will do.

## Normal coordinates

It will be clear from the foregoing that, although in principle any problem can be expressed in terms of almost any set of coordinates, the analysis proceeds much more easily if we choose the proper set. It would be perverse to define the lattice in terms of basis vectors other than those aligned with the natural axes. If other axes need to be introduced, the obvious procedure is to use the appropriate transformation; and we have implicitly done so.

This principle is common to many areas of mathematics, and we take the opportunity to state it explicitly. The first step is to define the functions appropriate to particular operators.

*Definition 4*: Let $T$ be any linear operator, and let

$$T(\phi)=\lambda\phi \qquad (23)$$

for some operand $\phi$ and some scalar $\lambda$. Then $\phi$ is an *eigenvector* of the operator $T$ (alternatively called an *eigenfunction* if defined in a function space) and $\lambda$ is an *eigenvalue*.

EXAMPLE  Let $T$ be the differential operator $d/dx$. Then (23) is the differential equation

$$\frac{d\phi}{dx} = \lambda\phi$$

with the solution

$$\phi(x) = ce^{\lambda x}$$

where $c$ is a non-zero constant. Here $e^{\lambda x}$ is an eigenfunction and $\lambda$ is its eigenvalue; the latter may be any real or complex number.

EXERCISE  (i) Find the eigenfunctions of the operator $d^2/dx^2$.
(ii) Find the eigenfunctions and eigenvalues of the same operator with the boundary conditions $\phi(0) = \phi(1) = 0$. (In this case, unlike the former, the eigenvalues are a discrete set.)

The widespread occurrence of exponential functions is due to their role as eigenfunctions of the differential operator. Using this property, differential equations can be transformed into algebraic equations; it is instructive to re-examine Theorem 2.3.7 with this point in mind. We shall encounter some more eigenfunctions of differential operators later in this chapter.

*Transformation matrices*  The other important category of operator in our field is the linear transformation expressed as a matrix multiplication (Definition 3.1.8). We have assumed that the transformation has an inverse (Definition 3.1.9). Geometrically, this implies that the variables $\mathbf{x}$ and $\mathbf{x}'$ have the same number of dimensions. A transformation such as

$$\mathbf{A} = \begin{bmatrix} 1 & 2 & 2 \\ 2 & 1 & 2 \\ 0 & 0 & 0 \end{bmatrix}$$

sets $x'_3 = 0$ identically; it projects a three-dimensional space $(x_1, x_2, x_3)$ on to a two-dimensional space $(x'_1, x'_2)$. Clearly this does not have an inverse; one cannot, unequivocally, project from two dimensions back into three. Algebraically, the inversion fails because the determinant $|A|$ is zero. A matrix which cannot be inverted is called *singular*; the vanishing of the determinant is a general criterion.

We shall assume all our square matrices to be non-singular. The rows and columns of a non-singular matrix are linearly independent; for otherwise the determinant vanishes. Geometrically this is clear since the columns of our transformation matrices are base vectors for an $n$-dimensional lattice.

Non-singular transformations can be combined by matrix multiplication. If $A$ and $C$ are non-singular matrices of the same dimension, then matrices such as $A^2$ ($=AA$), $AC$, $AC^{-1}$, $CAC^{-1}$, etc. are also non-singular transformations. Geometrically, we can perform operations in tandem; for example, a dilatation followed by a rotation is a spiral similarity (Figure 3.1.7(c)). The tandem operation of the form $CAC^{-1}$ is of special interest.

*Definition 5*: Let $A$, $C$ be non-singular matrices of the same dimension. Then $CAC^{-1}$ is a *similarity transformation* of $A$; the matrices $A$ and $CAC^{-1}$ are *similar*.

We interpret $C$ geometrically as a change of coordinates. Consider a system of coordinates $x'$ whose unit vectors are the columns of $C$, and suppose that we wish to make a transformation $A$ relative to this system. A point $x$ has $x'$-coordinates $C^{-1}x$, by Equation (1). A transformed point has $x'$-coordinates $AC^{-1}x$, and hence its $x$-coordinates are $CAC^{-1}x$.

EXAMPLE    Let $A$ be a scale change and $C$ a rotation

$$A = \begin{bmatrix} a & 0 \\ 0 & d \end{bmatrix} \qquad C = \begin{bmatrix} c & s \\ -s & c \end{bmatrix}$$

where $c, s$ signify $\cos \theta$, $\sin \theta$. The product

$$CAC^{-1} = \begin{bmatrix} ac^2 + ds^2 & (d-a)cs \\ (d-a)cs & as^2 + dc^2 \end{bmatrix}$$

is an inhomogeneous scale change whose principal axes are parallel to the unit vectors of $C$ (Figure 3.2.6). A circle is transformed into an ellipse whose eccentricity depends on $A$ and whose orientation depends on $C$.

The area of the transformed figure is, in this example, clearly independent of $C$; so the Jacobian must be invariant. This is a general property of similarity transformations, as can be seen from the algebraic identity

$$|CAC^{-1}| = |C| |A| |C^{-1}| = |A| \tag{24}$$

Generally speaking, similar matrices represent the same transfor-

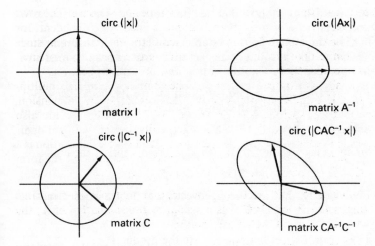

circ (|x|)

matrix I

circ (|Ax|)

matrix A⁻¹

circ (|C⁻¹x|)

matrix C

circ (|CAC⁻¹x|)

matrix CA⁻¹C⁻¹

*Figure 3.2.6 Similarity transformation*

mation in terms of different coordinate systems. Any non-singular matrix is a member of an equivalence class of similar matrices. As the above example suggests, one member of the equivalence class is a diagonal matrix. That is to say, there is a coordinate system in which the linear transformation reduces to a scale change. Such coordinates are called *normal coordinates*; they must be parallel to the eigenvectors of the matrix, which are by definition vectors whose directions are unchanged by the transformation.

EXERCISE  Show that the following transformations may be represented in the form $\mathbf{CAC}^{-1}$, where $\mathbf{A}$ is diagonal. Show that $\mathbf{A}$ is unique but $\mathbf{C}$ is not.

(i) Rotation through angle $\theta$ (Figure 3.1.7(b)). Suitable matrices are

$$\mathbf{A}=\begin{bmatrix} e^{j\theta} & 0 \\ 0 & e^{-j\theta} \end{bmatrix}, \qquad \mathbf{C}\begin{bmatrix} 1 & j \\ j & 1 \end{bmatrix}$$

(ii) Spiral similarity (Figure 3.1.7(c)).

(iii) Shear (Figure 3.1.7(d)). Suitable matrices are

$$A=\begin{bmatrix} 1 & 0 \\ 0 & \sec\theta \end{bmatrix}, \qquad C=\begin{bmatrix} 1 & -\tan\theta \\ 0 & \sec\theta-1 \end{bmatrix}$$

Note: cases (i) and (ii) show that real transformations may give rise to complex matrices.

The fundamental definition of an eigenvector must be augmented somewhat to take account of the fact that a matrix has two modes of operation, namely pre-multiplication and post-multiplication.

*Definition 6*: Let **M** be a non-singular matrix. Its *right eigenvectors* (which we shall often call simply *eigenvectors*) satisfy the equation

$$\mathbf{M}\mathbf{x} = \lambda_i \mathbf{x}_i \tag{25}$$

for some eigenvalue $\lambda_i$. The *left eigenvectors* satisfy the equation

$$(x_i^*)_t \mathbf{M} = \lambda_i (x_i^*)_t \tag{26}$$

Equivalently, they are the eigenvectors of the transposed matrix

$$\mathbf{M}_t \mathbf{x}_i^* = \lambda_i \mathbf{x}_i^* \tag{27}$$

The *spectral set* of matrices $A_i$ are the products

$$\mathbf{A}_i = \mathbf{x}_i (\mathbf{x}_i^*)_t \tag{28}$$

The notation anticipates two properties which we shall prove later, that the $\lambda_i$ are identical for the two sets of eigenvectors, and that the latter are reciprocal in the sense of Definition 3.1.11. In developing the theory we shall concentrate on transformations in $n$ dimensions giving rise to $n$ linearly independent eigenvectors. The eigenvectors are determined in direction but not in magnitude: it is clear from Equations (25)–(27) that they may be scaled by arbitrary constant multipliers, and we shall choose scale factors for local convenience.

Many of the significant properties can be deduced from the definition without actually calculating any eigenvalues or eigenvectors. However, it is perhaps more convincing to begin with a constructive procedure.

*Theorem 5*: The eigenvalues of the matrix **M** are the roots of

$$|\mathbf{M} - \lambda \mathbf{I}| = 0 \tag{29}$$

and are identical for left and right eigenvectors. Let $\mathbf{M}^{(k)} = \mathbf{M} - \lambda_k \mathbf{I}$; then the eigenvectors are solutions of the equations

$$\mathbf{M}^{(k)}\mathbf{x}_k = 0, \qquad \mathbf{M}_t^{(k)}\mathbf{x}_k^* = 0 \tag{30}$$

If the eigenvalues are distinct, the solutions are

$$\mathbf{x}_k = \text{any non-zero column of adj}\,\mathbf{M}^{(k)}$$

$$\mathbf{x}_k^* = \text{any non-zero row of adj}\,\mathbf{M}^{(k)} \tag{31}$$

where $\text{adj}\,\mathbf{M}^{(k)}$ is an adjoint matrix according to Definition 3.1.9.

*Proof*  The definition (25) implies that

$$(\mathbf{M} - \lambda \mathbf{I})\mathbf{x} = 0$$

and from the usual definition of matrix inversion (Definition 3.1.9) this can have a non-zero solution for $\mathbf{x}$ only if the determinant (29) is zero. Similarly from the definition (27)

$$(\mathbf{M}_t - \lambda \mathbf{I})\mathbf{x}^* = 0$$

and since the determinant is unchanged by transposition, Equation (29) still applies.

The first of Equations (30) follows directly from (25) and the definition of $\mathbf{M}^{(k)}$. Since $\lambda_k$ is a root of (29), $|\mathbf{M}^{(k)}| = 0$ and so from (3.1.43)

$$\mathbf{M}^{(k)} \operatorname{adj} \mathbf{M}^{(k)} = 0$$

It follows that each column of $\operatorname{adj} \mathbf{M}^{(k)}$ is either zero or a solution of (30); in the latter event it is a possible eigenvector $\mathbf{x}_k$. The $\mathbf{x}_k^*$, being eigenvectors of $\mathbf{M}_t$, can be derived in a similar way with all matrices transposed; in particular, they are columns of $(\operatorname{adj} \mathbf{M}^{(k)})_t$, and hence rows of $\operatorname{adj} \mathbf{M}^{(k)}$.

If the eigenvalues are not distinct, the formulation (31) does not apply; but eigenvectors may still be found as solutions of (30). Even when (31) is valid, it is not the only and may not be the best computational technique; for alternative methods, we refer to the mathematical literature, for instance Broyden (1).

EXAMPLE    (i) A rotation in the plane $x_1, x_2$ and a scaling of the $x_3$ axis, is represented by

$$\mathbf{M} = \begin{bmatrix} \cos\theta & \sin\theta & 0 \\ -\sin\theta & \cos\theta & 0 \\ 0 & 0 & a \end{bmatrix} \tag{32}$$

The eigenvalues follow from

$$|\mathbf{M} - \lambda \mathbf{I}| = (1 - 2\lambda\cos\theta - \lambda^2)(a - \lambda) = 0$$

and are

$$\lambda_1 = e^{j\theta}, \qquad \lambda_2 = e^{-j\theta}, \qquad \lambda_3 = a$$

The matrices $\mathbf{M}^{(k)}$ and $\operatorname{adj} \mathbf{M}^{(k)}$ are easily found. (We skip the details; it is an instructive exercise to fill them in.) The eigenvectors are

$$\mathbf{x}_1 = (\alpha, j\alpha, 0) \qquad \mathbf{x}_1^* = (\alpha, -j\alpha, 0)$$

$$\mathbf{x}_2 = (j\alpha, \alpha, 0) \qquad \mathbf{x}_2^* = (-j\alpha, \alpha, 0)$$

$$\mathbf{x}_3(0, 0, 1) \qquad \mathbf{x}_3^* = (0, 0, 1)$$

where $\alpha = 2^{-1/2}$; we have scaled them to have unit modulus.*

(ii) Consider the matrix

$$\mathbf{M} = \begin{bmatrix} \frac{1}{2} + \frac{1}{2}a & \frac{1}{2} - \frac{1}{2}a & 0 \\ \frac{1}{2} - \frac{1}{2}a & \frac{1}{2} + \frac{1}{2}a & 0 \\ 0 & 0 & 1 \end{bmatrix} \tag{33}$$

The eigenvalues are $\lambda_1 = \lambda_2 = 1$, $\lambda_3 = a$. Construction of adj$\mathbf{M}^{(3)}$ shows that $x_3 = x_3^* = (1, -1, 0)$. We cannot find the eigenvectors pertaining to the duplicated eigenvalue 1 by this method, because adj $\mathbf{M}^{(1)} = 0$ identically. However, there are two other ways of proceeding.

First, we attempt a direct solution of the Equation $\mathbf{M}^{(1)}\mathbf{x} = 0$ by writing out the equations corresponding to rows. It turns out that $\mathbf{x} = (p, p, q)$ satisfies the equations for arbitrary scalars $p, q$. The eigenvectors may lie anywhere in the plane $x_1 = x_2$. By choosing two linearly independent vectors in this plane, a set of three linearly independent eigenvectors can be constructed.

The second technique depends on Theorem 6 and will be given later.

For the further development of the theory, it is useful to have a succinct notation for the sets of eigenvalues and eigenvectors. The matrices $\mathbf{X}, \mathbf{X}^*$ have eigenvectors for columns:

$$\mathbf{X} = [\mathbf{x}_1 \mathbf{x}_2 \dots \mathbf{x}_n] \tag{34}$$

and similarly for $\mathbf{X}^*$. The matrix $\boldsymbol{\Lambda}$ is diagonal, and comprises the eigenvalues in order:

$$\boldsymbol{\Lambda} = \begin{bmatrix} \lambda_1 & 0 & 0 & \dots & 0 \\ 0 & \lambda_2 & 0 & \dots & 0 \\ 0 & 0 & \lambda_3 & \dots & 0 \\ 0 & 0 & 0 & \dots & \lambda_n \end{bmatrix} \tag{35}$$

---

* When dealing with complex-valued vectors, the modulus must be taken in the Hermitian sense; that is, its square is the scalar product of the vector and its complex conjugate.

In this notation

$$\mathbf{X}\boldsymbol{\Lambda} = [\lambda_1 \mathbf{x}_1 \; \lambda_2 \mathbf{x}_2 \ldots \lambda_n \mathbf{x}_n] \tag{36}$$

and the defining Equations (25), (27) become

$$\mathbf{MX} = \mathbf{X}\boldsymbol{\Lambda} \tag{37}$$

$$\mathbf{M}_t \mathbf{X}^* = \mathbf{X}^* \boldsymbol{\Lambda} \tag{38}$$

It follows that $\mathbf{M}$, $\boldsymbol{\Lambda}$ and $\mathbf{M}_t$ are similar, since

$$\mathbf{M} = \mathbf{X}\boldsymbol{\Lambda}\mathbf{X}^{-1} \tag{39}$$

$$\mathbf{M}_t = \mathbf{X}^* \boldsymbol{\Lambda} \mathbf{X}^{*-1} \tag{40}$$

There are several related properties of eigenvalues and eigenvectors which we gather together as a theorem.

*Theorem 6*: Let $\mathbf{M}$ be a non-singular matrix with a number of linearly independent eigenvectors equal to its dimension. Then the following statements are true:

(i) Any matrix $\mathbf{M}'$ related to $\mathbf{M}$ by a similarity transformation $\mathbf{M}' = \mathbf{CMC}^{-1}$ has the same eigenvalues as $\mathbf{M}$. Its right eigenvectors are the columns of $\mathbf{CX}$, and its left eigenvectors are the columns of $\mathbf{C}^* \mathbf{X}^*$, where $\mathbf{C}^*$ is reciprocal to $\mathbf{C}$.

(ii) The matrices $\mathbf{X}$ and $\mathbf{X}^*$ defining the right and left eigenvectors are reciprocal, save for an arbitrary scaling.

(iii) The power $\mathbf{M}'$ has eigenvalues $\lambda_k^r$ and the eigenvectors of $\mathbf{M}$; it may be represented as

$$\mathbf{M}' = \mathbf{X}\boldsymbol{\Lambda}'\mathbf{X}^{-1} \tag{41}$$

for any integer $r$.

(iv) The power $\mathbf{M}'$ may be represented in terms of the spectral set

$$\mathbf{M}' = \sum_k \lambda_k^r \mathbf{A}_k \tag{42}$$

*Proof*   (i) Premultiplying Equation (37) by $\mathbf{C}$ gives

$$(\mathbf{CMC}^{-1})(\mathbf{CX}) = (\mathbf{CX})\boldsymbol{\Lambda}$$

which shows that the similar matrix $\mathbf{CMC}^{-1}$ has eigenvalues $\boldsymbol{\Lambda}$ and eigenvectors $\mathbf{CX}$. The identity

$$(\mathbf{CMC}^{-1})_t = \mathbf{C}_t^{-1}\mathbf{M}_t\mathbf{C}_t$$

shows that the corresponding effect on $\mathbf{M}_t$ is a similarity transformation by $\mathbf{C}_t^{-1} = \mathbf{C}^*$, so the left eigenvectors are the columns of $\mathbf{C}^* \mathbf{X}^*$.

(ii) The matrix $\mathbf{M}$ is related by a similarity transformation to the diagonal matrix $\Lambda$. Its eigenvectors are therefore related to those of $\Lambda$ by the result (i) above. If the eigenvalues are distinct, the eigenvectors of $\Lambda$ (both left and right) are the columns of the identity' matrix $\mathbf{I}$ (with arbitrary scaling). If some eigenvalues are not distinct, the corresponding eigenvectors are incompletely determined but the scaled columns of $\mathbf{I}$ are among the valid sets of eigenvectors. Taking result (i) along with Equation (39), the left eigenvectors are $\mathbf{X}^*\mathbf{I} = \mathbf{X}^*$, where $\mathbf{X}^*$ is reciprocal to $\mathbf{X}$. These eigenvectors are always subject to an arbitrary scaling. However, we can always scale them for exact reciprocity, and indeed this is essential to the construction of the spectral set.

(iii) These properties are perhaps obvious from the definition. Formally, we deduce from (39) that

$$\mathbf{M}^r = (\mathbf{X}\Lambda\mathbf{X}^{-1})^r$$

Multiplying out and cancelling factors $\mathbf{X}^{-1}\mathbf{X}$ gives the result (41). Note that this formulation applies to both positive and negative powers, and defines the zeroth power as $\mathbf{M}^0 = \mathbf{I}$.

(iv) From the reciprocity of $\mathbf{X}$ and $\mathbf{X}^*$, the eigenvectors $\mathbf{x}^*$ are the rows of $\mathbf{X}^{-1}$. So we write (41) as

$$\mathbf{M}^r = [\lambda_1^r\mathbf{x}_1\ \lambda_2^r\mathbf{x}_2 \ldots] \begin{bmatrix} (\mathbf{x}_1^*)_t \\ (\mathbf{x}_2^*)_t \\ \vdots \end{bmatrix}$$

$$= \sum_k \lambda_k^r \mathbf{x}_k (\mathbf{x}_k^*)_t$$

By the definition (28) each term of the summation is a matrix of the spectral set, and the expression is identical with (42).

EXAMPLE    (i) Continuing our previous example, Equation (32), the eigenvector matrices are

$$\mathbf{X} = \begin{bmatrix} \alpha & j\alpha & 0 \\ j\alpha & \alpha & 0 \\ 0 & 0 & 1 \end{bmatrix} \quad \mathbf{X}^* = \begin{bmatrix} \alpha & -j\alpha & 0 \\ -j\alpha & \alpha & 0 \\ 0 & 0 & 1 \end{bmatrix}$$

It is easy to verify by multiplication that $\mathbf{X}\mathbf{X}_t^* = \mathbf{I}$ which demonstrates reciprocity. The spectral set is

$$\mathbf{A}_1 = \begin{bmatrix} \frac{1}{2} & -j\frac{1}{2} & 0 \\ j\frac{1}{2} & \frac{1}{2} & 0 \\ 0 & 0 & 0 \end{bmatrix} \quad \mathbf{A}_2 = \begin{bmatrix} \frac{1}{2} & j\frac{1}{2} & 0 \\ -j\frac{1}{2} & \frac{1}{2} & 0 \\ 0 & 0 & 0 \end{bmatrix} \quad \mathbf{A}_3 = \begin{bmatrix} 0 & 0 & 0 \\ 0 & 0 & 0 \\ 0 & 0 & 1 \end{bmatrix}$$

(ii) Continuining our previous example, Equation (33), we note that the matrix can be expressed as a similarity transformation

$$\mathbf{M} = \begin{bmatrix} \alpha & \alpha & 0 \\ -\alpha & \alpha & 0 \\ 0 & 0 & 1 \end{bmatrix} \begin{bmatrix} a & 0 & 0 \\ 0 & 1 & 0 \\ 0 & 0 & 1 \end{bmatrix} \begin{bmatrix} \alpha & -\alpha & 0 \\ \alpha & \alpha & 0 \\ 0 & 0 & 1 \end{bmatrix}$$

where $\mathbf{C}$ is a rotation by $\pi/4$ (again we use the notation $\alpha = 2^{-1/2}$).

This formulation gives as eigenvectors the columns of $\mathbf{C}$. One of these, namely $(\alpha, -\alpha, 0)$ is a normalised version of $x_3 = (1, -1, 0)$ which we found before. The other two, namely $(\alpha, \alpha, 0)$ and $(0, 0, 1)$, are orthogonal vectors in the plane $x_1 = x_2$.

It will be clear from the last example that much of the theory presented here, though usually stated only for the case of distinct eigenvalues, is in fact applicable with multiple eigenvalues so long as a complete set of linearly independent eigenvectors exists. It fails when the transformation is in effect a projection into a space of fewer dimensions.

EXERCISE (i) Verify expressions (41) and (42) for example (i) above.
(ii) Verify for example (i) the equations

$$\sum_i \mathbf{A}_i = \mathbf{I} \tag{43}$$

$$\mathbf{A}_i^2 = \mathbf{A}_i \tag{44}$$

$$\mathbf{A}_i \mathbf{A}_j = 0, \qquad i \neq j \tag{45}$$

Then prove them as general properties of a spectral set, using Theorem 6.
(iii) Prove that

$$\begin{bmatrix} \cosh \gamma & \sinh j \\ \sinh \gamma & \cosh j \end{bmatrix}^r = \begin{bmatrix} \cosh r\gamma & \sinh r\gamma \\ \sinh r\gamma & \cosh r\gamma \end{bmatrix} \tag{46}$$

It is now clear that the unit vectors of our earlier theory owe their convenience to their status as eigenvectors; and that the effect of the Fourier integral is to interchange the two reciprocal sets of eigenvectors usually associated with a linear transformation. These results are useful in many areas of applied mathematics; we employ them particularly in dealing with wave motion and multivariate probability distributions.

## 3.3 IMAGES AND SCANNING

In our first introduction to signal analysis (Chapter 2) the independent variable was taken as time, this being the physical dimension of most common concern in a one-dimensional theory. Our multidimensional theory has been developed in terms of mathematical variables whose physical counterparts have not been specified. The first application is to two-dimensional spatial patterns, which we shall call *images*. The obvious example is a visual image or picture; the intensity of emitted or reflected light is a function of position, and we shall write it as $h(x, y)$. It is to be assumed that $x, y$ are rectangular coordinates; they are commonly distances measured along a flat surface but can also be angular deflections, as for example in the case of a picture projected by a lens system.

It is a familiar fact that images may contain more or less detail; they may be reproduced with more or less resolution, and if the resolution is inadequate the detail may be obscured. We can represent these phenomena more precisely in the language of signal theory. Both detail and resolution can be quantified in terms of the *spatial frequency spectrum* which is the Fourier transform of the image function.

EXAMPLES   (i) A pattern of uniform black and white stripes (Figure 3.3.1(a)) extending to infinity in both dimensions:

$$h_1(x, y) = \text{rep}_b \, \text{rect}(2x/b) \tag{1}$$

$$H_1(u, v) = \{\tfrac{1}{2} \text{sinc}(\tfrac{1}{2}bu) \, \text{rep}_{1/b} \delta(u)\} \delta(v)$$

$$= \tfrac{1}{2}\delta(u)\delta(v) + \frac{\delta(v)}{\pi} \sum_{n=0}^{\infty} \frac{(-1)^n}{2n+1} \delta\left(u \pm \frac{2n+1}{b}\right) \tag{2}$$

(ii) A check pattern of black and white squares (Figure 3.3.1(b)), also extending to infinity

$$h_2(x, y) = 1 - \text{rep}_b \, \text{rect}(2x/b)$$

$$- \text{rep}_b \, \text{rect}(2y/b) + 2 \, \text{rep}_{b,b} \, \text{rect}(2x/b, 2y/b) \tag{3}$$

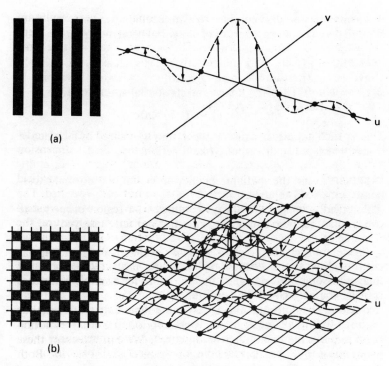

*Figure 3.3.1 Repeated patterns and their spectra*

$$H_2(u,v) = \delta(u,v) - \tfrac{1}{2}\operatorname{sinc}(\tfrac{1}{2}bu)\operatorname{rep}_{1/b}\delta(u)\delta(v)$$
$$- \tfrac{1}{2}\operatorname{sinc}(\tfrac{1}{2}bv)\operatorname{rep}_{1/b}\delta(v)\delta(u)$$
$$+ \tfrac{1}{2}\operatorname{sinc}(\tfrac{1}{2}bu, \tfrac{1}{2}bv)\operatorname{rep}_{1/b, \, 1/b}\delta(u,v)$$
$$= \tfrac{1}{2}\delta(u,v) + \frac{2}{\pi^2}\sum_{n=0}^{\infty}\sum_{m=0}^{\infty}\frac{(-1)^{n+m}}{(2n+1)(2m+1)}$$
$$\delta\left(u \pm \frac{2m+1}{b}, \, v \pm \frac{2n+1}{b}\right)$$

$$(4)$$

These spectra are discrete, because the images are periodic. The spatial frequencies are inversely proportional to the period of the image. The coefficients fall off slowly (as $u^{-1}$ and $u^{-1}v^{-1}$ respectively) because the images have discontinuities. All these features have familiar counterparts in the behaviour of waveforms and frequency spectra.

An image is normally confined to a finite region $\rho$ in the $(x, y)$ plane. We can deduce some properties of its spatial spectrum from this fact.

EXAMPLE    (iii) Let a periodic pattern $h(x, y)$ such as either example above be restricted to a region $\rho$, whose indicator function* is $\phi(x, y) \Rightarrow \Phi(u, v)$. Then the image and its spatial spectrum are

$$h(x, y)\phi(x, y) \Rightarrow H(u, v)*\Phi(u, v) \tag{5}$$

That is, each impulse in a discrete spectrum is replaced by a replica of $\Phi(u, v)$ which is usually a pulse-like function.

EXERCISE    Find the spatial frequency spectrum of a normal chessboard with $8 \times 8$ squares.

Practically, images are always confined to a region of moderate size, and so periodic components are not perfectly resolved.

*Image transfer characteristics*    The communication engineer is concerned with the formation, transmission or reproduction of images by some optical or electronic system. Such a system will have a transfer characteristic expressible in the domain of space or of spatial frequency. The limitations of a system are most apparent when it is required to display fine detail, such as a very small point. We analyse them in terms of the point spread function, a two-dimensional pulse which constitutes the smallest point the system can display; formally, it is analogous to impulse response.

*Definition 1*: let a point image $\delta(x, y)$ be applied to an image transmission system. The resulting output image $g(x, y)$ is characteristic of the system, and is called its point spread function.

Clearly, the response to any sufficiently fine spot will approximate this function. We may also use the point spread function to characterise display devices, which reconstruct an image from an input in another form; in this case, it may be difficult to assign a meaning to an impulsive input, and we take $g(x, y)$ as the smallest elementary spot which can be generated by the display.

*Definition 2*: let $g(x, y)$ have a Fourier transform $G(u, v)$. Then $G(u, v)$ is the spatial frequency response of the system.

We now suppose the system to be linear, so that images may be built up by superposition of elements. This may appear unwarranted, since

---

* We shall often use indicator functions and their transforms. It is important to recognise in which domain the function is an indicator; here, it is the $x$ domain, but in Theorem 3.2.3 it is the $u$ domain.

optical transducers are often non-linear. However, the dominant non-linearity is normally at the peripheries of a system; for example, in television transmission there is a substantially linear channel from the camera to the display cathode-ray tube, but the optical luminance generated is a non-linear monotonic function of the current in the c.r.t. The overall performance approximates closely to that of an ideally linear system, with monotonic nonlinearities at input and output only, and we may usefully apply linear theory to a wide range of problems.

With this reservation, we state

*Theorem 1*: let an image $h(x, y) \Rightarrow H(u, v)$ be applied to an image transmission system whose point spread function is $g(x, y) \Rightarrow G(u, v)$. Then the output image is $g(x, y)*h(x, y)$ and its spatial frequency spectrum is $G(u, v)H(u, v)$.

*Proof* is a two-dimensional variant of one-dimensional signal theory which we need not elaborate.

EXAMPLES   (i) A purely optical system comprising lenses, mirrors etc. when focussed as accurately as possible will produce a spot of perceptible diameter, usually brightest at the centre and fading more or less symmetrically. A lower bound to the size of spot, hence an approximate bound to the spatial frequency response, is set by *diffraction* which we study in section 3.7.

(ii) A cathode ray tube generates an imperfectly focussed electron beam whose profile constitutes a point-spread function, assuming there to be no other significant limitation. In television, both camera tubes and display tubes contribute to the overall response; there is also a frequency limitation in the transmission channel which translates to a spatial frequency limitation in the image, as we exhibit later in treating the theory of scanning. The overall spatial frequency response is the product of these three factors.

(iii) Optical and television systems are commonly tested by applying standard images (test charts) including bar and ray patterns of various spatial frequencies; the spatial cutoff of the system is then directly observable.

*Sampling of images*   The representation of images by discrete elements is familiar both in television, whose images are built up from lines of varying intensity, and from half-tone printing, whose images are built up from ink dots of varying size. The regularity of structure in such images makes them closely akin to the lattice-sampled

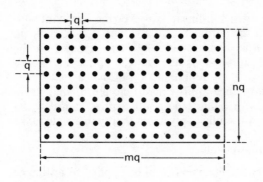

*Figure 3.3.2 Lattice sampling of image*

functions whose theory was developed in Section 3.2. Other discrete elements, such as the shadings, hatchings and line gradations used by artists and engravers, are less regular but depend for their effectiveness on the same phenomenon: the limited spatial bandwidth required to represent a recognisable image.

The spatial bandwidth of a source may be limited, i.e. it may contain no detail finer than some upper bound to spatial frequency. Whether this is the case or no, the human observer has eyes of limited acuity, and can resolve visual images only within a limited spatial bandwidth (expressed in cycles per radian subtended at the eye).*

Digital methods of transmitting, storing and processing images have led to an increasing interest in the representation of images by samples on a rectangular lattice (Figure 3.3.2). A sampling function, representing the action of taking ideal samples at such a set of points, is

$$s(x, y) = \operatorname{rep}_{q,q} \delta(x, y) \operatorname{rect}\left(\frac{x}{mq}, \frac{y}{nq}\right) \tag{6}$$

if the numbers $m, n$ are both odd, and the origin of coordinates be taken at the centre of the rectangular image. If an image $h(x, y)$ be sampled at these points, the sampled image and its Fourier transform

---

* Visual phenomena are, of course, too complex to be represented adequately by a simple low-pass filter, though qualitatively this is the important property for our present purpose. For a more detailed treatment of image analysis and related visual phenomena, see Pearson (1).

are

$$h(x, y)s(x, y) \Rightarrow H(u, v) * S(u, v)$$

$$= \frac{1}{q^2} \operatorname{rep}_{1/q, 1/q} H(u, v) \tag{7}$$

By Theorem 3.2.3, this sampling lattice is adequate if the spatial frequency spectrum of the original image has no components at spatial frequencies greater than $1/2q$. It may also be deemed adequate if a low-pass-filtered representation is acceptable; for example, if the stripes and checks of Figure 3.3.1 can be represented by an image with light and dark areas in appropriate positions but with blurred transitions between them, then a sampling interval of $q = \frac{1}{2}b$ may be adequate. A sample such as one of those in an adequate lattice is called a *picture element*, sometimes abbreviated *pixel* in the specialised literature.

EXERCISE   (i) Why is Equation (6) valid only for odd $m, n$? Find similar expressions for sampling functions with one or both of $m, n$ even. Show that

$$s(x, y) = \operatorname{rep}_{1,1} \delta\left(\frac{x}{q} - \frac{1}{2}, \; \frac{y}{q} - \frac{1}{2}\right) \operatorname{rect}\left(\frac{x}{mq} - \frac{1}{2}, \; \frac{y}{nq} - \frac{1}{2}\right) \tag{8}$$

is a valid sampling function for all $m, n$. Where is the origin of coordinates in Equation (8)?

(ii) Give a condition, not stated in the text, which must be satisfied if sampling at intervals $q = \frac{1}{2}b$ is to reproduce the stripes and checks of Figure 3.3.1.

*Moving images*   The foregoing remarks apply to an unchanging image, in whose description no time variable is necessary. An image which changes with the effluxion of time clearly needs for its analytical description a three-dimensional function

$$h(x, y, t) \Rightarrow H(u, v, f) \tag{9}$$

where $x, y$ are spatial dimensions transforming into spatial frequencies $u, v$; and $t$ is the time variable transforming into the (temporal) frequency $f$.

In general, the three-dimensional function will not be separable. If $h(x, y, t) = h_1(x, y)h_2(t)$ it follows that a stationary image is undergoing overall changes in brightness, a special case of little interest. Thus we shall normally need a full three-dimensional description of a changing image.

A cinematograph film consists of a sequence of exposures at regular intervals $\tau$. Each exposure yields a substantially instantaneous sample of a complete spatial field. Thus a cinematograph picture of a changing scene $h(x, y, t)$ is, analytically

$$h(x, y, t)\,\text{rep}_\tau\,\delta(t) \Rightarrow \tau^{-1}\,\text{rep}_{1/\tau}\,H(u, v, f) \qquad (10)$$

The same expression applies to stroboscopic observation, as often used on rotating machinery; illumination by a periodic flash presents to the observer a sequence of instantaneous samples. A human observer in either case sees a continuous picture, because his sense-organs have limited temporal resolution and contain the equivalent of a low-pass filter. If the changing scene $h(x, y, t)$ contains any periodic movements, then by the theory of sampling ambiguity (Theorem 2.5.5) many different periodicities are equivalent under sampling.

EXERCISE    Explain on the basis of sampling ambiguity (i) how stroboscopic illumination may be used to observe rapidly rotating or vibrating objects (ii) why in cinematograph films wheels may appear to rotate backwards.

Let us now suppose that each and every frame of a cinematograph film is sampled on a spatial lattice like Figure 3.3.2. The sampled sequence of images may be expressed analytically as

$$h(x, y, t)\,\text{rep}_{q,q,\tau}\,\delta(x, y, t) \Rightarrow \frac{1}{q^2\tau}\,\text{rep}_{1/q,1/q,1/\tau}\,H(u, v, f) \qquad (11)$$

The frequency limitations are now both spatial and temporal, in the $(u, v, f)$ domain. The human observer, as we have noted, has his bounds both to spatial and temporal resolution; it should now be added, that these interact, so that ideally the full three-dimensional domain is needed for their description.

## Scanning

For the purposes of communication, we almost always need to represent an image (which is inherently a 2- or 3-dimensional function) by a one-dimensional signal, a function of time which can be sent over a communication channel.

If an image be sampled on a three-dimensional lattice, as expressed by Equation (11), then in principle the conversion is simple. Signal samples may be stored by various means, and read out of store at any required speed. We can take the $mn$ samples which constitute one frame and arrange them in serial order for transmission over a time interval $\tau$. This process can be repeated for each frame, i.e. $1/\tau$ times per second. The sequence of samples can be conveyed by a uniform discrete signal (Section 2.5) whose rate is $mn/\tau$ bauds. In practice some supplementary information must be added, to identify the successive picture elements; but if the sequence is a simple and regular one, only a modest increase in signalling rate is needed.

Although this is a possible technique, the more usual method is to sample the image successively at various positions, proceeding systematically through the complete field: this is known as *scanning*.

*Definition 3*: Let $\xi = \xi(t)$ and $\eta = \eta(t)$ be single-valued functions of $t$, such that the variable point $(\xi, \eta)$ traverses the field of an image. Then a scanning function is defined as $\delta(x - \xi, y - \eta)$. A periodic scanning function $\mathrm{rep}_T\, \delta(x - \xi, y - \eta)$ performs repeated scans at uniform intervals $T$.

Like other sampling functions, this can be considered as multiplying a source function to produce a sampled signal. For example, a static image $h(x, y)$ yields on a single scan the signal

$$s(t) = h(x, y)\delta(x - \xi, y - \eta) = h\{\xi(t), \eta(t)\} \tag{12}$$

while a changing image $h(x, y, t)$ yields on repeated scanning the signal

$$s(t) = h(x, y, t)\,\mathrm{rep}_T\, \delta(x - \xi, y - \eta) \tag{13}$$

EXAMPLE   A simple quasi-rectangular scan, of the type used for television but without such complications as interlace, is shown in Figure 3.3.3. The scanning waveforms $\xi(t), \eta(t)$ shown at (b) cause the scanning spot to trace out a path in the $x, y$ plane as shown at (a). Bold lines denote lines of effective scan, faint lines the quasi-instantaneous 'flyback'. A three-dimensional representation of the $(x, y, t)$ domain is shown at (c); the faint lines here indicate a coordinate framework, while the bold lines are the scanning locus.

*Sampling the scanned signal*   The scanning process as described is itself a form of time sampling, since any point on the scanning locus is sampled every $T$ seconds. However, the signal generated by scanning is a continuous one. Let us suppose that this signal is time-sampled, at intervals $T/mn$ where $n$ is the number of lines and $m$ another integer (Figure 3.3.4). For comparison with rectangular sampling (Figure 3.3.2) we will also suppose that the vertical interval between lines, and the horizontal interval between samples, are equal: let their common value be $q$. The samples fall on the points of a skewed lattice, as shown in Figure 3.3.4.

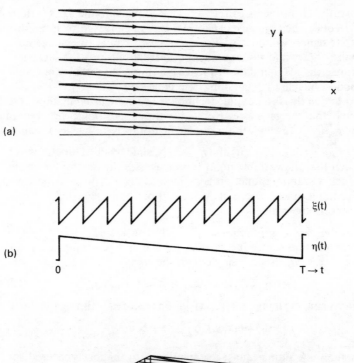

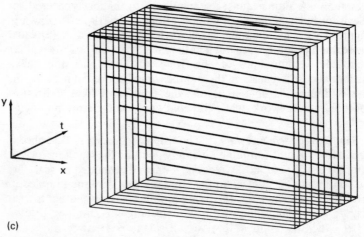

*Figure 3.3.3 Scanning. (a) The (x,y) plane; (b) Scanning waveforms; (c) The (x,y,t) lattice*

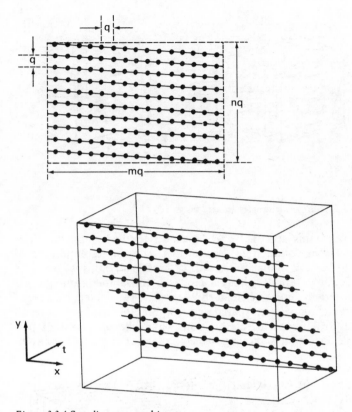

*Figure 3.3.4 Sampling a scanned image*

The sample lattice **B** and its reciprocal **B\*** (using the notation of Section 3.2) are

$$\mathbf{B} = \begin{bmatrix} q & 0 & 0 \\ -q/m & -q & 0 \\ T/mn & T/n & T \end{bmatrix} \qquad (14)$$

$$\mathbf{B^*} = \begin{bmatrix} 1/q & -1/qm & 0 \\ 0 & -1/q & 1/qn \\ 0 & 0 & 1/T \end{bmatrix} \qquad (15)$$

The unit vectors of these lattices are shown in Figure 3.3.5. The spectral repetition due to sampling is on the skewed lattice **B\***. The volume of

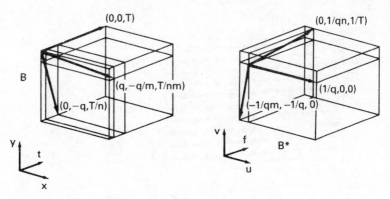

*Figure 3.3.5 Lattices for sampled scanned image*

a unit cell in this lattice is $1/q^2 T$, the same as for the rectangular lattice postulated in Equation (11), and at first sight the resolution would seem to be very similar in the two cases. Broadly, this is true if we consider only stationary images. However, the sampling ambiguity is significantly different when all three axes are considered, because of the interaction between spatial and temporal frequencies. The result is that stroboscopic effects are somewhat different, and that perceptible distortion of moving objects can occur in the scanned/sampled system.

EXERCISES   (i) Check that the lattices (14), (15) satisfy Equations (3.2.10–11).
(ii) Consider an image consisting of a vertical bar moving in a horizontal direction. Investigate the effects of sampling this image on (a) a rectangular lattice (b) the skewed lattice (14).
(iii) An image transmission system uses scanning and sampling as described above, but has non-trivial flyback times. Line flyback occupies a time equal to that of $m'$ samples, and frame flyback occupies a time equal to that of $n'$ lines. Show that the image spectrum is repeated on a lattice

$$
\mathbf{B}^* = \begin{bmatrix} \dfrac{1}{q} & \dfrac{-1}{q(m+m')} & 0 \\[2ex] 0 & -\dfrac{1}{q} & \dfrac{1}{q(n+n')} \\[2ex] 0 & 0 & \dfrac{1}{T} \end{bmatrix} \tag{16}
$$

*Resolution of a scanned image*   This will be affected both by the spatial point-spread functions of the devices and by the temporal resolution of the channel used to convey a signal of the form (12) or (13). Suppose a scanning spot to be moving in a straight line at velocity $c$: then an impulse response $f(t)$ in the signal path translates directly to a point-spread function $f(ct)$ in the direction of the line. For the normal television scan in which lines are almost horizontal, we can express horizontal resolution as

$$g(x) = g_1(x)*c^{-1}f(x/c)*g_2(x) \qquad (17a)$$

$$G(u) = G_1(u)F(cu)G_2(u) \qquad (17b)$$

where $g_1(x)$ and $g_2(x)$ are the horizontal point spreads of the source and display devices respectively. This composition is strictly valid only on the linearity assumption discussed previously.

## Image restoration

There are many ways in which images may become blurred in the course of storage or transmission. The general effect of limited resolution is summarised in Theorem 1: the point spread function here is the composition of several factors, as in (17). In principle, it might seem possible to remove the blurring by an inverse process. The frequency-domain formulation suggests that an inverse filter with spectrum $1/G(u,v)$ would restore the original image. Indeed some improvement may be made, but there are several impediments to simple inverse filtering.

(i) The spectrum $G(u,v)$ may have zeros, in which case the reciprocal diverges. Even if the zeros are outside the main frequency band, or if the spectrum has minima rather than zeros, the reciprocal msy have large peaks which are difficult to implement and sensitive to any variation in the signal or the filter.

(ii) The original image may be overlaid by noise: either temporal noise in transmission by electrical means, or spatial noise in the form of granularity, which can occur both in electro-optic and in photographic images. Attempts to restore resolution or contrast may enhance the noise to an unacceptable level.

(iii) Any type of processing carried out in optical form is constrained by the fact that optical intensity is a non-negative quantity: if restoration implies a filter function which in the time or space domain has oscillation or overshoot, this may not be feasible.

The best practical restoration filters have approximated $1/G(u,v)$ over a limited frequency region, while cutting off in regions where noise or divergence might be a problem. A systematic approach* is to use a recovery filter of the form

$$\frac{G(u,v)}{|G(u,v)|^2 + N(u,v)/S(u,v)} \qquad (18)$$

where $N(u,v)$ and $S(u,v)$ are the power spectra of the noise and the signal (image) respectively. This is one of the family of minimum-mean-square-error filters discussed in Section 4.8 (Vol. 2).

## 3.4 WAVE MOTION

Signals are conveyed through closed or open regions of space in the form of electromagnetic fluctuations known as *waves*. Wave motion is familiar from everyday observation: the surface of an expanse of water is rarely so free from disturbance as to fail to manifest it. The properties of such waves are apparent: (i) an oscillatory disturbance, and (ii) a translatory motion, not of the material medium, but of the oscillatory disturbance.

*Definition 1*: A travelling wave moving in the $x$ direction with velocity $c$ is a disturbance which can be expressed in the functional form

$$g(t,x) = g_w(t - x/c) \qquad (1)$$

where $g_w()$ is a functional form admitted as a signal waveform. Other spatial dimensions orthogonal to $x$ may or may not be significant: in any case the dimensionality of $g_w()$ is one less than that of $g()$.

EXAMPLES   (i) The two-dimensional sinusoid, Figure 3.1.6, is a sinusoidal travelling wave if one dimension is time and the other is space. It is redrawn in Figure 3.4.1 to illustrate some parameters of travelling waves: in particular the wavelength $\lambda$ and the wave number $k$ (the number of cycles per unit length). The velocity of the wave motion is

$$c = \frac{v}{k} = \frac{\lambda}{\tau} \qquad (2)$$

where $v$ is frequency and $\tau$ is the periodic time. The sinusoid drawn

---

* See Hunt (1) for a discussion and some illustrated examples.

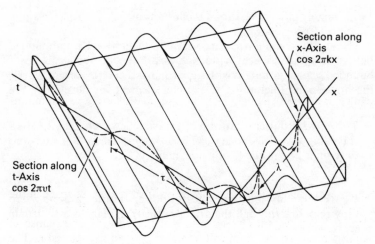

*Figure 3.4.1 Sinusoidal travelling wave* $\cos 2\pi(vt - kx)$, $k = wave\ number = 1/\lambda$, $v = frequency = 1/\tau$, *velocity* $c = v/k = \lambda/\tau$

can be written as

$$\cos 2\pi(vt - kx) = \cos 2\pi v(t - x/c) \tag{3}$$

which is clearly of the form (1).

(ii) A non-periodic travelling wave in the form of a pulse is shown in Figure 3.4.2. The section at $x = x_0$, namely $g(t - x_0/c)$, is a waveform illustrating the temporal fluctuation at a fixed point. The section at

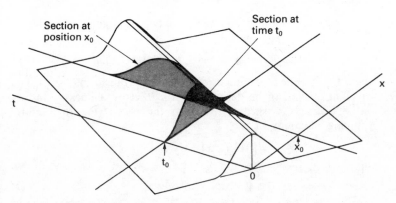

*Figure 3.4.2 Travelling pulse*

$t = t_0$, namely $g(t_0 - x/c)$, shows the instantaneous disturbance along the path of propagation.

The ideal travelling wave according to Definition 1 is unbounded both in time and in space: in practice, we are of course concerned with bounded segments, but (as with signal analysis in terms of sine waves) the unbounded fluctuation is a useful element for developing the theory.

*Theorem 1* (Fourier transform of a travelling wave): Let $g(t,x)$ be a travelling wave of velocity $c$. The Fourier transform is non-zero only on a line in the $(f, u)$ plane, namely

$$u + f/c = 0 \qquad (4)$$

Conversely, any function whose Fourier transform is non-zero only on a line through the origin of the $(f, u)$ plane is a travelling wave.

*First proof*    It is easily shown that for a sinusoidal travelling wave

$$e^{j2\pi(vt - kx)} \Rightarrow \delta(f - v, u + k)$$

(see Appendix, Table 4 or Figure 3.1.9(a)). Since $c = v/k$, the impulse lies on the line (4). Any admissible signal waveform can be represented as a superposition of sinusoids, therefore any travelling wave can be represented as a superposition of travelling sinusoids. If these have a common velocity $c$, they will all lie on the line (4).

Conversely, any element of a transform located at $(v, -k)$ corresponds to a travelling sinusoid of velocity $v/k$: so any union of such elements with a common value of $v/k$ is the transform of a travelling wave.

*Second proof*    Consider a function of two orthogonal variables $t,x$ having a section $g_w(t)$, namely

$$g_2(t,x) \equiv g_w(t)1 \Rightarrow G_w(f)\delta(u) \triangleq G_2(f,u)$$

where $G_w(f)$ is the (one-dimensional) Fourier transform of $g_w(t)$. The travelling wave can be derived from $g_2(t,x)$ by a linear transformation, namely a shear parallel to the $t$-axis (Figure 3.1.7(d)). Applying Theorem 3.1.5,

$$g_2(t - x/c, x) \Rightarrow G_2(f, u + f/c)$$

It follows that

$$g_w(t - x/c) \Rightarrow G_w(f)\delta(u + f/c) \qquad (5)$$

which implies both parts of the theorem.

The second proof is perhaps less intuitively obvious than the first, but it has two advantages. It gives a precise expression for the transform: and it leads naturally to certain applications, such as diffraction from a travelling wave which we discuss in Section 3.7.

We shall be concerned with the properties of several media which support travelling waves. Since the media of common interest are bilateral, and propagate waves equally well in opposite directions, they exemplify the following theorem.

*Theorem 2* (wave equation of a medium): Let $\phi(t,x) \Rightarrow \Phi(f,u)$ be an information-bearing variable in a medium supporting travelling waves of velocity $c$ in either the positive or the negative direction of the spatial variable $x$. Then the medium imposes the following (equivalent) conditions:

$$(u^2 - f^2/c^2)\Phi = 0 \tag{6}$$

$$\frac{d^2\phi}{dx^2} - \frac{1}{c^2}\frac{d^2\phi}{dt^2} = 0 \tag{7}$$

*Proof* By Theorem 1, waves of velocity $+c$ and $-c$ impose the conditions

$$(u + f/c)\Phi = 0$$

$$(u - f/c)\Phi = 0$$

and these are subsumed in Equation (6). Inverse Fourier transformation gives (7).

Equation (7) is a classical form of wave equation which in the present treatment we shall often encounter in the transformed version (6).

EXAMPLE   An obvious solution of Equations (6) and (7) is the sinusoidal travelling wave

$$e^{j2\pi(vt \pm kx)} \tag{8}$$

with $c = v/k$. We shall use this as an elementary wave in many media to be discussed later.

Waves in practical media such as cables, waveguides and optical fibres exhibit three further phenomena which we shall analyse: attenuation, dispersion and reflection. Dissipative media absorb energy from a travelling wave: a mathematical expression such as (3) is then multiplied by a factor $e^{-\alpha x}$ where $\alpha$ is the *attenuation constant*. We shall derive this property in detail for a TEM line later in this section. *Reflection* occurs at a boundary or discontinuity in the transmission medium: we shall study this in several different media. *Dispersion* is a form of linear distortion in the medium. A travelling wave in the sense of Definition 1 has a waveform which is invariant under translation because its frequency components travel at the same velocity. So a path which propagates such waves with arbitrary form is a distortionless channel in the sense of Definition 2.3.5: it provides equal loss and equal delay at all frequencies. Many practical media exhibit a dependence of velocity on frequency: and this introduces several new concepts.

*Definition 2*: A medium whose wave velocity varies with frequency exhibits *dispersion*. In such a medium, a sinusoidal wave $e^{j2\pi(vt-kx)}$ has a wave number $k = k(v)$ which varies with frequency. The *phase velocity* at any frequency $v$ is $v_p = v/k$. The *group velocity* at any frequency $v$ is $v_g = dv/dk$. In a dispersive medium the two velocities are in general different (save possibly at one or more discrete frequencies). Dispersion is *normal* if $v_g < v_p$ and *anomalous* if $v_p < v_g$.

The phase velocity is the velocity of a point of constant phase in a sinusoidal travelling wave of single frequency $v$. The group velocity is the velocity of the envelope of a group of frequency components centred on a frequency $v$: it is therefore the effective velocity of propagation of a modulated signal. This is consistent with our definition 2.3.6 for group delay, and the envelope delay is derived mathematically in section 2.3. In a normally-dispersive medium, the modulating signal travels more slowly than the carrier, but if sufficiently narrow-band may suffer little or no distortion. A wide-band signal in a dispersive medium always suffers phase distortion.

The terms 'normal' and 'anomalous' have a historical justification, but are a little unfortunate in our present context where both types are of common occurrence. A distinction often used is that dispersion is normal if phase velocity decreases with increasing frequency, and anomalous if it increases. These properties are consistent with Definition 2, as may be seen from the equation

$$\frac{dv_p}{dv} = \frac{d}{dv}\left(\frac{v}{k}\right) = \frac{1}{k}\left(1 - \frac{v}{k}\frac{dk}{dv}\right) = \frac{1}{k}\left(1 - \frac{v_p}{v_g}\right) \tag{9}$$

It follows that our definition is consistent with that used in optical physics, namely that dispersion is normal if refractive index increases with increasing frequency and anomalous if it decreases.*

---

* See for example Born and Wolf, pp. 92–3.

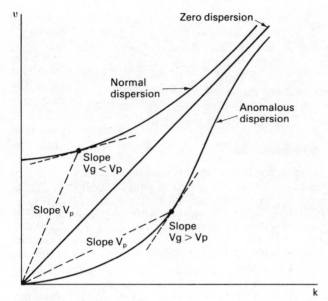

*Figure 3.4.3 Dispersion*

Figure 3.4.3 shows examples of the relationship between frequency $v$ and wave-number $k$ for

(i) zero dispersion (linear relationship)

(ii) normal dispersion (the example is typical for a hollow metallic waveguide)

(iii) anomalous dispersion (the example is typical for a lossy TEM line)

The phase velocity $v_p$ corresponding to any point $(v, k)$ is the slope of the radius vector: the group velocity is the slope of the tangent.

The $(v, k)$ diagram of Figure 3.4.3 gives an important generalisation of the concept introduced in Theorem 1, that the Fourier transform of a wave travelling in the $x$-direction is confined to a line in the $(f, u)$ plane. In the theorem, the line is a straight line through the origin; and by implication, in a dispersionless medium, all frequencies are admissible. In a dispersive medium, the line is not straight, and does not necessarily embrace the whole semi-infinite range either of frequency or of wave-number. The frequency/wave-number relationship is an important description of a wave-bearing medium, defining the velocities, delays, dispersion and frequency range of wave propagation.

Similarly we can generalise Theorem 2 to include the effects of dispersion. In a bilateral medium, dispersion effects are the same for positively- and negatively-directed waves. The proof therefore holds, without any formal change, for the case where $c$ is not constant but is a function of $f$ (or, equivalently, of $u$). Our procedure in analysing specific wave-bearing media will be to formulate a wave equation in either the original domain (7) or the transform domain (6), and to deduce the $(v, k)$ relationship of the solution.

## The TEM transmission line

A form of transmission line commonly used for frequencies from zero up to about 1 GHz consists of a pair of parallel conductors, either with bilateral symmetry (Figure 3.4.4(a)) or concentric (Figure 3.4.4(b)). The flow of current in the line will be accompanied by an electromagnetic field in its vicinity. If the transverse dimensions are

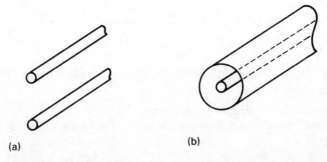

(a)                              (b)

*Figure 3.4.4 TEM transmission line. (a) Symmetrical paired conductors; (b) coaxial conductors*

small enough (we shall see later what is meant by this loosely-phrased condition) then the field is wholly transverse: the electric field is directed betwen the conductors, and the magnetic field encircles them. In this *transverse electromagnetic* mode, the field configuration is constant, and may be calculated from the geometrical properties of a cross-section of the line: it does not vary either with time, or along the length of the line. The strengths of the electric and magnetic fields, however, are functions of time and of linear position. They are proportional, respectively, to the potential difference between conductors, and the (equal and opposite) currents in the conductors.

We shall take as our primary variables the potential difference $e$ and the current $i$. These are explicit functions of time and position.

They have two-dimensional Fourier transforms

$$e(t,x) \Rightarrow E(f,u)$$
$$i(t,x) \Rightarrow I(f,u) \tag{10}$$

We shall also use two-dimensional functions which have been transformed in the time domain only, while retaining the original spatial variable:

$$e(t,x) \Rightarrow E_1(f,x)$$
$$i(t,x) \Rightarrow I_1(f,x) \tag{11}$$

The TEM line can be analysed in terms of distributed impedance and admittance parameters. Consider an infinitesimal element of length $dx$. Associated with the conductors is a series impedance

$$Zdx = (R + j2\pi fL)dx \tag{12}$$

Associated with the intervening dielectric is a shunt admittance

$$Ydx = (G + j2\pi fC)dx \tag{13}$$

The behaviour of a line element can be analysed by the methods of lumped-circuit theory, and the line treated as a tandem combination of elements.

*Theorem 3*: A TEM line supports attenuated travelling waves of the form

$$e^{-\alpha x}e^{j2\pi(vt-kx)} \tag{14a}$$

or

$$e^{\alpha x}e^{j2\pi(vt+kx)} \tag{14b}$$

the attenuation constant $\alpha$ being zero if $R = G = 0$. A non-sinusoidal wave comprising a superposition of such components suffers anomalous dispersion, unless the 'distortionless' condition

$$LG - RC = 0 \tag{15}$$

is satisfied. In general, the attenuation constant is

$$\alpha = \{\tfrac{1}{2}(RG - 4\pi^2 v^2 LC) + \tfrac{1}{2}[(RG + 4\pi^2 v^2 LC)^2 + 4\pi^2 v^2 (LG - RC)^2]^{1/2}\}^{1/2} \tag{16}$$

and the wave number is

$$k = \frac{1}{2\pi}\{\tfrac{1}{2}(4\pi^2 v^2 LC - RG) + \tfrac{1}{2}[(RG + 4\pi^2 v^2 LC)^2 + 4\pi^2 v^2 (LG - RC)^2]^{1/2}\}^{1/2} \tag{17}$$

If the wave is travelling in one direction only, its ratio of voltage to current is

$$\frac{E}{I} = \frac{E_1}{I_1} = \pm \left(\frac{R + j2\pi vL}{G + j2\pi vC}\right)^{1/2} \equiv \pm Z_0 \qquad (18)$$

the sign being positive for the positive direction of propagation (Equation 14a) and negative for the negative direction (Equation 14b).

*Proof* Consider an infinitesimal section of line with series impedance (12) and shunt admittance (13). Application of Kirchhoff's laws to the equivalent circuit Figure 3.4.5 gives

$$E_1(f, x + dx) - E_1(f, x) = -ZI_1(f, x)dx$$

$$I_1(f, x + dx) - I_1(f, x) = -YE_1(f, x + dx)dx$$

In the limit as $dx \rightarrow 0$

$$\frac{dE_1}{dx} = -ZI_1$$

$$\frac{dI_1}{dx} = -YE_1 \qquad (19)$$

Transformation in the spatial domain gives

$$j2\pi uE = -ZI$$

$$j2\pi uI = -YE$$

These simultaneous equations imply that

$$[(j2\pi u)^2 - \gamma^2]\Phi = 0 \qquad (20)$$

where $\Phi$ is either $E$ or $I$, and

$$\gamma = \gamma(f) = (ZY)^{1/2} = \{(R + j2\pi fL)(G + j2\pi fC)\}^{1/2} \qquad (21)$$

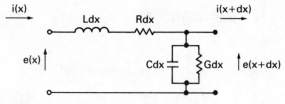

*Figure 3.4.5 Equivalent circuit of line section*

Equation (20) can be factorised to yield

$$(j2\pi u \pm \gamma)\Phi = 0$$

which on transformation back to the spatial domain gives

$$\frac{d\Phi_1}{dx} \pm \gamma\Phi_1 = 0$$

where $\Phi_1$ is either $E_1$ or $I_1$. This has the solution (save for an arbitrary constant multiplier)

$$\Phi_1(f, x) = e^{\mp \gamma x} \qquad (22)$$

A sinusoid $e^{j2\pi vt}$ therefore has the coefficient

$$\Phi_1(v, x) = e^{\pm \gamma(v)x} \equiv e^{\pm \alpha x} e^{\pm j2\pi kx}$$

It is easily verified that the real and imaginary parts of $\gamma$ yield $\alpha$ and $2\pi k$ according to Equations (16) and (17).

Substitution of (15) gives $\alpha = (RG)^{1/2}$ and $k = v(LC)^{1/2}$ which corresponds to constant attenuation and delay. To verify that dispersion when it occurs is anomalous, we express $v_p$ in terms of $y = 1/4\pi^2 v^2$ as follows:

$$\frac{1}{v_p^2} = \tfrac{1}{2}LC - \tfrac{1}{2}RGy + \tfrac{1}{2}\{(LC + RGy)^2 + (LG - RC)^2 y\}$$

The derivative of this, after a little manipulation, is

$$\frac{d}{dy}\left(\frac{1}{v_p^2}\right) = \frac{RG}{2}\left\{-1 + \left[1 + \frac{\dfrac{LC}{RG}(LG - RC)^2 + \dfrac{(LG - RC)^2}{4R^2G^2}}{(LC + RGy)^2 + (LG - RC)^2 y}\right]^{1/2}\right\}$$

The quantity under the square root sign is clearly $\geqslant 1$, the equality being attained only for $LG - RC = 0$ (the condition for zero dispersion) or for $v = 0$: consequently $v_p$ increases with $v$ for all positive $v$, whence from (9) $v_g > v_p$ which is the criterion for anomalous dispersion.

To find the voltage/current ratio, we use either of Equations (19), for example the second, which gives

$$\frac{E_1}{I_1} = \frac{-1}{Y}\frac{dI_1/dx}{I_1}$$

and note that with solutions of the form (22)

$$\frac{dI_1}{I_1} = \mp\gamma = \mp(ZY)^{1/2}$$

This yields $E_1/I_1$ according to (18): since the ratio is independent of $x$, it applies also to $E/I$.

If we assume the parameters $L$, $C$, $R$, $G$ to be independent of frequency, then at high frequencies the phase velocity tends towards $(LC)^{-1/2}$ and the impedance $Z_0$ towards $(L/C)^{1/2}$. In practice, $R$ rises with frequency*: but the rise is slow, and the foregoing statements remain broadly true. Dispersion and impedance variation in cables are predominantly low-frequency problems. The general nature of the dispersion is illustrated by the 'anomalous' curve in Figure 3.4.3.

EXERCISES   (i) Assuming the line parameters to be independent of frequency, show that the phase velocity of the TEM line satisfies the inequalities

$$\frac{(LC)^{-1/2}}{\frac{1}{2}\left(\sqrt{\frac{LG}{RC}}+\sqrt{\frac{RC}{LG}}\right)} \leqslant v_p \leqslant (LC)^{-1/2}$$

(ii)  The parameters of a 4.5 mm diameter coaxial cable are typically, in the frequency range of interest

$$L=0.26\,\mathrm{mH/km}, \qquad C=4.9\,\mathrm{nF/km}$$

$$R=20.5\,\Omega/\mathrm{km}, \qquad G \text{ negligibly small}$$

When such a cable is used for carrier telephony, the normal practice is to translate all signals to frequencies above 60 kHz. Examine the impedance and dispersion characteristics of the cable, and see whether you think that they justify the frequency allocation.

The quantity $Z_0$ of Theorem 3 is known as the *characteristic impedance* and is an important property of the line. It was derived on the assumption that waves were travelling in one direction only. If waves travelling in opposite directions be superposed, then the ratio of voltage to current departs from $Z_0$. Conversely, if a local ratio other than $Z_0$ be imposed, then waves in both directions must be present. If a wave travelling along a line encounters a terminating impedance not equal to $Z_0$, then a *reflected wave* is generated (Figure 3.4.6(a)).

*Theorem 4*: Let a line of characteristic impedance $Z_0$ be terminated in an impedance $Z_T$. Then a travelling wave of unit magnitude incident upon the termination will generate a reflected wave, in the

---

* Due to 'skin effect', not treated here. For a full derivation of the line parameters with typical structures, see specialised texts on electromagnetism such as Ramo, Whinnery and Van Duzer: or Johnk.

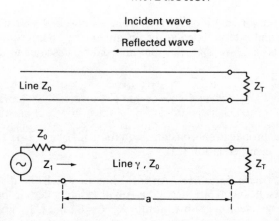

Figure 3.4.6 Terminated line section. (a) Reflection at a mismatched termination; (b) Input impedance of terminated line

opposite direction, of magnitude

$$\Gamma = \frac{Z_T - Z_0}{Z_T + Z_0} \tag{23}$$

If $Z_0$ and/or $Z_T$ vary with frequency, then this expression applies separately to each sinusoidal component of a composite wave.

*Proof* The termination imposes the boundary condition $e/i = Z_T$ which must be satisfied by a superposition of travelling waves. Let us suppose a unit incident wave, and a reflected wave of (voltage) magnitude $\Gamma$. We note from the proof of Theorem 3 that the ratio of voltage to current is $+Z_0$ and $-Z_0$ for the incident and reflected waves respectively. Adding components of the two waves, the ratio of voltage to current at the point of termination is

$$\frac{e}{i} = \left(\frac{1 + \Gamma}{1 - \Gamma}\right) Z_0$$

Equating this to $Z_T$ gives the result (23).

The *reflection coefficient* $\Gamma$ is zero only for $Z_T = Z_0$. Its magnitude is bounded by $|\Gamma| \leqslant 1$: it attains the values $+1$ and $-1$ for open-circuit and short-circuit termination respectively. Travelling waves in one direction exist only on a uniform line which is either of infinite extent or terminated in $Z_0$: any irregularity or mismatch — a break, an improper termination, a lumped shunt impedance, a joint between two lines of different impedance — will give rise to a reflection.

EXERCISE   A line or length $a$ is driven from a sinusoidal source of impedance $Z_0$ and is terminated at the distant end by an impedance $Z_T$ (Figure 3.4.6(b)). Show that the input impedance presented to the source is

$$Z_1 = Z_0 \left( \frac{1 + \Gamma e^{-2\gamma a}}{1 - \Gamma e^{-2\gamma a}} \right) \tag{24}$$

where $\gamma$ is the propagation constant, equation (21), and $\Gamma$ is the reflection coefficient, equation (23).

*The lossless transmission line*   An ideal line in which the dissipative elements $R$ and $G$ are negligibly small exhibits certain line properties very clearly. Substituting $R = G = 0$ in (21) gives $\gamma = j2\pi f (LC)^{1/2}$, in which case (20) reduces to the wave equation (6) with $c = (LC)^{-1/2}$: the line is distortionless, both phase and group velocity having this value, and the attenuation $\alpha$ being zero. The characteristic impedance (18) is a pure resistance $Z_0 = (L/C)^{1/2}$. The impedance and velocity of the lossless line are constant, and equal to the high-frequency asymptotic values for the general line. Simple lossless theory gives a vivid picture of some useful properties of short line sections, both in the time domain and in the frequency domain.

EXAMPLES   (i) Short pulses for radar and other purposes can be generated by switching an e.m.f. to a short-circuited line of delay time equal to half the pulse width (Figure 3.4.7). Similar effects have been used in time-division switching by means of resonant transfer (Cattermole (2)).
(ii) At a single frequency (or, in practice, over a narrow band) line sections can be used to match sources and loads of different impedance. A well-known example is the quarter-wave transformer (Figure 3.4.8). Let the length be $c/4v$, and let $Z_0^2 = Z_1 Z_2$. Then the line section is matched at each end.

EXERCISE   Prove the property of the quarter-wave transformer cited in Example (ii).

*Standing waves*   Let us consider a lossless line with a forward wave of voltage amplitude $A$ and a backward wave of voltage amplitude $B$, both of frequency $v$. With suitable origin the total line voltage is

$$e^{j2\pi vt}(A e^{-j2\pi kx} + B e^{j2\pi kx})$$

At any point $x$, there is a (temporal) sinusoidal oscillation of

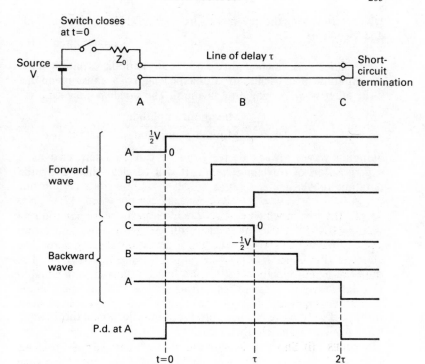

*Figure 3.4.7 Pulse generation*

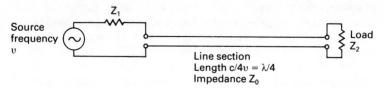

*Figure 3.4.8 Quarter-wave transformer*

magnitude

$$|Ae^{-j2\pi kx} + Be^{j2\pi kx}| = (A^2 + B^2 + 2AB\cos 4\pi kx)^{1/2} \qquad (25)$$

which as one moves along the line varies between $A + B$ and $A - B$. Similarly, the total line current exhibits a sinusoidal oscillation with magnitude

$$\frac{1}{Z_0}|Ae^{-j2\pi kx} - Be^{j2\pi kx}| = \frac{1}{Z_0}(A^2 + B^2 - 2AB\cos 4\pi kx)^{1/2} \qquad (26)$$

which varies along the line, having its maxima at the voltage minima, and vice versa.

*Definition 3*: A *standing wave* is a spatially periodic variation in the amplitude of an oscillation, along the length of a transmission line or other wave-propagating medium. The *standing-wave ratio* is

$$S = \frac{\text{Maximum amplitude}}{\text{Minimum amplitude}}$$

Standing waves always derive from or can be interpreted as a superposition of travelling waves. It will be clear that, using the notation above,

$$S = \frac{|A| + |B|}{|A| - |B|} \tag{27}$$

whence

$$\frac{|B|}{|A|} = \frac{S - 1}{S + 1} \tag{28a}$$

If the backward wave has been produced by reflection of the forward wave from a mismatch, then clearly

$$|\Gamma| = \frac{S - 1}{S + 1} \tag{28b}$$

Measurements of current or of voltage will give the same value of $S$, but as noted above the peaks of voltage and of current are interleaved. The spacing between similar peaks is half the wavelength of a travelling wave, as can be seen from (25) or (26).

Some examples of standing wave patterns are shown in Figure 3.4.9. Note particularly (c), which shows some of the many modes of standing wave possible on a lossless line section with short-circuits at each end. Stable patterns exist with $v = nc/2a$ for $n = 1, 2, 3 \ldots$: this is the basis of multiple resonance in waveguides and cavities, and of multi-mode propagation in waveguides (Section 3.5).

EXERCISE   Derive a general expression for the ratio voltage/current as a function of position, in the presence of standing waves. Use this to study the quarter-wave transformer (Figures 3.4.8 and 3.4.9(b)). Investigate the impedance transformations possible with a line section of one-eighth wavelength.

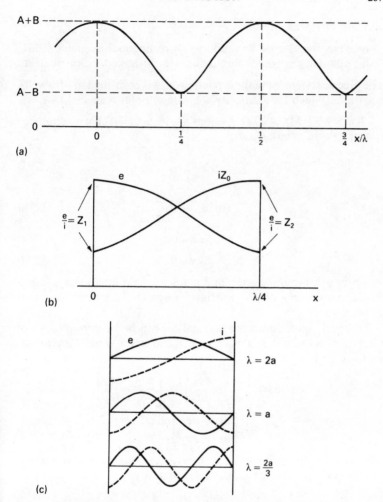

Figure 3.4.9 Standing waves. (a) General (A and B real and positive); (b) quarter-wave transformer; (c) resonance

## Maxwell's equations for the electromagnetic field

The one-dimensional analysis of travelling waves generalises readily to the three dimensions of normal Euclidean space. The key relationships of electromagnetism, first established experimentally and then developed into a theoretical structure of imposing power and completeness, are that

(i) changing electric flux induces an orthogonal magnetic field
(ii) changing magnetic flux induces an orthogonal electric field.

The precise statement of these relationships is enshrined in Maxwell's equations, which for simplicity we state only for a special case.

*Definition 4*: Maxwell's equations in a linear, isotropic medium free from electric charge are

$$\text{curl}\,\mathbf{h} = \varepsilon \frac{d\mathbf{e}}{dt} \tag{29a}$$

$$\text{curl}\,\mathbf{e} = -\mu \frac{d\mathbf{h}}{dt} \tag{29b}$$

$$\text{div}\,\mathbf{h} = 0 \tag{29c}$$

$$\text{div}\,\mathbf{e} = 0 \tag{29d}$$

where $\mathbf{e}$, $\mathbf{h}$ are the electric and magnetic field intensities and $\varepsilon$, $\mu$ are parameters of the medium, respectively permittivity and permeability.*

The 'curl' operation of vector analysis can be written in terms of Cartesian coordinates $\mathbf{x} = (x_1, x_2, x_3)$ and gives when applied to $\mathbf{e} = (e_1, e_2, e_3)$

$$\text{curl}\,\mathbf{e} = \mathbf{i}_1 \left[ \frac{de_3}{dx_2} - \frac{de_2}{dx_3} \right] + \mathbf{i}_2 \left[ \frac{de_1}{dx_3} - \frac{de_3}{dx_1} \right]$$
$$+ \mathbf{i}_3 \left[ \frac{de_2}{dx_1} - \frac{de_1}{dx_2} \right] \tag{30}$$

where $\mathbf{i}_1, \mathbf{i}_2, \mathbf{i}_3$ are unit vectors in the $x_1, x_2, x_3$ directions respectively.

The 'div' operator gives the scalar quantity

$$\text{div}\,\mathbf{e} = \frac{de_1}{dx_1} + \frac{de_2}{dx_2} + \frac{de_3}{dx_3} \tag{31}$$

We shall suppose that the electric and magnetic field components can be represented by 4-dimensional Fourier-transformable

---

* The reader is assumed to be moderately familiar with basic electromagnetism. There are many textbooks available, at different levels of sophistication and with the bias alternatively towards physics or engineering. Two texts which combine good basic exposition with engineering applications are Ramo-Whinnery-Van Duzer, and Johnk. Maxwell's original treatise (whose third edition of 1891 is available in a modern reprint) remains remarkably clear, sound and accessible to the modern reader.

functions of the form

$$e_i(t, \mathbf{x}) \Rightarrow E_i(f, \mathbf{u})$$
$$h_i(t, \mathbf{x}) \Rightarrow H_i(f, \mathbf{u}) \tag{32}$$

We shall assemble the field components together as vectors

$$\mathbf{E} = (E_1, E_2, E_3)$$
$$\mathbf{H} = (H_1, H_2, H_3) \tag{33}$$

and develop the theory in terms of these vector transforms.

Maxwell's equations for the linear isotropic charge-free medium become

$$\begin{bmatrix} 0 & -u_3 & u_2 \\ u_3 & 0 & -u_1 \\ -u_2 & u_1 & 0 \\ u_1 & u_2 & u_3 \end{bmatrix} \begin{bmatrix} H_1 \\ H_2 \\ H_3 \end{bmatrix} = \varepsilon f \begin{bmatrix} E_1 \\ E_2 \\ E_3 \\ 0 \end{bmatrix} \tag{34a}$$

$$\begin{bmatrix} 0 & -u_3 & u_2 \\ u_3 & 0 & -u_1 \\ -u_2 & u_1 & 0 \\ u_1 & u_2 & u_3 \end{bmatrix} \begin{bmatrix} E_1 \\ E_2 \\ E_3 \end{bmatrix} = -\mu f \begin{bmatrix} H_1 \\ H_2 \\ H_3 \\ 0 \end{bmatrix} \tag{34b}$$

The first three rows of each matrix equation follow from Equation (29a, b) using the curl definition (30) together with the differentiation theorem for the Fourier transform: $d/dx_i$ transforms into multiplication by $u_i$ and $d/dt$ transforms into multiplication by $f$ (omitting common factors of $j2\pi$). Similarly, the last row follows from (29c, d) using the div definition (31) and the differentiation theorem.

Our most fundamental theorem in this section is that the electromagnetic medium can support travelling waves.

*Theorem 5*: The linear isotropic charge-free electromagnetic medium imposes the following (equivalent) conditions on fluctuations of the electric and magnetic field intensities **E** and **H**:

$$(u_1^2 + u_2^2 + u_3^2 - \mu \varepsilon f^2)\Phi = 0 \tag{35}$$

$$\frac{d^2\phi}{dx_1^2} + \frac{d^2\phi}{dx_2^2} + \frac{d^2\phi}{dx_3^2} - \mu\varepsilon \frac{d^2\phi}{dt^2} = 0 \tag{36}$$

where $\phi \Rightarrow \Phi$ is any field component $e_i$ or $h_i$. It supports travelling waves of characteristic velocity $c = (\mu\varepsilon)^{-1/2}$, specifically

$$\phi = e^{j2\pi(vt - \mathbf{k} \cdot \mathbf{x})} \tag{37}$$

subject to the condition

$$k^2 \equiv |\mathbf{k}|^2 = \mu\varepsilon v^2 \tag{38}$$

where $\mathbf{k} = (k_1, k_2, k_3)$ is a wave-number vector.

*Proof* We define the extended vector $\mathbf{H}_0 = (H_1, H_2, H_3, 0)$ and similarly for $\mathbf{E}_0$. Then Equations (34) can be written

$$\mathbf{W}\mathbf{H}_0 = \varepsilon f \mathbf{E}_0$$

$$\mathbf{W}\mathbf{E}_0 = -\mu f \mathbf{H}_0$$

where $\mathbf{W}$ is the matrix in (34) extended by the addition of an arbitrary fourth column. It follows that

$$(\mathbf{W}^2 + \mu\varepsilon f^2)\mathbf{H}_0 = 0$$

$$(\mathbf{W}^2 + \mu\varepsilon f^2)\mathbf{E}_0 = 0$$

Squaring of a matrix $\mathbf{W}$ with an arbitrary fourth column reveals that the structure is simplified if we choose

$$\mathbf{W} = \begin{bmatrix} 0 & -u_3 & u_2 & -u_1 \\ u_3 & 0 & -u_1 & -u_2 \\ -u_2 & u_1 & 0 & -u_3 \\ u_1 & u_2 & u_3 & 0 \end{bmatrix} \tag{39}$$

for which

$$\mathbf{W}^2 = -(u_1^2 + u_2^2 + u_3^2)\mathbf{I}$$

where $\mathbf{I}$ is the $4 \times 4$ identity matrix. This yields directly equation (35) applied to each and every component $E_i, H_i$. Inverse Fourier transformation gives (36).

The sinusoidal solution (37) implies

$$\Phi = \delta(f - v, u_1 + k_1, u_2 + k_2, u_3 + k_3)$$

which is clearly consistent with (35) under the condition (38). It may also be verified directly that (37) with (38) satisfies the differential equation (36).

*Plane waves* An important ideal case is a wave whose field components are all uniform over any plane normal to the direction of propagation. Analysis of the plane wave reveals that the electromagnetic medium has a characteristic impedance, and that there can be two independent modes of wave propagation along the same axis.

*Theorem 6*: The linear isotropic medium supports plane travelling waves of velocity $c = (\mu\varepsilon)^{-1/2}$. The electric and magnetic fields are wholly orthogonal to the direction of propagation, and there are two independent modes each with its electric field orthogonal to its magnetic field. The medium has a characteristic impedance $Z_0 = (\mu/\varepsilon)^{1/2}$ relating the electric to the magnetic field of each mode. Specifically, if the direction of propagation is along the (positive) $x_3$ axis,

$$E_3 = H_3 = 0 \tag{40}$$

$$\frac{E_1}{H_2} = -\frac{E_2}{H_1} = \left(\frac{\mu}{\varepsilon}\right)^{1/2} \tag{41}$$

*Proof* Constancy in the $x_1, x_2$ axes transforms to impulses on the $u_1, u_2$ axes: so for a plane wave along $x_3$ it follows that $u_1 = u_2 = 0$. Equation (35) then reduces to

$$(u_3^2 - \mu\varepsilon f^2)\Phi = 0$$

for any non-zero $E$ or $H$ component: this is the wave equation (6) with $c = (\mu\varepsilon)^{-1/2}$. Equations (34) with $u_1 = u_2 = 0$ give

$$\mu f \mathbf{H} = u_3 \begin{bmatrix} E_2 \\ -E_1 \\ 0 \end{bmatrix}, \qquad \varepsilon f \mathbf{E} = u_3 \begin{bmatrix} -H_2 \\ H_1 \\ 0 \end{bmatrix} \tag{42}$$

the last rows of which give (40) directly. The non-zero variables fall into two sets, namely $\{E_1, H_2\}$ and $\{H_1, E_2\}$: each variable is coupled by two equations to the other in its own set, but is independent of variables in the other set. Thus there are two independent modes as stated.

To show the impedance relationship, we note from (42) that

$$\frac{E_1}{H_2} = -\frac{\mu f}{u_3} = -\frac{u_3}{\varepsilon f} = \pm\left(\frac{\mu}{\varepsilon}\right)^{1/2}$$

For a positive-going wave $u_3 + f(\mu\varepsilon)^{1/2} = 0$ and this defines the positive sign (for a negative-going wave the sign is reversed): which proves the first equation of (41). Proof of the second equation is similar.

It is interesting to compare these results with the corresponding properties of a TEM line, Theorem 3\*. The isotropic medium has a characteristic velocity $(\mu\varepsilon)^{-1/2}$ analogous to the line velocity $(LC)^{-1/2}$: and a characteristic impedance $(\mu/\varepsilon)^{1/2}$ analogous to the line impedance $(L/C)^{1/2}$. In free space, the velocity is almost exactly $3 \times 10^8$ m/s (the 'velocity of light') and the impedance is $120\,\pi \approx 377\,\Omega$ (the 'intrinsic wave impedance').

*Polarisation*   The two independent modes revealed by Theorem 6 differ in the orientation of their $E$ and $H$ vectors; this is in the usual language a difference of polarisation.

*Definition 5*: A *linearly-polarised* plane wave has its $E$ vector confined to one direction normal to the axis of propagation (whence by Theorem 6 its $H$ vector is confined to an orthogonal direction also normal to the axis of propagation). The direction of polarisation is described by the direction of the $E$ field vector. A *circularly-polarised* wave comprises two linearly-polarised waves of the same magnitude and frequency propagating in the same direction, but orthogonally polarised and in phase quadrature: there are two senses of circular polarisation, known as *right hand* and *left hand*. Superpositions of waves with the same frequency and direction but unrestricted as to relative magnitude, phase and polarisation are known as *elliptically polarised*.

The intrinsic justification for such terms as 'circular' and 'elliptical' emerges from the following analysis. Consider a superposition of two plane waves, with the same direction $x_3$ and frequency $v$ but with orthogonal polarisations along $x_1$ and $x_2$ respectively. The electric vectors of the components are (assuming arbitrary amplitudes $A_i$ and phases $\phi_i$)

$$e_1 = A_1 \cos\{2\pi v(t - x_3/c) - \phi_1\}$$
$$e_2 = A_2 \cos\{2\pi v(t - x_3/c) - \phi_2\}$$

The resultant electric vector lies in a plane normal to $x_3$. At any given spatial point it varies with time; its locus is in general an ellipse, of the form shown in Figure 3.4.10. This reduces to a circle if $A_1 = A_2$ and $\phi_1 - \phi_2 = \pm \pi/2$, and to a straight line if $\phi_2 - \phi_1 = 0$ or $\pi$.

EXERCISE   Show that an arbitrary elliptically polarised wave can be

---

\* The similarity is of course fundamental: the TEM line properties are governed by Maxwell's equations and may be derived by field analysis. See for example Johnk (1) Chapter 9.

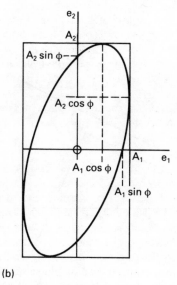

(b)

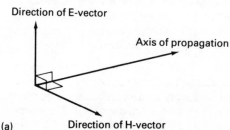

(a)

Direction of E-vector

Axis of propagation

Direction of H-vector

*Figure 3.4.10 Polarisation. (a) Plane polarisation; (b) Elliptical polarisation. (Note: $\phi = \phi_2 - \phi_1$, example drawn for $0 < \phi < \pi/2$)*

represented as the sum of two circularly polarised components with opposite senses of rotation (i.e. phase differences $\pm\pi/2$).

In Theorem 6 we have for convenience taken the direction of the plane wave as an axis, but in an isotropic medium waves may propagate equally well in any direction. In general, the wave number is a vector $\mathbf{k} = (k_1, k_2, k_3)$ as stated in Theorem 5. Figure 3.4.11 illustrates the wave-number vector of an inclined wave in the $(x_1, x_3)$ plane. The wavefronts, i.e. the loci of constant phase, are planes separated by $\lambda = 1/k$ whose intercepts on the $x_i$ axis are spaced at intervals $1/k_i$. Expressions for the several variables may be found either by a formal rotation of the coordinate frame as discussed in

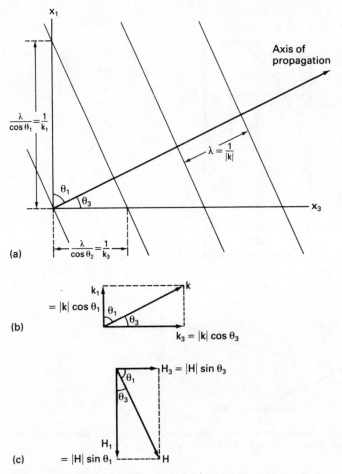

*Figure 3.4.11 Inclined plane waves. (a) Wavefronts; (b) Wave number vector. (c) H-vector of an $x_2$-polarised wave*

Section 3.1, or by resolution of vector components as shown in Figure 3.4.11. Specifically, we have for this example

$$k_i = k \cos \theta_i = \frac{v}{c} \cos \theta_i \tag{43}$$

where $\theta_i$ are the angles between the direction of propagation and the

$x_i$ axes. For a unit wave polarised in the $x_2$ direction

$$e_2 = e^{j2\pi(vt - \mathbf{k} \cdot \mathbf{x})}$$
$$Z_0 h_1 = -\sin\theta_1 . e^{j2\pi(vt - \mathbf{k} \cdot \mathbf{x})} \tag{44}$$
$$Z_0 h_3 = -\sin\theta_3 . e^{j2\pi(vt - \mathbf{k} \cdot \mathbf{x})}$$

For a wave polarised orthogonally to $x_2$

$$Z_0 h_2 = e^{j2\pi(vt - \mathbf{k} \cdot \mathbf{x})}$$
$$e_1 = \sin\theta_1 . e^{j2\pi(vt - \mathbf{k} \cdot \mathbf{x})} \tag{45}$$
$$e_3 = \sin\theta_3 . e^{j2\pi(vt - \mathbf{k} \cdot \mathbf{x})}$$

where as usual $Z_0 = (\mu/\varepsilon)^{1/2}$ and $c = (\mu\varepsilon)^{-1/2}$. Waves with other polarisations may be expressed as the superposition of components with these two forms.

EXERCISE    Consider the superposition of two plane waves of the same amplitude and frequency, with their axes of propagation in the $(x_1, x_3)$ plane inclined at equal and opposite angles $\pm\theta_3$ to the $x_3$ axis. Show that with polarisation in the direction $x_2$ the total field is given by

$$\tfrac{1}{2}e_2 = \cos 2\pi k_1 x_1 . e^{j2\pi(vt - k_3 x_3)}$$
$$\tfrac{1}{2}Z_0 h_1 = -\cos\theta_3 . \cos 2\pi k_1 x_1 . e^{j2\pi(vt - k_3 x_3)} \tag{46}$$
$$\tfrac{1}{2}Z_0 h_3 = j\sin\theta_3 . \sin 2\pi k_1 x_1 . e^{j2\pi(vt - k_3 x_3)}$$

Show that with the orthogonal polarisation the field is given by

$$\tfrac{1}{2}Z_0 h_2 = \cos 2\pi k_1 x_1 . e^{j2\pi(vt - k_3 x_3)}$$
$$\tfrac{1}{2}e_1 = \cos\theta_3 . \cos 2\pi k_1 x_1 . e^{j2\pi(vt - k_3 x_3)} \tag{47}$$
$$\tfrac{1}{2}e_3 = -j\sin\theta_3 . \sin 2\pi k_1 x_1 . e^{j2\pi(vt - k_3 x_3)}$$

Interpret these expressions as travelling waves along one axis and standing waves along another.

## 3.5 METALLIC WAVEGUIDES

Waves may be confined, guided or modified by material structures of several kinds. We begin by analysing the effect of metallic structures which we suppose to be perfectly conductive. This ideal assumption reveals some of the principal features of waveguide propagation very clearly, and is a good approximation for many practical purposes. No electric field can exist in a perfect conductor, and so a wave cannot penetrate its surface. Thus the field in the vicinity of a metallic conductor must satisfy Maxwell's equations in the electromagnetic medium together with the boundary condition $e = 0$ over the metallic surface.

The simplest metallic structure is a single planar sheet. Let us suppose a plane travelling wave, generated by some remote source, to be incident on the sheet. The boundary condition $e = 0$ can be satisfied only if the incident wave be accompanied by a reflected wave which cancels the electric field along the surface. If the incidence is normal, then the behaviour is precisely analogous to reflection from a short-circuit termination to a TEM line, which by Theorem 3.4.4 has a reflection coefficient $-1$. For a general solution in three dimensions, we must take into account the angle of incidence and the plane of polarisation. It is not difficult to prove the law of reflection familiar from geometrical optics. An optical ray is a wave propagating along a rectilinear axis, with a wavefront sufficiently wide in relation to wavelength that it can be considered as plane within most of the illuminated region. The reflected ray lies in the plane of incidence, at an angle to the reflecting surface equal and opposite to that of the incident ray.

EXERCISE    (i) Prove that a plane wave is reflected from a perfectly conducting surface in accordance with the reflection law of geometrical optics (a) by using expressions (3.4.46–7) for the superposition of two plane waves, showing that the boundary condition of zero tangential electric field at the reflecting surface can be satisfied (b) by postulating incident and reflected waves of arbitrary wave-number vectors, and showing that only the stated result satisfies the boundary condition. Show that if incident (and reflected) waves are polarised in the plane of incidence, there is no phase change on reflection: and that if they are polarised normal to the plane of incidence, there is a phase reversal.

(ii) Consider the space between two conducting planes of infinite extent, parallel to the $(x_2, x_3)$ plane and separated by distance $2a$ (Figure 3.5.1(a)). Show that superposed waves of the forms (3.4.46) and (3.4.47) can satisfy boundary conditions at both planes. Show that a necessary condition is

$$4\pi k_1 a = N\pi \qquad (N = 1, 2, 3 \ldots) \qquad (1)$$

Hence interpret the field between the two planes as (a) a travelling wave along the axis $x_3$ combined with a standing wave along the axis

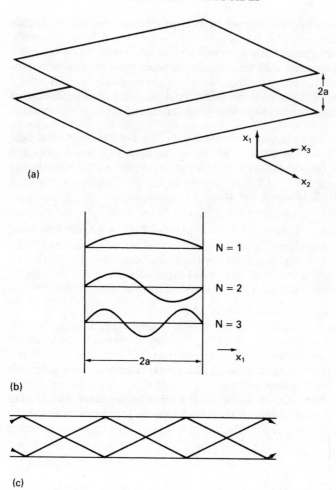

*Figure 3.5.1 Planar waveguide. (a) Planar structure; (b) Standing waves (E-field component); (c) Ray model*

$x_1$, the latter according to Figure 3.5.1(b): (b) a system of reflected rays as in Figure 3.5.1(c).

We shall develop a general theory of wave propagation in metallic guides which interacts with the reflected-ray model in two ways. Firstly, the reflection properties stated above will emerge as a special case of Theorems 1 and 2. Secondly, the field distribution within waveguides may be interpreted as a superposition of reflected plane waves.

Examination of the superposed waves in (3.4.46) and (3.4.47) shows that, according to the relationship between the direction of polarisation and the plane of reflection, either the longitudinal electric field $e_3$ or the longitudinal magnetic field $h_3$ may be annulled. This observation prompts the following definition.

> *Definition 1*: A *transverse electric* (TE) wave has its electric field vector normal to the axis of propagation but has a non-zero magnetic field along the axis. A *transverse magnetic* (TM) wave has its magnetic field vector normal to the axis but has a non-zero electric field along the axis.

*General properties of uniform guides* Let us consider a wave propagating along the $x_3$ axis, in a structure which extends indefinitely in this dimension but has a uniform cross-section in the $(x_1, x_2)$ plane; typical examples are metal pipes of rectangular or circular cross-section. We shall show that structures of this family

(i) support travelling waves of TE and TM types

(ii) have a series of discrete modes of each type, differing in their transverse field pattern and in the cut-off frequency above which waves propagate

(iii) exhibit in each mode characteristic velocities $v_p > c$ and $v_g < c$ with normal dispersion

(iv) exhibit in each mode a characteristic impedance which is the ratio of orthogonal transverse electric and magnetic fields.

We begin by investigating the general properties of the wave equation in such structures. Let there be a solution of (3.4.35–6) in the form of a travelling wave in the $x_3$ direction, with a separable transverse distribution:

$$\phi = \phi_{12}(x_1, x_2)e^{j2\pi(vt - k_3 x_3)} \tag{2a}$$

$$\Phi = \Phi_{12}(u_1, u_2)\delta(f - v, u_3 + k_3) \tag{2b}$$

From the first two rows of 3.4.34a–b) we can write

$$\begin{bmatrix} k_3 & -\mu v \\ \varepsilon v & -k_3 \end{bmatrix} \begin{bmatrix} E_1 \\ H_2 \end{bmatrix} = \begin{bmatrix} -u_1 E_3 \\ u_2 H_3 \end{bmatrix}$$

$$\begin{bmatrix} k_3 & \mu v \\ -\varepsilon v & -k_3 \end{bmatrix} \begin{bmatrix} E_2 \\ H_1 \end{bmatrix} = \begin{bmatrix} -u_2 E_3 \\ u_1 H_3 \end{bmatrix}$$

These can be solved to give the transverse components in terms of the longitudinal,

$$
\begin{bmatrix}
E_1 \\
H_2 \\
E_2 \\
H_1
\end{bmatrix}
= \frac{1}{\varepsilon\mu v^2 - k_3^2}
\begin{bmatrix}
k_3 u_1 & \mu v u_2 \\
\varepsilon v u_1 & k_3 u_2 \\
k_3 u_2 & -\mu v u_1 \\
-\varepsilon v u_2 & k_3 u_1
\end{bmatrix}
\begin{bmatrix}
E_3 \\
H_3
\end{bmatrix}
\tag{3}
$$

It is convenient to use the notations

$$
k^2 = \varepsilon\mu v^2 = v^2/c^2
$$
$$
Z_0^2 = \mu/\varepsilon
$$

introduced in Theorems 3.4.5 and 3.4.6 respectively. In these terms,

$$
\begin{bmatrix}
E_1 \\
H_2 \\
E_2 \\
H_1
\end{bmatrix}
= \frac{1}{k^2 - k_3^2}
\begin{bmatrix}
k_3 u_1 & k Z_0 u_2 \\
k u_1/Z_0 & k_3 u_2 \\
k_3 u_2 & -k Z_0 u_1 \\
-k u_2/Z_0 & k_3 u_1
\end{bmatrix}
\begin{bmatrix}
E_3 \\
H_3
\end{bmatrix}
\tag{4}
$$

This equation gives all the transverse field components in terms of the longitudinal components and the longitudinal wave number $k_3$: it remains to find a solution for these.

We now turn to the transverse distribution $\phi_{12} \Rightarrow \Phi_{12}$. From the transform-domain equation (3.4.35) it is immediately obvious that $\Phi_{12}$ can be non-zero only on the set defined by

$$
u_1^2 + u_2^2 = k^2 - k_3^2 \tag{5}
$$

and we shall use this property to find solutions. A more classical approach starts with the original-domain equation (3.4.36), which yields

$$
\left( \frac{d^2}{dx_1^2} + \frac{d^2}{dx_2^2} \right)\phi_{12} = -4\pi(k^2 - k_3^2)\phi_{12} \tag{6}
$$

Then $\phi_{12}$ is an eigenfunction, in the sense of Definition 3.2.4, and $(k^2 - k_3^2)$ is an eigenvalue.

As the exercise following Definition 3.2.4 illustrates, the set of eigenfunctions and eigenvalues for any operator may be reduced by imposition of boundary conditions. Let us impose the condition $\phi_{12} = 0$ along a set in the form of a linear contour (the waveguide wall, or part of it) whose indicator function is

$$
a(x_1, x_2) \Rightarrow A(u_1, u_2) \tag{7}
$$

Zeros of $\phi(x)$        Indicator of $\Phi_{12}(u)$

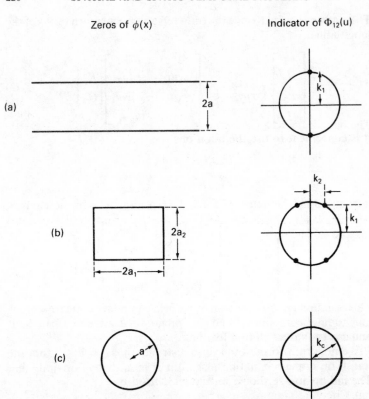

*Figure 3.5.2 Transverse distribution functions in metallic waveguide. (a) Planar,*
$k_1^2 = k^2 - k_3^2$; *(b) Rectangular* $k_1^2 + k_2^2 = k^3 - k_3^2$; *(c) Circular* $k_c^2 = k^2 - k_3^2$

Some examples are shown in Figure 3.5.2, on the left-hand side. The combination of Equation (5) with the boundary condition on the set (7) defines the eigenfunctions and eigenvalues of the system: that is, the transverse distribution and the transverse wave-number appropriate to the given form of waveguide.

EXAMPLES   (i) Planar boundaries. Consider the region between two infinite conducting plants at $x_1 = 0, x_1 = 2a$. The indicator function is uniform in the $x_2$ dimension, so $u_2 = 0$. The eigenfunctions are exponentials $e^{j2\pi k_1 x_1}$ subject to the constraint

$$k_1^2 = k^2 - k_3^2 \tag{8}$$

With zeros at the two planes, the set of eigenfunctions is reduced to

$$\phi_{12}(x_1, x_2) = \sin 2\pi k_1 x_1 = \frac{e^{j2\pi k_1 x_1} - e^{-j2\pi k_1 x_1}}{2j} \qquad (9a)$$

with eigenvalues

$$k_1 = N/4a \qquad (N = 1, 2, 3 \dots) \qquad (9b)$$

The boundaries and the indicator of $\Phi_{12}(u_1, u_2)$ are shown in Figure 3.5.2(a). Note that the condition (9b) is identical with (1).

(ii) Rectangular boundaries, say at

$$x_1 = 0 \qquad x_1 = 2a_1$$
$$x_2 = 0 \qquad x_2 = 2a_2$$

After the last example, it is clear that the two orthogonal conditions may be satisfied by

$$\phi_{12}(x_1, x_2) = \sin 2\pi k_1 x_1 \cdot \sin 2\pi k_2 x_2 \qquad (10a)$$

with

$$k_1 = N/4a_1 \qquad (10b)$$
$$k_2 = M/4a_2 \qquad (10c)$$

and integer values of $M, N$. In this case

$$k_1^2 + k_2^2 = k^2 - k_3^2 \qquad (11)$$

The indicators are shown in Figure 3.5.2(b).

(iii) Circular boundary, say $r = a$. Solutions will have circular or rotational symmetry, so we transform to polar coordinates. The constraint then shows that

$$\Phi_{12}(u_1, u_2) = \Phi_0(\phi)\delta(q - k_c) \qquad (12a)$$

where

$$k_c^2 = k^2 - k_3^2 \qquad (12b)$$

The factor $\Phi_0$ is necessarily periodic in $\phi$, so can be written as a Fourier series. Consider the term of periodicity $N$. By Theorem 3.1.7

$$e^{jN\phi}\delta(q - k_c) \Rightarrow (-j)^N e^{jN\theta} 2\pi J_N(2\pi k_c r) \qquad (13)$$

Consequently we can take as eigenfunctions

$$\phi_{12}(x_1, x_2) = e^{\pm jN\theta} J_N(2\pi k_c r) \qquad (14a)$$

and define the eigenvalues $k_c$ by the equation

$$J_N(2\pi k_c a) = 0 \qquad (14b)$$

The Bessel functions $J_N$ being oscillatory, there is an infinite series of non-zero solutions for $k_c$. The indicators for this example are shown in Figure 3.5.2(c).

EXERCISES    (i) Consider a boundary in the form of a single conducting sheet at $x_1 = 0$. Show that the eigenfunctions are of the form (9a) but with a continuous set of eigenvalues $k_1 > 0$. Deduce the reflection properties of geometric optics as stated at the beginning of this section.

(ii) Find a set of eigenfunctions which vanish on the boundary of a regular hexagon. Consider the symmetries of the indicator function of their Fourier transform.

If a waveguide is propagating in a TM mode, it is clearly necessary thst $e_3$ vanishes on the walls; we shall see, after Theorem 1, that the eigenfunctions given above are indeed examples of TM transverse field distributions. For TE modes, we shall see in Theorem 2 that certain derivatives of the distribution of $h_3$ must vanish on the walls. The eigenfunctions for any specific geometry remain within the same general class (e.g. trigonometric functions for rectangular guides, Bessel functions for circular guides) with differences of detail which will emerge.

*Theorem 1*: Let a perfectly-conducting hollow metallic cylinder have a cross-section such that some function $\phi_{12}(x_1, x_2)$ of its transverse coordinates is zero on the wall, while its Fourier transform $\Phi_{12}(u_1, u_2)$ is non-zero only on the set defined by

$$u_1^2 + u_2^2 = Q^2 \qquad (15)$$

for some constant $Q$. Then the cylinder is a waveguide, and will support TM travelling waves along the axis $x_3$. The longitudinal field has the form

$$e_3 = \phi_{12}(x_1, x_2)e^{j2\pi(vt - k_3 x_3)} \qquad (16)$$

where

$$k_3^2 = k^2 - Q^2 \qquad (17)$$

Waves propagate only for frequencies above a cut-off frequency

$$v > v_c = Qc \qquad (18)$$

The phase velocity is

$$v_p = \frac{v}{k_3} = c\left(1 - \frac{v_c^2}{v^2}\right)^{-1/2} \qquad (19)$$

and the group velocity is

$$v_g = \frac{dv}{dk_3} = c \left(1 - \frac{v_c^2}{v^2}\right)^{1/2} \tag{20}$$

dispersion being normal in the sense of Definition 3.4.2. The characteristic impedance relating the orthogonal transverse electric and magnetic fields is

$$\frac{E_1}{H_2} = -\frac{E_2}{H_1} = \frac{k_3 Z_0}{k} = Z_0 \left(1 - \frac{v_c^2}{v^2}\right)^{1/2} \tag{21}$$

*Proof* From the wave equation (3.4.35) it follows immediately that any solution in the form (16) has a transverse wave-number constraint (15): we have already remarked on this in connection with Equation (5). It remains to be shown that the solution satisfies the boundary conditions at the waveguide wall, which are that all tangential components of electric field are zero. The stipulation that $\phi_{12}$ vanishes on the wall ensures that the longitudinal component $e_3$ is zero. For a TM wave $h_3$ is zero, and in this case Equation (4) yields immediately

$$\begin{bmatrix} E_1 \\ E_2 \end{bmatrix} = \frac{k_3}{Q^2} \begin{bmatrix} u_1 \\ u_2 \end{bmatrix} E_3 \tag{22}$$

That is, $e_1$ is proportional to $de_3/dx_1$ and $e_2$ to $de_3/dx_2$. More generally, the transverse $e$ field in any direction is proportional to the derivative of $e_3$ in that direction. Since $e_3$ is zero at all points on the wall, its derivative tangential to the wall is also zero. Thus, the tangential $e$ field vanishes as required.

Equation (4) also yields

$$\begin{bmatrix} H_2 \\ H_1 \end{bmatrix} = \frac{k}{Q^2 Z_0} \begin{bmatrix} u_1 \\ -u_2 \end{bmatrix} E_3 \tag{23}$$

which in conjunction with (22) gives the impedances (21) in the first form. Noting that $k = v/c$, we see from (17) that $k_3$ is real and non-zero only if $v^2 > c^2 Q^2$ which gives the cut-off frequency (18). It follows from (17) and (18) that

$$k_3^2 = \frac{v^2}{c^2} - \frac{v_c^2}{c^2}$$

which gives (19) directly and (20) on differentiation. From these expressions for the velocities

$$\frac{v_g}{v_p} = 1 - \frac{v_c^2}{v^2} < 1$$

which shows that dispersion is normal. Equations (17) and (18) also yield

$$\frac{k_3^2}{k^2} = 1 - \frac{v_c^2}{v^2}$$

which gives the impedances (21) in the second form.

*Corollary 1*   A planar waveguide comprising two parallel conducting sheets separated by a distance $2a$ supports TM waves in an infinite series of independent modes, designated $TM_{N0}$ ($N = 1, 2, 3 \ldots$), with the transverse distribution of $e_3$

$$\phi_{12}(x_1, x_2) = \sin 2\pi k_1 x_1 \qquad (24a)$$

and transverse wave-number

$$k_1 = Q = \frac{N}{4a} \qquad (24b)$$

*Corollary 2*   A rectangular waveguide with dimensions $2a_1, 2a_2$ supports TM waves in a doubly infinite series of independent modes, designated $TM_{NM}$ ($N, M = 1, 2, 3 \ldots$) with the transverse distribution of $e_3$

$$\phi_{12}(x_1, x_2) = \sin 2\pi k_1 x_1 . \sin 2\pi k_2 x_2 \qquad (25a)$$

and the transverse wave-number

$$k_1 = N/4a_1 \qquad (25b)$$

$$k_2 = M/4a_2 \qquad (25c)$$

$$Q = (k_1^2 + k_2^2)^{1/2} \qquad (25d)$$

*Corollary 3*   A circular waveguide with radius $a$ supports TM waves in a doubly infinite series of independent modes designated $TM_{NM}$ ($N = 0, 1, 2 \ldots : M = 1, 2, 3 \ldots$) with the transverse distribution of $e_3$

$$\phi_{12}(x_1, x_2) = J_N(2\pi k_c r) \begin{Bmatrix} \cos N\theta \\ \sin N\theta \end{Bmatrix} \qquad (26a)$$

with the transverse wave-number $k_c = Q$ defined as the $M$th non-zero solution of

$$J_N(2\pi k_c a) = 0 \tag{26b}$$

*Corollary 4* Transverse field components may be deduced directly from equations used in the proof of Theorem 1. Equation (22) transformed to the original domain gives the transverse distributions of $e_1$ and $e_2$

$$(e_1) \qquad \frac{k_3}{Q^2} \cdot \frac{1}{j2\pi} \cdot \frac{d\phi_{12}}{dx_1} \tag{27a}$$

$$(e_2) \qquad \frac{k_3}{Q^2} \cdot \frac{1}{j2\pi} \cdot \frac{d\phi_{12}}{dx_2} \tag{27b}$$

The transverse distributions of $h_1$ and $h_2$ follow either from applying similar reasoning to Equation (23), or from the impedance relationship (21). The results for rectangular and circular waveguide are given on the left-hand side of Tables 3.5.1 and 3.5.2.

**Table 3.5.1** RECTANGULAR-WAVEGUIDE MODES
All field components have a factor $e^{j2\pi(vt - k_3 x_3)}$ not included in the entries. Transverse wave-numbers: $k_1 = N/4a_1$, $k_2 = N/4a_2$. General notation: $k = v(\varepsilon\mu)^{1/2}$, $Z_0 = (\mu/\varepsilon)^{1/2}$, $v_c^2/v^2 = (k_1^2 + k_2^2)/k^2 = 1 - k_3^2/k^2$. Rectangular waveguide has $TE_{NM}$ and $TM_{NM}$ modes for all $N, M \geqslant 1$: also $TE_{N0}$ and $TE_{0M}$ modes. Planar waveguide has $TE_{N0}$ and $TM_{N0}$ modes only, similar to those given below but without $x_2$ variation.

| | $TM_{NM}$ | | $TE_{NM}$ | |
|---|---|---|---|---|
| $e_3$ | $\sin 2\pi k_1 x_1 \sin 2\pi k_2 x_2$ | | 0 | |
| $h_3$ | 0 | | $\cos 2\pi k_1 x_1 \cos 2\pi k_2 x_2$ | |
| $e_1$ | $j\left(\dfrac{k_1 k_3}{k_1^2 + k_2^2}\right)$ | $\cos 2\pi k_1 x_1 \sin 2\pi k_2 x_2$ | $jZ_0\left(\dfrac{k_2 k}{k_1^2 + k_2^2}\right)$ | $\cos 2\pi k_1 x_1 \sin 2\pi k_2 x_2$ |
| $h_1$ | $\dfrac{j}{Z_0}\left(\dfrac{k_2 k}{k_1^2 + k_2^2}\right)$ | $\sin 2\pi k_1 x_1 \cos 2\pi k_2 x_2$ | $-j\left(\dfrac{k_1 k_3}{k_1^2 + k_2^2}\right)$ | $\sin 2\pi k_1 x_1 \cos 2\pi k_2 x_2$ |
| $e_2$ | $j\left(\dfrac{k_2 k_3}{k_1^2 + k_2^2}\right)$ | $\sin 2\pi k_1 x_1 \cos 2\pi k_2 x_2$ | $-jZ_0\left(\dfrac{k_1 k}{k_1^2 + k_2^2}\right)$ | $\sin 2\pi k_1 x_1 \cos 2\pi k_2 x_2$ |
| $h_2$ | $\dfrac{-j}{Z_0}\left(\dfrac{k_1 k}{k_1^2 + k_2^2}\right)$ | $\cos 2\pi k_1 x_1 \sin 2\pi k_2 x_2$ | $-j\left(\dfrac{k_2 k_3}{k_1^2 + k_2^2}\right)$ | $\cos 2\pi k_1 x_1 \sin 2\pi k_2 x_2$ |

**Table 3.5.2** CIRCULAR-WAVEGUIDE MODES

All field components have a factor $e^{j2\pi(vt-k_3x_3)}$ not included in the entries. Circular wave-number $k_c$ such that $2\pi a k_c$ is the Mth zero of $J_N$ (for $TM$ modes) or $J_N'$ (for $TE$ modes). General notation: $k = v(\varepsilon\mu)^{1/2}$, $Z_0 = (\mu/\varepsilon)^{1/2}$, $v_c^2/v^2 = k_c^2/k^2 = 1 - k_3^2/k^2$. Circular waveguide has $TE_{NM}$ and $TM_{NM}$ modes for all $N \geqslant 0$, $M \geqslant 1$.

| | $TM_{NM}$ | | $TE_{NM}$ | |
|---|---|---|---|---|
| $e_3$ | | $J_N(2\pi k_c r)\cos N\theta$ | | 0 |
| $h_3$ | | 0 | | $J_N(2\pi k_c r)\cos N\theta$ |
| $e_r$ | $j\dfrac{k_3}{k_c}$ | $J_N'(2\pi k_c r)\cos N\theta$ | $-Z_0\dfrac{k}{k_c^2}\dfrac{N}{2\pi r}$ | $J_N(2\pi k_c r)\sin N\theta$ |
| $h_r$ | $\dfrac{1}{Z_0}\dfrac{k}{k_c^2}\dfrac{N}{2\pi r}$ | $J_N(2\pi k_c r)\sin N\theta$ | $j\dfrac{k_3}{k_c}$ | $J_N'(2\pi k_c r)\cos N\theta$ |
| $e_\theta$ | $-\dfrac{k_3}{k_c^2}\dfrac{N}{2\pi r}$ | $J_N(2\pi k_c r)\sin N\theta$ | $-jZ_0\dfrac{k}{k_c}$ | $J_N'(2\pi k_c r)\cos N\theta$ |
| $h_\theta$ | $\dfrac{j}{Z_0}\dfrac{k}{k_c}$ | $J_N'(2\pi k_c r)\cos N\theta$ | $-\dfrac{k_3}{k_c^2}\dfrac{N}{2\pi r}$ | $J_N(2\pi k_c r)\sin N\theta$ |

EXERCISE Derive the transverse components for a planar waveguide. Check that boundary conditions are satisfied. Compare your results with those for rectangular guide, given in Table 3.5.1. Apply a coordinate transformation to Equations (27) in order to justify the circular-waveguide expressions in Table 3.5.2.

*Theorem 2* Let a perfectly-conducting hollow metallic cylinder have a cross-section such that the normal derivative of some function $\phi_{12}(x_1, x_2)$ is zero on the wall, while the Fourier transform is non-zero only on the set defined by

$$u_1^2 + u_2^2 = Q^2 \tag{28}$$

for some constant $Q$. Then the cylinder is a waveguide, and will support $TE$ travelling waves along the axis $x_3$. The longitudinal magnetic field has the form

$$h_3 = \phi_{12}(x_1, x_2)e^{j2\pi(vt-k_3x_3)} \tag{29}$$

where

$$k_3^2 = k^2 - Q^2 \tag{30}$$

Waves propagate only for frequencies above a cut-off frequency

$$v > v_c = Qc \tag{31}$$

Dispersion is normal, with phase and group velocities

$$v_p = c\left(1 - \frac{v_c^2}{v^2}\right)^{-1/2} \tag{32}$$

$$v_g = c\left(1 - \frac{v_c^2}{v^2}\right)^{1/2} \tag{33}$$

The characteristic impedance relating the orthogonal transverse electric and magnetic fields is

$$\frac{E_1}{H_2} = -\frac{E_2}{H_1} = \frac{kZ_0}{k_3} = Z_0\left(1 - \frac{v_c^2}{v^2}\right)^{-1/2} \tag{34}$$

*Proof* The arguments for the wavenumber constraint, the velocities and the character of the dispersion are the same as in Theorem 1.

The boundary conditions are that tangential components of the electric field are zero at the wall. For a $TE$ wave, $e_3$ is zero and so only transverse components need be considered. In this case, Equation (4) yields immediately

$$\begin{bmatrix} E_1 \\ E_2 \end{bmatrix} = \frac{kZ_0}{Q^2}\begin{bmatrix} u_2 \\ -u_1 \end{bmatrix} H_3 \tag{35}$$

That is, $e_1$ is proportional to $dh_3/dx_2$ and $e_2$ to $-dh_3/dx_1$. More generally, the transverse $e$ field in any direction is proportional to the derivative of $h_3$ normal to that direction. The stipulation for $\phi_{12}$ is that the derivative normal to the walls shall vanish, so the tangential electric field vanishes as required.

Equation (4) also yields

$$\begin{bmatrix} H_2 \\ H_1 \end{bmatrix} = \frac{k_3}{Q^2}\begin{bmatrix} u_2 \\ u_1 \end{bmatrix} H_3 \tag{36}$$

which in conjunction with (35) gives the impedances (34) in the first form. The second form follows as in Theorem 1.

*Corollary 1* A planar waveguide with separation $2a$ supports $TE$ waves in an infinite series of independent modes designated $TE_{N0}$ ($N = 1, 2, 3 \ldots$) with the transverse distribution of $h_3$

$$\phi_{12}(x_1, x_2) = \cos 2\pi k_1 x_1 \tag{37a}$$

and the transverse wave number

$$k_1 = Q = \frac{N}{4a} \tag{37b}$$

Comparing this with (9) and (24), we note that the eigenfunction $\cos 2\pi k_1 x_1$ has zeros of its derivative at points where the eigenfunction $\sin 2\pi k_1 x_1$ itself vanishes: the eigenvalues $N/4a$ are the same.

*Corollary 2* A rectangular waveguide with dimensions $2a_1, 2a_2$ supports $TE$ waves in a doubly infinite series of independent modes designated $TE_{NM}$ ($N, M = 1, 2, 3 \ldots$: also $N$ or $M = 0$, provided that the other is non-zero) with the transverse distribution of $h_3$

$$\phi_{12}(x_1, x_2) = \cos 2\pi k_1 x_1 \cdot \cos 2\pi k_2 x_2 \tag{38a}$$

and the transverse wave numbers

$$k_1 = N/4a_1 \tag{38b}$$

$$k_2 = M/4a_2 \tag{38c}$$

$$Q = (k_1^2 + k_2^2)^{1/2} \tag{38d}$$

*Corollary 3* A circular waveguide with radius $a$ supports $TE$ waves in a doubly infinite series of independent modes designated $TE_{NM}$ ($N = 0, 1, 2 \ldots$: $M = 1, 2, 3 \ldots$) with the transverse distribution of $h_3$

$$\phi_{12}(x_1, x_2) = J_N(2\pi k_c r) \begin{Bmatrix} \cos N\theta \\ \sin N\theta \end{Bmatrix} \tag{39a}$$

with the transverse wave-number $k_c = Q$ defined as the $M$th non-zero solution of

$$J'_N(2\pi k_c a) = 0 \tag{39b}$$

Comparing this with (14) and (26), we note that the eigenfunction $J_N(2\pi k_c r)$ is the same, but the eigenvalues $k_c$ are different, being defined by the zeros of the derivative.

*Corollary 4* Transverse field components may be deduced directly from equations used in the proof of Theorem 2. Equation (36) transformed to the original domain gives the transverse distributions of $h_1$ and $h_2$:

$$(h_1) \qquad \frac{k_3}{Q^2} \frac{1}{j2\pi} \cdot \frac{d\phi_{12}}{dx_1} \tag{40a}$$

$$(h_2) \qquad \frac{k_3}{Q^2} \frac{1}{j2\pi} \cdot \frac{d\phi_{12}}{dx_2} \qquad\qquad (40b)$$

The transverse distributions of $e_1$ and $e_2$ follow either from applying similar reasoning to equation (35), or from the impedance relationship (34).

The results for rectangular and circular waveguides are given in the right-hand side of Tables 3.5.1 and 3.5.2 respectively.

*Waveguide dispersion* To illustrate some topics in dispersion theory we will take a specific example, namely the planar metallic waveguide, and study it in detail. It is convenient to use normalised variables,* respectively a function of wave-number $k_3$

$$b = \frac{k_3^2}{k^2} = 1 - \frac{Q^2}{k^2} \qquad\qquad (41)$$

and a function of frequency

$$g = 2\pi a v/c \qquad\qquad (42)$$

The phase delay per unit length is, quite generally,

$$\frac{1}{v_p} = \frac{k_3}{v} = \frac{b^{1/2}}{c} \qquad\qquad (43)$$

and the group delay per unit length, again quite generally

$$\frac{1}{v_g} = \frac{dk_3}{dv} = \frac{1}{c} \frac{d}{dv}(vb^{1/2})$$

$$= \frac{1}{cb^{1/2}} \left\{ b + \frac{v}{2} \frac{db}{dv} \right\} \qquad\qquad (44)$$

In all metallic waveguides, the last bracketed expression reduces to unity, so that

$$\frac{1}{v_g} = \frac{1}{cb^{1/2}} = \frac{v_p}{c^2} \qquad\qquad (45)$$

consistently with (19—20) and (32–33).

In the specific case of planar guide, substitution of (24b) or (37b)

---

* These may be generalised to deal with other types of waveguide, for example circular tubes, and dielectric films and fibres: the latter are treated in Section 3.6.

gives the relationship

$$b = 1 - \frac{N^2 \pi^2}{4g^2} \tag{46}$$

The delays (43) and (45) may be calculated in terms of the normalised frequency $g$. Some typical results are plotted in Figure 3.5.3.

The dispersion shown will cause a signal in the form of a pulse to be broadened as it travels along a waveguide, even though it utilises only a single mode. Another form of pulse broadening can be caused by *multi-mode transmission*. If the signal frequency band lies above the cut-off frequency of the $N$th order modes, it will lie in the propagating

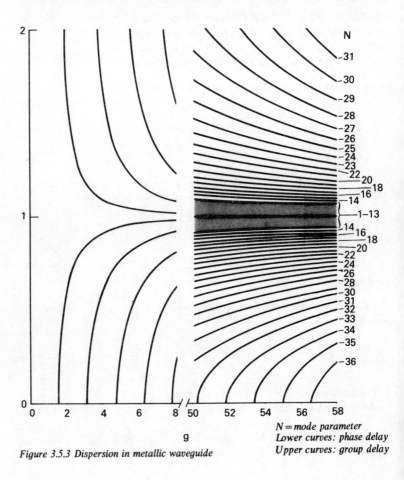

*Figure 3.5.3 Dispersion in metallic waveguide*

$N = mode\ parameter$
*Lower curves: phase delay*
*Upper curves: group delay*

range for all modes of lower order. These modes travel at different velocities, so if several modes are excited by the transmitter they will contribute to the received signal with different delays. Many practical waveguide systems are designed to use a single mode only, thereby avoiding this form of dispersion: but some systems are intentionally multi-mode, and in any case unintended couplings between modes may occur due to the departure of the guide from strict uniformity. Single-mode operation is ensured if the operating frequency lies between the cut-offs of the first two modes: in this region, as Figure 3.5.3 shows, the dispersion of the first-order mode is at its greatest. Rectangular waveguides are normally used only over short distances.

Practical rectangular waveguides have different dimensions $a_1$ and $a_2$, so we must distinguish $TE_{N0}$ modes (with $N$ antinodes along the $x_1$ axis but uniform along the $x_2$ axis) from $TE_{0M}$ modes (with $M$ antinodes along the $x_2$ axis, but uniform along $x_1$). There are also $TE_{NM}$ and $TM_{NM}$ modes for $N, M \geqslant 1$. The $TE_{10}$ mode is often used in practical guides because it may, over a useful frequency range, be the unique propagating mode, so that multi-mode dispersion is eliminated.

EXERCISE One type of practical rectangular waveguide has $2a_1 = 2.418$ in, $2a_2 = 1.273$ in. Calculate the first few cut-off frequencies, and show that there is a frequency band in the 4 GHz region for which only one mode will propagate.

*The ray interpretation of waveguides* The solution for the planar metallic guide exhibits travelling-wave behaviour longitudinally, combined with standing-wave behaviour transversely. The result is identical with the superposition of two inclined waves, with equal $k_3$ and equal and opposite $k_1$. A transverse distribution such as (9) is equivalent to a standing-wave pattern such as Figure 3.4.9(c) or 3.5.1(b). Thus the waveguide modes correspond precisely to the appropriate superpositions of plane waves. The $TE$ and $TM$ modes correspond to two orthogonal polarisations of the plane waves: the modes of different order correspond to different angles of inclination.

This approach suggests a ray model, using the ideas of geometrical optics. A ray inclined to the axis at an angle $\theta$ is reflected between the planes, and progresses along the guide in a zig-zag path (Figure 3.5.4(a)). This is a useful model for some purposes: but we need an admixture of wave theory to explain why only certain discrete values of $\theta$ are permissible. A ray is the axis of a plane wave, and we must consider a wave front. Points $A$ and $E$ in Figure 3.5.4(b) lie on the same wavefront. Tracing ray paths forwards from these points, we

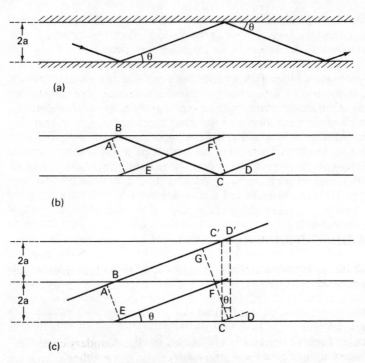

*Figure 3.5.4 Ray model of waveguide. (a) Ray path in waveguide; (b) Two rays with common normals; (c) Calculation of path difference*

arrive at the points $D$ and $F$ which lie on a common normal to both ray paths. If a travelling wave is to be sustained, points $D$ and $F$ must be in phase despite their obvious difference of path length. (If they are not, destructive interference will attenuate the wave.) We calculate the path length difference with the aid of Figure 3.5.4(c), in which reflections are unfolded: it is

$$AD - EF = AD' - AG = 4a \sin \theta = 4ak_1/k \tag{47}$$

Waves at $D$ and $F$ will be in phase if this path difference is $N\lambda = N/k$. (Note that ray $AD$ has suffered two reflections, at $B$ and $C$; so this criterion applied whether there is a phase reversal on reflection or not.) It follows that for stable wave propagation $k_1 = N/4a_1$, as required by Theorems 1 and 2, Corollary 1.

EXERCISE  (i) On the ray model, the longitudinal component of velocity is clearly $c \cos \theta$. Show that this is equal to the group velocity

(20). (Corollary: multi-mode dispersion can be calculated from the ray model.)

(ii) Sketch a ray model for rectangular waveguide.

Propagation in circular waveguides can also be visualised in terms of a ray theory. The $(0, M)$ modes correspond to meridional rays; that is, rays which lie in a plane through the central axis of the waveguide. The $N > 0$ modes correspond to skew rays: that is, to rays which do not lie in such a plane. Whereas the ray theory for planar and rectangular guides is exact, for circular guides it is only approximate, because reflection from a curved surface does not lead to a strictly plane wave. However, if the guide dimensions are large compared with the wavelength (normally the case in guides supporting modes of large $M$) then the picture is a reasonable one.*

## 3.6 DIELECTRIC WAVEGUIDES

The second kind of material structure which we shall consider is made from perfectly lossless dielectric materials. Two different materials are required, the wave being confined by the boundary between them. The ideal lossless model reveals the principal features of dielectric waveguides very clearly, and is a good approximation to optical fibres as used for long-distance communication. The boundary conditions amount to matching the electromagnetic fields on either side of the interface in an appropriate way: this is somewhat more complex than the boundary condition for a metallic waveguide. We also have to consider the field configurations in both media: in practical waveguides, one medium carries travelling waves in modes reminiscent of metallic-waveguide modes, while the other medium exhibits an evanescent field (that is, one which decays rapidly in one or more dimensions). An exact analysis of dielectric waveguide is very complex: we shall concentrate here on the so-called weakly-guiding waveguide, a special case approximating very closely to practical optical fibres, and permitting some simplification of the theory.†

The simplest form of interface between two dielectrics is an infinite plane. Let us suppose a plane travelling wave, generated by a remote source in one medium, to be incident on such an interface. It is well known that, in general, there are two resultants: a transmitted wave

---

* Adams (1) pp. 214–20 discusses the comparison at some length, and shows that the accuracy of the ray model increases rapidly with $M$ (our $M$ being $N + 1$ in his notation).

† For a more detailed treatment and an introduction to the specialised literature, the text by Adams (1) is strongly recommended.

proceeding into the second medium, and a reflected wave. The boundary conditions which enable the properties of these waves to be calculated are that (i) tangential electric field must be continuous across the interface (ii) tangential magnetic field must be continuous across the interface. In the context of guided waves, we emphasise the case of shallow incidence, which gives rise to a dominant reflected component. In the context of optics, we shall characterise a dielectric by its *refractive index n*, which is inversely proportional to wave velocity. If $\varepsilon_0$, $\mu_0$ are the permittivity and permeability of free space, then the typical dielectric has $\mu = \mu_0$ and $\varepsilon > \varepsilon_0$; the velocity of plane waves in the medium is then

$$v = (\varepsilon \mu_0)^{-1/2} = (\varepsilon_0 \mu_0)^{-1/2} (\varepsilon_0/\varepsilon)^{1/2} = c/n \tag{1}$$

where $c$ is the velocity in free space. The magnitude of the wave-number vector is

$$k = \frac{v}{v} = \frac{vn}{c} \tag{2}$$

and the characteristic impedance is

$$Z = \left(\frac{\mu_0}{\varepsilon}\right)^{1/2} = \left(\frac{\mu_0}{\varepsilon_0}\right)^{1/2} \left(\frac{\varepsilon_0}{\varepsilon}\right)^{1/2} = \frac{Z_0}{n} \tag{3}$$

Throughout the following treatment we shall be dealing with two materials of refractive indices $n_1$ and $n_2$, and wave-number vectors $\mathbf{k}$ and $\mathbf{h}$ respectively: numerically $n_1 > n_2$ and $k > h$.

The interface does not strictly confine the field, but one medium usually exhibits an evanescent field which decays with increasing distance from the interface. An evanescent field component may be represented by a complex or imaginary wave-number. For example, in developing the theory of planar films we shall use a wave-number vector of the form

$$\mathbf{h} = (h_1, 0, k_3): \qquad h_1 = -j\alpha \tag{4a}$$

Substituting this in a wave expression of the form (3.4.37) gives

$$\phi = e^{-2\pi\alpha x_1} \cdot e^{j2\pi(vt - k_3 x_3)} \tag{4b}$$

which is a travelling wave in the $x_3$ direction, attenuating exponentially with increasing $x_1$.

An optical fibre waveguide comprises a central circular *core* of refractive index $n_1$ surrounded by a *cladding* of refractive index $n_2$. The appropriate eigenfunctions for the core include a radial component $J_N(2\pi k_c r)$, for the same reasons as in metallic waveguide.* The radial component in the cladding is defined in terms of the *modified Bessel functions* $K_N(z)$ which are closely related to ordinary Bessel functions of imaginary argument. The modified Bessel function of the first kind

$$I_N(z) = e^{-j\frac{1}{2}N\pi} J_N(jz) \tag{5}$$

increases without bound as $z \to \infty$ and so does not meet the conditions for a guided field. However, a wave equation leading to an imaginary wave-number would be satisfied by any linear combination of $J_{\pm N}(\pm jz)$. A suitable combination is the modified function of the second kind

$$K_N(z) = \frac{1}{2}\pi \left\{ \frac{I_{-N}(z) - I_N(z)}{\sin N\pi} \right\} \tag{6}$$

which converges to zero as $z \to \infty$. (It diverges as $z \to 0$, but as we shall use it only in the exterior of a cylinder this is no problem.) Asymptotically, for large $z$

$$K_N(z) \approx \left( \frac{\pi}{2z} \right)^{1/2} e^{-z} \tag{7}$$

EXERCISE    Use the asymptotic expression for the ordinary Bessel function, Equation (2.4.30), together with Equations (5) and (6) to derive the asymptotic expression (7).

The cladding of an optical waveguide is of finite extent, but since evanescent fields decay rapidly the outer boundary may usually be ignored. We shall analyse the planar and circular structures of Figure 3.6.1 on this assumption.

A dielectric waveguide supports travelling waves in an infinite series of modes, each with normal dispersion. In certain special cases, these modes may be *TE* or *TM*: more generally, they are *hybrid modes* in which the longitudinal electric and magnetic field components are both non-zero but have a characteristic ratio.

In the theorems to follow, we shall use the following notations:

| | |
|---|---|
| $\phi_1, \phi_2$ | transverse eigenfunctions for the core and cladding regions respectively |
| $\phi_1^{(t)}, \phi_2^{(t)}$ | derivatives of $\phi_1$ and $\phi_2$ in the transverse direction tangential to the interface |
| $\phi_1^{(n)}, \phi_2^{(n)}$ | derivatives of $\phi_1$ and $\phi_2$ in the transverse direction normal to the interface. |

* See the argument leading to Equation (3.5.14(a)).

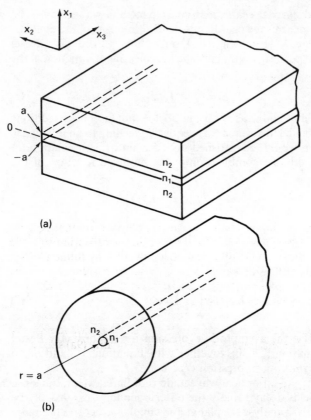

*Figure 3.6.1 Dielectric waveguide structures. (a) Planar; (b) Circular*

*Theorem 1*: Let a waveguide structure consist of two lossless dielectric materials of wave-numbers $k, h$ with an interface of uniform cross-section. Let there be two eigenfunctions appropriate to the inner and outer regions respectively, such that

$\phi_1(x_1, x_2)$ has a constant value $\phi_1(\mathbf{a})$ on the interface
$\Phi_1(u_1, u_2)$ is non-zero only on the set $u_1^2 + u_2^2 = Q^2$
$\phi_2(x_1, x_2)$ has a constant value $\phi_2(\mathbf{a})$ on the interface
$\Phi_2(u_1, u_2)$ is non-zero only on the set $u_1^2 + u_2^2 = Q^2 + h^2 - k^2$

Then the structure will support $TE$ travelling waves along the axis

$x_3$, with longitudinal components of the form

$$h_3 = \frac{\phi_i(x_1, x_2)}{\phi_i(\mathbf{a})} \cdot e^{j2\pi(vt - k_3 x_3)} \tag{8}$$

The wave-number $k_3$ satisfies

$$h < k_3 < k \tag{9a}$$

$$k_3^2 = k^2 - Q^2 \tag{9b}$$

The longitudinal and transverse wave-numbers are defined implicitly by solution of the equation

$$\frac{\phi_1^{(n)}}{(k^2 - k_3^2)\phi_1} = \frac{\phi_2^{(n)}}{(h^2 - k_3^2)\phi_2} \tag{10}$$

*Proof* The boundary conditions at the interface are that tangential electric and magnetic fields shall be continuous. Continuity of the longitudinal component $h_3$ implies that (i) the longitudinal wave-number $k_3$ is the same in both media (ii) the amplitudes of the longitudinal components are the same in both media: the latter is ensured by normalising the eigenfunctions as in (8).

Guidance by the core requires that the field in the cladding be evanescent, which is true if and only if $k_3^2 > h^2$. A real wave-number vector in the core requires that $k_3^2 < k^2$. The inequality (9a) subsumes these conditions, for positively-directed waves.

From the wave equation (3.4.35) it follows that any solution in the form (8) must satisfy

$$u_1^2 + u_2^2 = k^2 - k_3^2 \qquad \text{in the core}$$

$$= h^2 - k_3^2 \qquad \text{in the cladding}$$

and the constraints on $\Phi_1, \Phi_2$ stated in the theorem are equivalent to these, with $Q^2 = k^2 - k_3^2$.

General relationships between longitudinal and transverse components are deduced in the proofs of Theorems 3.5.1 and 3.5.2. The tangential transverse magnetic field is proportional to the tangential transverse derivative of $h_3$, hence to $\phi_i^{(t)}$. Amending Equations (3.5.40) to allow for the refractive indices gives

$$\frac{k_3}{k^2 - k_3^2} \cdot \frac{1}{j2\pi} \cdot \frac{\phi_1^{(t)}}{\phi_1(\mathbf{a})} \qquad \text{in the core}$$

$$\frac{k_3}{h^2 - k_3^2} \cdot \frac{1}{j2\pi} \cdot \frac{\phi_2^{(t)}}{\phi_2(\mathbf{a})} \qquad \text{in the cladding}$$

and by the transverse boundary condition these must be equal. But by the longitudinal condition, the factors $\phi_i^{(n)}/\phi_i(\mathbf{a})$ must be equal. These conditions are inconsistent save in the special case $\phi_i^{(t)} = 0$. The stipulation in the theorem that the $\phi_i$ shall be constant over the interface is therefore necessary.

The tangential transverse electric field is proportional to the normal transverse derivative of $h_3$, hence to $\phi_i^{(n)}$. Amending Equations (3.5.35) to allow for the refractive indices gives

$$\frac{kZ_0/n_1}{k^2 - k_3^2} \cdot \frac{1}{j2\pi} \cdot \frac{\phi_1^{(n)}}{\phi_1(\mathbf{a})} \qquad \text{in the core}$$

$$\frac{hZ_0/n_2}{h^2 - k_3^2} \cdot \frac{1}{j2\pi} \cdot \frac{\phi_2^{(n)}}{\phi_2(\mathbf{a})} \qquad \text{in the cladding}$$

Recalling from (2) that $k/n_1 = h/n_2$, we see that the transverse electric condition implies Equation (10). This is a single equation in a single variable $k_3$ (under the conditions of this theorem, the transverse wavenumbers are all uniquely related to $k_3$) and is in general soluble to yield a $TE$ mode.

*Corollary 1*   The planar waveguide supports an infinite series of $TE$ modes, designated $TE_N$ ($N = 0, 1, 2 \ldots$). The core eigenfunctions are

$$\phi_1(x_1) = \begin{Bmatrix} \cos \\ \sin \end{Bmatrix} 2\pi k_1 x_1, \qquad k_1^2 = k^2 - k_3^2 \tag{11}$$

and the cladding eigenfunctions are

$$\phi_2(x_1) = e^{-2\pi\alpha x_1}, \qquad \alpha^2 = k_3^2 - h^2 \tag{12}$$

(for justification, see the argument leading to Equation 3.6.4(b)).

Equation (10) then becomes

$$\begin{Bmatrix} -\cot \\ \tan \end{Bmatrix} 2\pi k_1 a = \frac{\alpha}{k_1} \tag{13a}$$

Allowing for the periodicity of the cot and tan functions, and the relationship between them, all cases are subsumed in the equation

$$2\pi a k_1 - \tan^{-1}\left(\frac{\alpha}{k_1}\right) = N\pi/2 \tag{13b}$$

$$(N = 0, 1, 2 \ldots)$$

taking the inverse tangent in the first quadrant. We shall later examine the solutions for $k_1$, the distribution of field over the cross-section, and the waveguide dispersion.

*Corollary 2* The circular waveguide supports an infinite series of *TE* modes with no angular variation, designated $TE_{0M}$ ($M = 1, 2, 3 \ldots$). The core eigenfunctions are

$$\phi_1(r) = J_0(2\pi k_c r), \qquad k_c^2 = k^2 - k_3^2 \tag{14}$$

and the cladding eigenfunctions are

$$\phi_2(r) = K_0(2\pi h_c r), \qquad h_c^2 = k_3^2 - h^2 \tag{15}$$

The determining equation is in this case

$$\frac{J_0'(2\pi k_c a)}{k_c J_0(2\pi k_c a)} = -\frac{K_0'(2\pi h_c a)}{h_c K_0(2\pi h_c a)} \tag{16}$$

which may be solved numerically to obtain values of $k_c$: the function $J_0$ being oscillatory and $K_0$ monotonically decreasing, there is an infinity of solutions.

*Theorem 2*: Under the general conditions of Theorem 1, the dielectric waveguide will also support *TM* travelling waves, with a longitudinal component of the form

$$e_3 = \frac{\phi_i(x_1, x_2)}{\phi_i(\mathbf{a})} e^{j2\pi(vt - k_3 x_3)} \tag{17}$$

and wave-number restrictions (9). The longitudinal and transverse wave-numbers are defined implicitly by solution of the equation

$$\frac{n_1^2 \phi_1^{(n)}}{(k^2 - k_3^2)\phi_1} = \frac{n_2^2 \phi_2^{(n)}}{(h^2 - k_3^2)\phi_2} \tag{18}$$

over the interface.

*Proof* is similar to that of Theorem 1, and we indicate only the differences. The tangential transverse electric field is proportional to the tangential transverse derivative of $e_3$, hence to $\phi_i^{(t)}$. Amending Equation (3.5.27) to allow for the refractive indices gives

$$\frac{k_3}{k^2 - k_3^2} \frac{1}{j2\pi} \frac{\phi_1^{(t)}}{\phi_1(\mathbf{a})} \qquad \text{in the core}$$

$$\frac{k_3}{h^2 - k_3^2} \frac{1}{j2\pi} \frac{\phi_2^{(t)}}{\phi_2(\mathbf{a})} \qquad \text{in the cladding}$$

and by the transverse boundary condition these must be equal. But by the longitudinal condition the factors $\phi_n^{(t)}/\phi_i(\mathbf{a})$ must be equal. These conditions are inconsistent save in the special case $\phi_i^{(t)} = 0$, so again the stipulation that the $\phi_i$ shall be constant over the interface is necessary.

The tangential transverse magnetic field is proportional to the normal transverse derivative of $e_3$, hence to $\phi_i^{(n)}$. Amending Equations (3.5.23) to allow for the refractive indices gives

$$\frac{k}{(k^2 - k_3^2)Z_0/n_1} \frac{1}{j2\pi} \frac{\phi_1^{(n)}}{\phi_1(\mathbf{a})} \quad \text{in the core}$$

$$\frac{h}{(h^2 - k_3^2)Z_0/n_2} \frac{1}{j2\pi} \frac{\phi_2^{(n)}}{\phi_2(\mathbf{a})} \quad \text{in the cladding}$$

Recalling from (2) that $k/n_1 = h/n_2$, we see that the transverse magnetic condition implies equation (18), which is in general soluble to yield a *TM* mode.

*Corollary 1* The planar and circular dielectric waveguides support *TM* modes with eigenfunctions similar to the *TE* case (corollaries to Theorem 1) but with eigenvalue equations modified by the factor $n_1^2/n_2^2$.

*Corollary 2* In the weakly-guiding case where $n_1 \approx n_2$, the *TE* and *TM* modes approach degeneracy, with similar velocities, cut-off frequencies and field patterns.

Dielectric waveguide differs from metallic waveguide in that pure *TE* and *TM* waves exist only in a more restricted set of modes, and in a more restricted class of structures: those whose symmetries permit the tangential transverse derivative to be zero. Basically, the dielectric guide imposes more boundary conditions, and these can be satisfied only in special cases (as above) or by absorbing an additional degree of freedom as in the hybrid modes.

*Definition 1*: A *hybrid mode* is a travelling wave mode in which the longitudinal electric and magnetic components are both non-zero and are constrained by the boundary conditions to assume a definite ratio characteristic of the waveguide structure.

Note that the relationships between longitudinal and transverse components invoked in the proofs of Theorems 1 and 2 still apply. A hybrid mode may be considered as the superposition of *TE* and *TM* type field patterns in definite proportions. Hybrid modes are possible in a great variety of structures: we shall prove their existence and properties only for the important special case of a circular waveguide such as an optical fibre.

*Theorem 3*: The lossless circular dielectric waveguide will support travelling waves in hybrid modes of two kinds, designated *EH* and *HE*. There is a series of independent modes of each type, with *N*-fold angular periodicity ($N = 1, 2, 3 \ldots$). The eigenfunctions defining the field distributions are, in the core

$$\phi_1(x_1, x_2) = \frac{J_N(2\pi k_c r)}{J_N(2\pi k_c a)} \begin{Bmatrix} \cos N\theta \\ \sin N\theta \end{Bmatrix} \tag{19a}$$

and in the cladding

$$\phi_2(x_1, x_2) = \frac{K_N(2\pi h_c r)}{K_N(2\pi h_c a)} \begin{Bmatrix} \cos N\theta \\ \sin N\theta \end{Bmatrix} \tag{19b}$$

the denominator being for normalisation. The wave-numbers are defined implicitly by the solutions of

$$\left( \frac{J_N'}{k_c J_N} + \frac{K_N'}{h_c K_N} \right) \left( n_1^2 \frac{J_N'}{k_c J_N} + n_2^2 \frac{K_N'}{h_c K_N} \right) = \left( \frac{Nck_3}{2\pi va} \right)^2 \left( \frac{1}{k_c^2} + \frac{1}{h_c^2} \right)^2 \tag{20}$$

where the argument of each *J* is $2\pi k_c a$ and the argument of each *K* is $2\pi h_c a$, and

$$k_c^2 + h_c^2 = k^2 - h^2 \tag{21}$$

The ratio of the longitudinal *e* field to the longitudinal *h* field at the interface is

$$\pm jZ_0 \left\{ \frac{\dfrac{J_N'}{k_c J_N} + \dfrac{K_N'}{h_c K_N}}{\dfrac{n_1^2 J_N'}{k_c J_N} + \dfrac{n_2^2 K_N'}{h_c K_N}} \right\}^{1/2} \tag{22}$$

the two modal types *EH* and *HE* differing in sign.

*Proof*  We express the hybrid wave as the superposition of *TE* and *TM* waves with longitudinal components $h_3$ and $e_3$ respectively, in proportions to be determined: specifically, we write the sum as

$$\mathscr{E} \, (TM \text{ wave}) + \mathscr{H}(TE \text{ wave})$$

and show that with suitable ratio $\mathscr{E}/\mathscr{H}$ this can satisfy the boundary conditions at the interface. An arbitrary angular distribution can be expressed as a Fourier series, and $N$-fold periodicity is associated with the radial eigenfunction $J_N$ (see Theorem 3.1.7, and its application to metallic waveguides in Section 3.5): so (19a) is a suitable set of eigenfunctions for the core. By extension of the argument to imaginary wave-numbers, (19b) is a suitable set of eigenfunctions for the cladding.

The transverse components are related to the longitudinal components as stated in the proofs of Theorems 1 and 2. The tangential magnetic field, in this case $h_\theta$, depends on the tangential derivative of $h_3$ and the normal derivative of $e_3$. Continuity at the interface requires that

$$\mathscr{H}\frac{k_3 N}{2\pi a}\left(\frac{1}{k_c^2}+\frac{1}{h_c^2}\right)+\mathscr{E}\frac{v}{jcZ_0}\left(\frac{n_1^2 J_N'}{k_c J_N}+\frac{n_2^2 K_N'}{h_c K_N}\right)=0 \tag{23}$$

assuming an angular factor $e^{jN\theta}$. Similarly, the tangential electric field, in this case $e_\theta$, depends on the tangential derivative of $e_3$ and the normal derivative of $h_3$. Continuity requires that

$$\mathscr{E}\frac{k_3 N}{2\pi a}\left(\frac{1}{k_c^2}+\frac{1}{h_c^2}\right)+\mathscr{H}\frac{jZ_0 v}{c}\left(\frac{J_N'}{k_c J_N}+\frac{K_N'}{h_c K_N}\right)=0 \tag{24}$$

Elimination of the ratio $\mathscr{E}/\mathscr{H}$ between Equations (23) and (24) gives (20). If $N=0$, the right-hand side is zero, and the two factors of the left-hand side give independent criteria which are those of Equation (10) for $TE$ waves and its counterpart for $TM$ waves (see Theorem 1, Corollary 2 and Theorem 2, Corollary 1). Otherwise, the equation may be solved to obtain a series of values for $k_c$, each corresponding to two modes. The existence of two modes, and the ratio $e_3/h_3$ for each, follows from solving Equations (23) and (24) for $\mathscr{E}/\mathscr{H}$. The result is

$$\left(\frac{\mathscr{E}}{\mathscr{H}}\right)^2=-Z_0^2\left\{\frac{\dfrac{J_N'}{k_c J_N}+\dfrac{K_N'}{h_c K_N}}{\dfrac{n_1^2 J_N'}{k_c J_N}+\dfrac{n_2^2 K_N'}{h_c K_N}}\right\} \tag{25}$$

which gives the two solutions (22). Alternatively, the two solutions follow on noting that $e^{jN\theta}$ and $e^{-jN\theta}$ are equally valid angular distributions. These distributions can be superposed to obtain real independent angular distributions $\cos N\theta$ and $\sin N\theta$ as in equations (19).

*Corollary 1* Under the weakly-guiding condition $n_2 \approx n_1$ there is a further degeneracy of modes, since the two factors on the left-hand side of (20) are annulled by substantially the same condition. Allowing for the fact that $k_3 \approx k = vn_1/c$ this may be written as

$$\frac{J'_N}{k_c J_N} + \frac{K'_N}{h_c K_N} = \pm \frac{N}{2\pi a}\left(\frac{1}{k_c^2} + \frac{1}{h_c^2}\right) \qquad (26)$$

The ratio of longitudinal electric to magnetic field is in this case

$$\frac{\mathscr{E}}{\mathscr{H}} \approx \pm \frac{jZ_0}{n_1} \qquad (27)$$

(i.e. the characteristic impedance of the medium). To prove this last statement we note that for $N \neq 0$ neither numerator nor denominator of (25) is zero, and their ratio approaches $1/n_1^2$.

*Corollary 2* There are several equivalent forms of the eigenvalue equation (26), including the following. (Throughout the argument of any $J$ is $2\pi k_c a$, and of any $K$ is $2\pi h_c a$.)

$$\frac{J_{N+1}}{k_c J_N} + \frac{K_{N+1}}{h_c K_N} = 0, \qquad N \geqslant 0 \qquad (28)$$

$$\frac{J_{N-1}}{k_c J_N} - \frac{K_{N-1}}{h_c K_N} = 0, \qquad N \geqslant 1 \qquad (29)$$

$$\frac{J_{N-2}}{J_N} + \frac{K_{N-2}}{K_N} = 0, \qquad N \geqslant 2 \qquad (30)$$

These expressions turn out to be useful in the discussion of cut-off frequencies and dispersion. Equation (28) with $N = 0$ applies to $TE$ and $TM$ modes: with $N \geqslant 1$ it applies to the hybrid modes conventionally designated $EH$. Equations (29) and (30), which are equivalent for $N \geqslant 2$, apply to the modes conventionally designated $HE$. For further information on these modes, and on their reduction to linearly-polarised pseudo-modes, see Adams (1).

EXERCISE Derive Equations (28–30) from (26). The following Bessel-function relationships, quoted from Abramowitz and Stegun (1), will be found useful:

$$J'_N(z) = J_{N-1}(z) - \frac{N}{z}J_N(z) = -J_{N+1}(z) + \frac{N}{z}J_N(z) \qquad (31)$$

$$K'_N(z) = -K_{N-1}(z) - \frac{N}{z}K_N(z) = -K_{N+1}(z) + \frac{N}{z}K_N(z) \qquad (32)$$

### Cut-off and dispersion in dielectric waveguides

We take as our primary example $TE$ waves in planar guide (Theorem 1, Corollary 1) which illustrate the main phenomena without too much analytical complexity. It is convenient to use normalised variables.*

In place of wave-number $k_3$ we use

$$b = \frac{k_3^2 - h^2}{k^2 - h^2} \qquad (33)$$

which varies from 0 to 1 as $k_3$ varies between its lower bound $h$ and its upper bound $k$. In place of frequency $v$ we use the scaled value

$$g = 2\pi a \frac{v}{c}(n_1^2 - n_2^2) \qquad (34)$$

In these terms, the eigenvalue equation (13b) for the $TE_N$ mode becomes

$$g = \frac{1}{(1-b)^{1/2}}\left\{\tan^{-1}\left(\frac{b}{1-b}\right)^{1/2} + \tfrac{1}{2}N\pi\right\} \qquad (35)$$

with the arctan taken in the first quadrant. Each mode has a lower cut-off frequency at $b=0$, namely

$$g_c = \tfrac{1}{2}N\pi \qquad (36)$$

The phase delay per unit length is $1/v_p = k_3/v$, given by

$$\left(\frac{c}{v_p}\right)^2 = n_2^2 + b(n_1^2 - n_2^2) \qquad (37a)$$

In the weakly-guiding case this is approximated by

$$\frac{c}{v_p} \approx n_2 + b(n_1 - n_2) \qquad (37b)$$

The group delay per unit length is $1/v_g = dk_3/dv$, which may be deduced from

$$\frac{c^2}{v_p v_g} = c^2\left(\frac{k_3}{v} \cdot \frac{dk_3}{dv}\right) = \frac{1}{2v}\frac{d}{dv}\left(v^2\frac{c^2}{v_p^2}\right)$$

* Compare equations (3.5.41) and (3.5.42)

To evaluate this we require the derivative

$$\frac{dg}{db} = \frac{g + b^{-1/2}}{2(1-b)}$$

which may be obtained by differentiating equation (35). The results are conveniently expressed in terms of a parameter

$$B = \frac{g + b^{1/2}}{g + b^{-1/2}} \tag{38}$$

The group delay follows from

$$\frac{c^2}{v_p v_g} = n_2^2 + B(n_1^2 - n_2^2) \tag{39a}$$

in general, and in the weakly-guiding case from

$$\frac{c}{v_g} \approx n_2 + (2B - b)(n_1 - n_2) \tag{39b}$$

It is readily shown that $0 \leqslant b \leqslant B \leqslant 1$, whence

$$n_2^2 \leqslant \frac{c^2}{v_p^2} \leqslant \frac{c^2}{v_p v_g} \leqslant n_1^2 \tag{40}$$

Thus dispersion is normal, and the velocity $v_p$ is intermediate between the characteristic velocities of the media $c/n_1$ and $c/n_2$.

Some curves of $b$ and $2B - b$ against $g$ are shown in Figure 3.6.2: these indicate the behaviour of phase and group delay respectively. At frequencies well above cut-off, phase and group velocities approach $c/n_1$, and their geometric mean approaches it even more rapidly as may be seen from (39). The distribution of field strength varies with frequency; at high frequencies the field is concentrated in the core, near to cut-off it penetrates further into the cladding. Some examples are shown in Figure 3.6.3. The velocities and the field distribution are related: the parameter $B$ in Equations (38-9) is equal to the proportion of power in the core.*

*Circular guide cut-off frequencies* Broadly similar properties are exhibited by $TE$ and $TM$ modes in planar guide and by $TE$, $TM$ and hybrid modes in circular guide. The cut-off frequencies in circular

---

* It is beyond the scope of the present section to prove this statement. See Adams (1) for a full derivation and discussion.

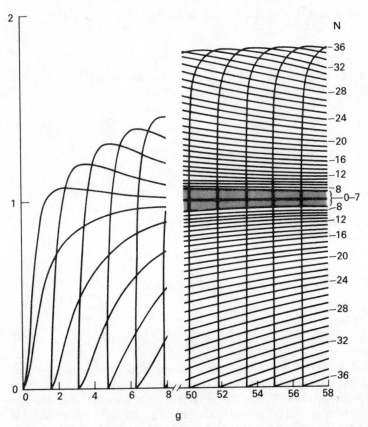

*Figure 3.6.2 Dispersion in dielectric waveguide.* N = *mode parameter. Lower curves:* b *(phase delay). Upper curves:* 2B − b *(group delay)*

guide may be deduced from the versions of the eigenvalue equation given in Corollary 2 to Theorem 3. At cut-off, the cladding wave-number $h_c$ approaches zero: so the argument $2\pi a h_c$ of all the modified Bessel functions does likewise. It may be shown that in consequence $K_{N+1}/h_c K_N \to \infty$. Also, the argument $2\pi a k_c$ of the core Bessel functions approaches $2\pi a(k^2 - h^2)^{1/2} = g$. The cut-off frequency in the modes governed by Equation (28) is given by

$$J_N(g) = 0, \qquad J_{N+1}(g) \neq 0 \qquad\qquad (41)$$

so there is a series of modes, indicated by all the zeros of $J_N$ other than zero. For modes governed by Equation (30), we note that

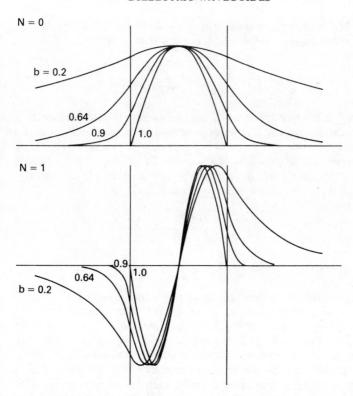

*Figure 3.6.3 Field distribution in dielectric waveguide*

$K_{N-2}/K_N \to 0$, so

$$J_{N-2}(g) = 0, \qquad J_N(g) \neq 0 \tag{42}$$

which again indicates an infinite series of modes, whose cut-offs are determined by all the zeros of $J_{N-2}(g)$ other than zero. The only remaining case to be considered is Equation (29) with $N = 1$. It may be shown that $K_0/h_c K_1 \to \infty$ as $h_c \to 0$, so the solutions are

$$J_1(g) = 0, \qquad J_0(g) \neq 0 \tag{43}$$

which admits all the zeros of $J_1(g)$ including the one at the origin.

*Single-mode operation* As with metallic waveguides, it is possible to select a combination of frequency and transverse dimension such that only one mode will propagate. In planar guide the mode is $TE_0$

(or $TM_0$) which has cut-off frequency zero: the condition is that $g < \pi/2$ (see Equation (36)) which implies that

$$a < \frac{c}{4v(n_1^2 - n_2^2)^{1/2}} = \frac{\lambda}{4(n_1^2 - n_2^2)^{1/2}} \tag{44}$$

(where $\lambda$ is the free-space wavelength). In circular guide the mode is $HE_{11}$, the first in the $HE$ series governed by Equation (29) and the only hybrid mode with zero cut-off frequency (see Equations (41–43)). The next lowest cut-off is that of the $TE_{01}$ (and $TM_{01}$) modes defined by the first zero of $J_0(g)$ which is $g = 2.405$ (see Equation (41)). The condition for single-mode operation is therefore

$$a < \frac{0.383\lambda}{(n_1^2 - n_2^2)^{1/2}} \tag{45}$$

For typical optical fibres this implies a rather small diameter ($< 10^{-5}$ m).

Single-mode operation also implies that the waveguide dispersion of the unique propagating mode is substantial, and that a non-trivial fraction of the power travels in the cladding; for planar guide this is clear from Figures 3.6.2–3, and circular guide is qualitatively similar.

Waveguide dispersion is calculated above for nominally unchanging refractive indices. In practical materials, the refractive indices change with frequency: this is called *material dispersion*. In some optical fibres, the material and waveguide dispersion terms are of opposite sign: the resulting cancellation can yield very low total dispersion at suitable wavelengths.

*Multi-mode operation*    Many practical guides are of larger dimensions and support numerous modes. The right-hand side of Figure 3.6.2 shows a typical sample of a multi-mode region, in this case with 32–36 modes. It is clear that the difference of delay between modes vastly exceeds the variation in any one mode over the small fractional bandwidth used for communication. The difference between maximum and minimum phase delay per unit length is approximately

$$\delta t = \frac{n_1 - n_2}{c} \tag{46}$$

The difference in group delay is about the same, save for the immediate vicinity of mode cut-off.

## The ray interpretation

The ray model, applied to metallic waveguides in Section 3.5, is also applicable to dielectric waveguides. The dielectric interface can reflect plane waves, so that a planar waveguide propagates by successive reflections as in Figure 3.5.4(a). The differences from the metallic waveguide are that (i) reflection occurs only if the angle of incidence exceeds a critical value (ii) there is a phase change on reflection (iii) the electromagnetic field penetrates into the cladding material. The precise properties are stated without proof in the following theorem.

*Theorem 4*: Let two dielectric media separated by a plane boundary $x_1 = 0$ have refractive indices $n_1, n_2$ $(< n_1)$ and corresponding wave-number magnitudes $k, h$. Let a plane wave in the denser material be incident on the boundary, with its axis in the plane $x_2 = 0$, and with angle of incidence

$$\phi = \sin^{-1}(k_3/k) > \phi_c = \sin^{-1}(h/k) \qquad (47)$$

Then a reflected wave is generated whose axis lies in the plane $x_2 = 0$. The angle of reflection equals the angle of incidence, and the magnitudes of incident and reflected waves are equal. There is a phase shift on reflection, the lead being

$$2\tan^{-1}\left\{\frac{k_3^2 - h^2}{k^2 - k_3^2}\right\}^{1/2} = 2\tan^{-1}\left\{\frac{(\sin^2 \phi - \sin^2 \phi_c)^{1/2}}{\cos \phi}\right\} \qquad (48)$$

if the incident (and reflected) waves are linearly polarised normal to the plane of incidence: it is

$$2\tan^{-1}\left\{\left(\frac{k_3^2 - h^2}{k^2 - k_3^2}\right)^{1/2}\frac{k^2}{h^2}\right\} = 2\tan^{-1}\left\{\frac{(\sin^2 \phi - \sin^2 \phi_c)^{1/2}}{\cos \phi}\frac{n_1^2}{n_2^2}\right\} \qquad (49)$$

if the incident (and reflected) waves are linearly polarised in the plane of incidence. The field in the second medium is evanescent, and decays as

$$e^{-2\pi\alpha x_1} \qquad (50a)$$

where

$$\alpha = (k_3^2 - h^2)^{1/2} = \frac{vn_1}{c}(\sin^2 \phi - \sin^2 \phi_c)^{1/2} \qquad (50b)$$

EXERCISES (i) Prove Theorem 4 by matching the tangential electric and magnetic fields across the interface.

(ii) Give an alternative proof of Theorem 4, based on Theorems 1 and 2.

(iii) In Section 3.5 we used the ray model to deduce eigenvalues for a planar metallic waveguide (see especially Figure 3.5.4 and Equation 3.5.47). Extend this model to deal with planar dielectric waveguide by taking account of the phase change on reflection. Show that the resulting eigenvalues agree with those of Equation (13). Deduce the transverse distribution of the field, and compare your results with Figure 3.6.3.

(iv) Estimate the dispersion of a weakly-guiding optical waveguide by comparing the axial velocities of (a) an axial ray (b) an extreme ray reflected at the critical angle. Show that your result is in agreement with Equation (46).

*Graded-index waveguides.* It is possible to make optical wave-guides whose refractive index varies more or less continuously: these are known as *graded-index* guides, in distinction from the step-index guides which exhibit discontinuous change as in the structures of Theorems 1–3. Graded-index optical fibres are valuable for long-distance transmission, since they can be made to have low dispersion. Practical fibres are of course circular in cross-section, but for simplicity we will exhibit the principle in a planar structure.

A refractive-index profile of parabolic or near-parabolic form has properties of especial interest.

*Theorem 5*: Let a planar dielectric structure have its refractive index continuously graded, with the profile

$$n^2 = n_1^2(1 - a^2 x_1^2) \tag{51}$$

over a region wide enough to contain all the light rays of interest. Then the structure will support travelling waves along an axis normal to $x_1$. The ray paths corresponding to these waves are sinusoidal, and undulate symmetrically about the axis of propagation. Let the local refractive index at the points of maximum excursion from the axis be $n_1(1 - \delta)$. Then the mean phase delay per unit length over a long-distance path, is

$$\frac{n_1}{c}\{1 + \tfrac{1}{2}\delta^2 + O(\delta^3)\} \tag{52}$$

within the limits of applicability of ray theory.*

* Primarily, so long as the refractive index changes are small and are graduated over a transverse dimension which is a large multiple of wavelength and extends well beyond the nominal ray paths.

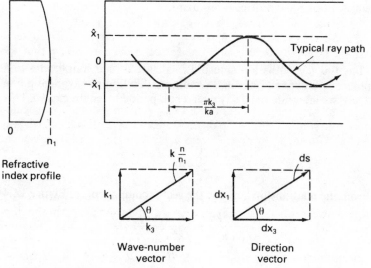

*Figure 3.6.4 Graded-index waveguide*

*Proof* Within the limits of ray theory, a ray at an angle $\theta$ to the axis has a wave-number vector as shown in Figure 3.6.4 with a magnitude

$$\frac{kn}{n_1} = k(1 - a^2 x_1^2)^{1/2}$$

where as before $k = vn_1/c$. It has a direction vector as also shown in Figure 3.6.4. Using the relationship between vector components, we can write the differential equation of the ray path as

$$\frac{dx_3}{dx_1} = \frac{k_3}{k_1} = \frac{k_3}{(k^2 n^2/n_1^2 - k_3^2)^{1/2}} = \frac{k_3}{(k^2 - k_3^2 - k^2 a^2 x_1^2)^{1/2}}$$

Integrating gives (with a suitable origin)

$$x_3 = \frac{k_3}{ka} \sin^{-1} \left\{ \frac{kax_1}{(k^2 - k_3^2)^{1/2}} \right\}$$

or equivalently

$$x_1 = \hat{x}_1 \sin \left( \frac{kax_3}{k_3} \right)$$

which is a sinusoid of peak excursion

$$\hat{x}_1 = \frac{(k^2 - k_3^2)^{1/2}}{ka}$$

Thus the ray paths are sinusoids, as stated: their amplitudes and phases will depend on initial conditions. To find the average phase delay, we integrate the delay over a half-period of length $\pi k_3/ka$. This is

$$\tau = \int_{-\hat{x}_1}^{\hat{x}_1} \frac{n}{c} \frac{ds}{dx_1} dx_1$$

From the relationship between the vector components in Figure 3.6.4

$$\frac{ds}{dx_1} = \frac{kn}{k_1 n_1} = \frac{kn/n_1}{\left(\dfrac{k^2 n^2}{n_1^2} - k_3^2\right)^{1/2}}$$

and introducing the parabolic profile as above gives

$$\frac{ds}{dx_1} = \frac{k(1 - a^2 x_1^2)^{1/2}}{(k^2 - k_3^2 - k^2 a^2 x_1^2)^{1/2}}$$

The delay is then

$$\tau = \frac{n_1}{ca} \int_{-\hat{x}_1}^{\hat{x}_1} \frac{(1 - a^2 x_1^2)}{(\hat{x}_1^2 - x_1^2)} dx_1 = \frac{\pi n_1}{ca}\left(1 - \frac{a^2 \hat{x}_1^2}{2}\right)$$

$$= \frac{\pi n_1}{2ca}\left(1 + \frac{k_3^2}{k^2}\right)$$

The mean delay per unit length over the half-period is

$$\frac{\tau ka}{\pi k_3} = \frac{n_1}{2c}\left(\frac{k}{k_3} + \frac{k_3}{k}\right)$$

and this is also the mean delay per unit length over a path which is much longer than the period of the sinusoidal ray.

If the local refractive index on the ray path is bounded by $n_1 \geqslant n \geqslant n_1(1 - \delta)$ then

$$1 - \delta = (1 - a^2 \hat{x}_1^2)^{1/2} = \frac{k_3}{k}$$

and the mean delay per unit length is

$$\frac{n_1}{2c}\left(1-\delta+\frac{1}{1-\delta}\right)=\frac{n_1}{c}\left(1+\frac{\frac{1}{2}\delta^2}{1-\delta}\right)$$

which proves (52).*

The fractional dispersion of order $\frac{1}{2}\delta^2$ may be compared with the fractional dispersion of a step-index guide with the same refractive index range, which by Equation (46) (or by a simple ray-optics argument) is of order $\delta$. With typical refractive index values, the ideal graded-index guide has a lower dispersion, hence a higher bandwidth, than a step-index guide by a factor of several hundreds. In practice, the bandwidth limit may be set by inaccuracy of profile and other constructional parameters; but the nominally parabolic-index circular guide is still superior to a step-index guide by a large factor.

## 3.7 DIFFRACTION

In the last two sections, we studied the propagation of waves along a guiding structure. The other type of wave motion significant in communication engineering is the radiation of waves from a finite source into an unbounded medium. We shall emphasise the relationship between the radiation pattern in the unbounded medium and the field in a small radiating aperture. This problem is common to the theory of microwave antennas, and to radiation from optical sources: in the latter context especially, it is known as *diffraction*.

The radiating aperture must be defined by a material structure, normally metallic or dielectric: and the fields both near and distant must be solutions of Maxwell's equations with boundary conditions defined by the properties of the structure. This approach turns out to be mathematically complicated for all but a few special cases, and it is usual to employ a simplified theory. There are several modes of simplification, including

(i) Formulate the problem fairly rigorously, and obtain an approximate solution
(ii) Formulate the problem in terms of approximate boundary conditions, and obtain a more or less rigorous solution to the new problem

---

* The reader familiar with optical physics may invoke Fermat's principle, along with the constancy of ray-path period, to deduce zero dispersion. The discrepancy shows, of course, that ray theory in inhomogeneous media is not sufficiently accurate to yield answers more precise than $O(\delta^2)$.

(iii) As (ii) with the further simplification, that polarisation effects are ignored and a solution obtained in terms of *scalar waves* only.

The second approach has two advantages. Firstly, both the simplifications and the major phenomena have a clear physical interpretation which assists understanding. Secondly, the method yields abundant results with the aid of familiar mathematical techniques, and especially in the scalar case the results are both simple and general in form. So we shall confine our treatment to this type of approximation.*

There are two particularly simple types of travelling wave: *plane waves*, introduced in Section 3.4, and *spherical waves*, which emanate symmetrically from a centre. The basic principle of our treatment is that a wide repertoire of practical field patterns may be represented, exactly or approximately, by superpositions of plane waves or of spherical waves: and further, that in small regions sufficiently distant from the centres of symmetry, the two representations are asymptotically equivalent.

We begin by defining a superposition of plane waves in a convenient form. Let the medium be isotropic and capable of supporting waves of the form

$$\phi = e^{j2\pi(vt - \mathbf{k} \cdot \mathbf{x})}$$

where $v/|\mathbf{k}|$ is the characteristic velocity, and the direction is that of the wave-number vector $\mathbf{k}$ (Figure 3.4.11). We take the axis $x_3$ as reference direction (it may be, for example, the principal axis of an antenna or an optical system) and suppose that an aperture in the plane $x_3 = 0$ is radiating in the positive direction. The relationship between rays and plane waves was introduced in Section 3.5 and is equally relevant here: a beam fanning out from the aperture will be represented by the superposition of plane wave components whose axes of propagation are inclined to the $x_3$ axis. The angle of inclination may be specified, for given $k$, by the lateral components of the wave-number $(k_1, k_2)$. A component in a given direction has a specific amplitude and phase which can be represented by a complex number $G(k_1, k_2)$.

*Definition 1*: the *angular spectrum* of a field is the function $G(k_1, k_2)$ defining magnitude and phase of plane wave components as a function of angular direction. Each component is of form

$$G(k_1, k_2)e^{j2\pi(vt - \mathbf{k} \cdot \mathbf{x})} \tag{1a}$$

The factor $e^{j2\pi vt}$ is common, and we shall usually characterise the

* It is also a useful introduction for readers who ultimately wish to pursue more exact methods. For a second course in the topic, see the book by Jull.

component by its spatial variation

$$G(k_1, k_2)e^{-j2\pi \mathbf{k} \cdot \mathbf{x}} \qquad (1b)$$

Note that for the time being we have used only a scalar wave representation: a full field description requires two orthogonally-polarised components.

If a wave is to propagate without attenuation and to carry power, its wave-number components must be real, which implies the limitation

$$k_1^2 + k_2^2 < k^2 \qquad (2)$$

If this is not satisfied then $k_3$ is imaginary, corresponding to an evanescent wave decaying exponentially in the $x_3$ direction (see Section 3.6). In general, we shall ignore the evanescent waves, which are clearly unimportant if the radiation pattern of interest is the far field.*

There is a simple relationship between the angular spectrum of the radiation and the field in the plane of the aperture.

*Theorem 1*: Let the field in the plane of a radiating aperture be $g(x_1, x_2)e^{j2\pi vt}$ and the angular spectrum of the far-field radiation be $G(k_1, k_2)$. Then the aperture distribution and the angular spectrum are related as Fourier transforms,

$$G(k_1, k_2) \Rightarrow g(x_1, x_2) \qquad (3)$$

This relationship is derived from an approximate theory whose limitations are discussed below.

*Proof*  The superposition of all the plane wave components is

$$e^{j2\pi vt} \iint_R G(k_1, k_2)e^{-2\pi \mathbf{k} \cdot \mathbf{x}} dk_1 dk_2$$

where the region $R$ is the interior of a circle $k_1^2 + k_2^2 < k^2$. If evanescent waves be ignored, $G$ may be taken as zero outside the region $R$, so the integral is effectively between infinite limits. The field in the aperture is found by setting $x_3 = 0$, giving

$$g(x_1, x_2) = \int_{-\infty}^{\infty} \int_{-\infty}^{\infty} G(k_1, k_2)e^{-j2\pi(k_1 x_1 + k_2 x_2)} dk_1 dk_2$$

which is the Fourier transform relationship (3).

* Evanescent waves may be essential to satisfy boundary conditions precisely, and are important in analysis of the driving-point impedance of antennas, to which they contribute a reactive component.

There are two limitations, both obvious from the proof.

(i) We have used only scalar wave representations. As we shall remark later in this section, this may be remedied by introduction of polarised components each analysed in this way.

(ii) The equation of the integral over $R$ to the infinite integral, which we have justified by concentrating on the far field and ignoring evanescent waves, always introduces some inaccuracy in practice. Truncation in the **k** domain implies infinite support in the **x** domain (see the discussion of asymptotic behaviour in Section 2.8). However, in practice we normally use the theorem to study the radiation from finite apertures, thereby assuming a truncation in the **x** domain. There will usually be some small but non-zero field in the aperture plane but outside the main aperture: effectively this is being ignored.

Practically, this theory is fairly accurate for the far field and at small angles to the $x_3$ axis: for small $x_3$ and at larger angles, it is incomplete.

EXAMPLES   (i) Optical diffraction from a slit. Let uniform illumination fall on a slit of width $a$ in an opaque screen (Figure 3.7.1). Assuming uniformity in the $x_2$ direction we analyse in one dimension. Uniform field in the aperture (physically plausible, but not strictly accurate for the satisfaction of boundary conditions) gives

$$g(x_1) = \text{rect}(x_1/a) \tag{4a}$$

whence

$$G(k_1) = a \,\text{sinc}(ak_1) \tag{4b}$$

If $\theta$ is the inclination of the ray to the axis

$$k_1 = k \sin \theta = \lambda^{-1} \sin \theta \tag{5}$$

(see Figure 3.7.1). The angular spectrum is sketched in polar coordinates in Figure 3.7.1(c). The polar diagram has a main lobe in the forward direction, and a series of side lobes separated by nulls: these features are common to most polar diagrams of radiating systems, for reasons which should be obvious given the Fourier transform relationship (3). The position of the first nulls, a useful approximate measure of the beam width, is given by

$$\frac{\lambda}{a} = \sin \theta_0 \approx \theta_0 \tag{6}$$

the last approximation holding for small angles. Thus the width of the main lobe is inversely proportional to aperture width.

(ii) Microwave antennas. These are often in the form of circular

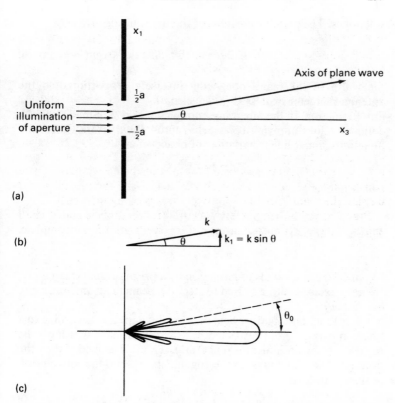

*Figure 3.7.1 Diffraction. (a) Illuminated slit; (b) Wave-number vector; (c) Polar diagram*

parabolic reflectors, illuminated symmetrically by a central feed. If the feed produces a uniform illumination over the whole aperture of the reflector with diameter $d$

$$g(x_1, x_2) = \text{circ}(2r/d) \tag{7a}$$

whence

$$G(k_1, k_2) = \frac{d^2}{4q} J_1(\pi q d) \tag{7b}$$

where $r, q$ are radial variables in the $\mathbf{x}$ and $\mathbf{k}$ domains respectively. (See Equations 3.1.28–29.) The transform (7b) is a decaying oscillating function (see Figure 3.1.8) so again there is a main lobe and a series of side lobes. The angular position of the first nulls is given by

$$1.22\frac{\lambda}{d} = \sin\theta_0 \approx \theta_0 \tag{8}$$

the width of the main lobe being inversely proportional to the antenna diameter expressed in wavelengths.

(iii) Refraction. In the foregoing examples, $g$ in real; it may also take complex values, implying a phase shift across the aperture. Consider a one-dimensional linear variation of phase

$$g(x_1) = e^{-j2\pi\psi x_1} \tag{9a}$$

which implies

$$G(k_1) = \delta(k_1 - \psi) \tag{9b}$$

This is an angular deviation of

$$\sin^{-1}(\lambda\psi) \approx \lambda\psi \tag{9c}$$

In optics, it corresponds to refraction by a prism or similar structure. In radio, phase-shifting is used to steer the beam of an antenna array (see below).

(iv) Masking. The aperture field may exhibit variation according to a function $g_1(x_1, x_2)$ but restricted in extent by a mask which can be represented by an indicator function $g_2(x_1, x_2)$. The field is then the product of two functions, so the angular spectrum is the convolution of their transforms:

$$g_1(x_1, x_2)g_2(x_1, x_2) \Leftarrow G_1(k_1, k_2)*G_2(k_1, k_2) \tag{10}$$

(Compare the treatment of finite images in Section 3.3.) For example, if the phase variation (9a) extends over the width of a slit (4a) then

$$g(x_1) = e^{-j2\pi\psi x_1} \operatorname{rect}(x_1/a) \tag{11a}$$

whence

$$G(k_1) = \delta(k_1 - \psi)*a\operatorname{sinc}(ak_1) = a\operatorname{sinc}\{a(k_1 - \psi)\} \tag{11b}$$

That is to say, there is a main lobe of angular width $\approx \lambda/a$ deflected through an angle $\approx \lambda\psi$.

EXERCISES   (i) Find the angular spectrum resulting from uniform illumination of an aperture in the form of (a) a rectangle (b) a rhombus: and compare your results with similar problems in Section 3.1.

(ii) It is common practice in microwave antennas to reduce the sidelobes in relation to the main lobe by tapering the excitation: that is, by designing the feed so that the field strength is lower at the edges of the aperture than at the centre. Use the convolution principle, Equation (10), to explain the effect. Compare with the problem of shaping digital signals so as to minimise band spread, and with the asymptotic properties discussed in Section 2.8.

*Arrays* Many radiating structures use a multiplicity of similar elements. In optics, diffraction gratings are used for deflection, spectral analysis and filtering; in radio, antenna arrays are used to achieve high directivity, beam steering or both. We will define a property of the array geometry which combines with the properties of the individual element to yield the overall performance of the array.

*Definition 2.* Let $N$ identical radiating elements, similarly and coherently excited, be located at sites $(a_i, b_i)$, $i = 1, 2, \ldots N$ in the $(x_1, x_2)$ plane. Then the *array factor* is

$$G_a(k_1, k_2) = \sum_{i=1}^{N} e^{j2\pi(a_i k_1 + b_i k_2)} \tag{12}$$

**EXAMPLE**   Let the $N$ elements lie on the line $x_2 = 0$, at intervals $A$, and symmetrically located around $x_1 = 0$. Then

$$a_i = A(-\tfrac{1}{2}N - \tfrac{1}{2} + i) \qquad i = 1, 2, \ldots N$$

$$b_i = 0$$

and

$$G_a(k_1, k_2) = \frac{\sin \pi N A k_1}{\sin \pi A k_1} \tag{13}$$

This is a periodic function with peaks of height $N$ at $Ak_1 = 0$, $\pm 1$, $\pm 2 \ldots$ (Figure 3.7.2). The signs of the peaks alternate, for even $N$; this is immaterial if, as usual in this context, we are mainly concerned with magnitudes.

*Theorem 2*: Let one element of an array have an angular spectrum $G_e(k_1, k_2) \Rightarrow g_e(x_1, x_2)$, and let the array factor be $G_a(k_1, k_2)$. Then the angular spectrum of the array is

$$G(k_1, k_2) = G_e(k_1, k_2) G_a(k_1, k_2) \tag{14}$$

*Proof*   The field in the aperture plane is the sum of contributions

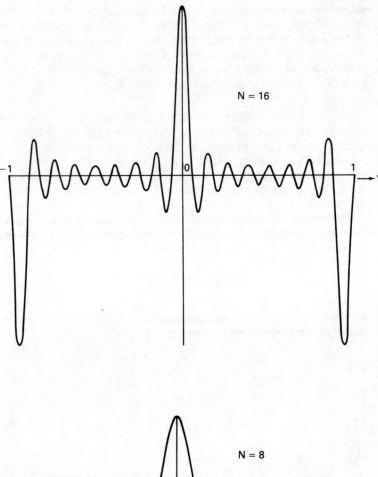

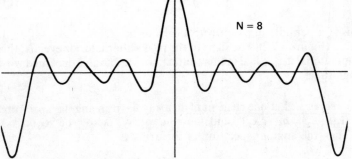

*Figure 3.7.2 Array factor* $\sin \pi Ny/\sin \pi y$

due to the elements, namely

$$g(x_1, x_2) = \sum_{i=1}^{N} g_e(x_1 - a_i, x_2 - b_i)$$

$$= g_e(x_1, x_2) * \sum_{i=1}^{N} \delta(x_1 - a_i, x_2 - b_i)$$

The Fourier transform of the right-hand sum is

$$\sum_{i=1}^{N} e^{j2\pi(a_i k_1 + b_i k_2)} = G_a(k_1, k_2)$$

The convolution transforms into a product, giving the result (14).

EXAMPLES  (i) Directivity of antennas. An array of elements has a narrower main lobe than any one element, as shown qualitatively in Figure 3.7.3 for a linear array of 5 elements. In fact, the width of the main lobe depends principally on the spacing of the extreme elements, which is clearly much greater than the width of one element.

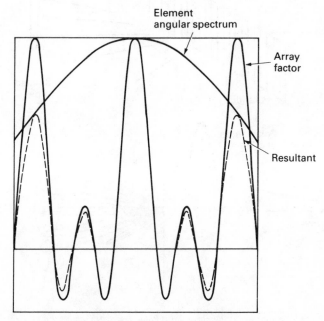

*Figure 3.7.3 Antenna array properties*

However, there are numerous side lobes, whose position and magnitude depend on the number and size of elements.

(ii) Diffraction gratings. The 'side lobes' are put to practical use if deflection is desired, as in virtually all applications of gratings. In its simplest form, a grating consists of a series of slits of width $a$ at regular intervals $A$ ($>a$). Let us imagine an infinitely long grating. Its aperture field is

$$g(x_1) = \text{rep}_A \text{rect}(x_1/a) = \text{rect}(x_1/a)* \text{rep}_A \delta(x_1) \qquad (15a)$$

so its angular spectrum is (by Theorem 2.4.3)

$$G(k_1) = \frac{a}{A} \text{sinc}(ak_1) \text{rep}_{1/A} \delta(k_1) \qquad (15b)$$

This is illustrated in Figure 3.7.4(b). In practice the grating is of limited extent, say $NA$ in width embracing $N$ slits. We can either

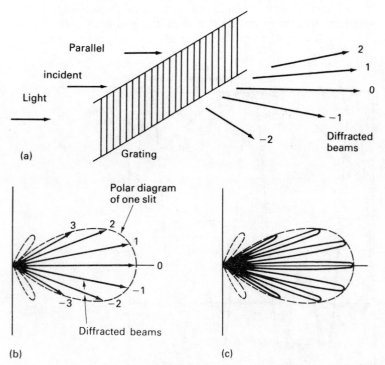

Figure 3.7.4 Diffraction grating. (a) Illuminated; (b) Polar diagram of infinite grating; (c) Polar diagram of finite grating

truncate (15a) to obtain the aperture field

$$\{\text{rep}_A \text{rect}(x_1/a)\}\text{rect}(x_1/NA)$$

$$\Rightarrow \{Na\,\text{sinc}(ak_1)\,\text{rep}_{1/A}\,\delta(k_1)\}*\text{sinc}(NAk_1) \qquad (16)$$

(it is implicit in this formulation that $N$ is odd) or we can use the array factor (13) to obtain directly

$$G(k_1) = a\,\text{sinc}(ak_1)\frac{\sin \pi NAk_1}{\sin \pi Ak_1} \qquad (17)$$

It is intuitively clear from either of these approaches that the lines in the angular spectrum are broadened into lobes of approximate width $\lambda/NA$ radians, as shown in the polar diagram Figure 3.7.4(c).

EXERCISE   (i) Show that the two versions of the diffraction grating output, Equations (16) and (17) above, are equivalent. Compare with the theory of truncated Fourier series, Theorem 2.4.6. Show that the position of the lobes depends only on the pitch of the grating, but that their magnitudes depend on slit width.
(ii) A radio-telescope was required to observe 1420 MHz emissions from the sun, which at the earth subtends an angle of about 34′. The instrument built uses 32 circular dishes, each of diameter 2.2 m and spaced at 6 m intervals in a linear array. Investigate its polar diagram. Show in particular that (a) the width of the mainlobe is much less than a solar diameter (b) the spacing between lobes of maximum amplitude is more than a solar diameter.

*Reciprocity*   Our discussion so far has been of the radiation pattern from an aperture, assuming it to be excited by a source of power. In communication engineering, the receiver is as important as the transmitter, and we need to know the response of an antenna to incoming waves. It is plausible that an antenna which radiates predominantly in a certain direction will be preferentially sensitive to waves incoming from that direction. There is a sense in which radiating systems of the kind discussed here are reciprocal, as the next theorem shows.

*Theorem 3* (reciprocity): Let a plane wave be incoming from a specified direction, to an aperture in the plane $x_3 = 0$ whose angular spectrum as an emitter is $G(k_1, k_2) \Rightarrow g(x_1, x_2)$. Let the field in the aperture be integrated with weight function $g(x_1, x_2)$ to constitute a received signal. Then this received signal is proportional to the angular spectrum in the direction of incidence.

Note that if $g(x_1,x_2)$ is a simple indicator function of an aperture, the receiver is merely required to integrate over the same region as is used for emission. If there is a gradation of amplitude or phase, these are to be the same in both cases. In practical antennas this would normally be the case; the exception being if non-reciprocal devices (using, for example, polarisation rotation) had been deliberately inserted.

*Proof* An incoming wave is travelling in the opposite sense to the outgoing waves of Equation (1), so its spatial factor may be written as $e^{j2\pi\mathbf{k}\cdot\mathbf{x}}$. In the aperture plane $x_3=0$ so the field is $e^{j2\pi(k_1x_1+k_2x_2)}$; the weighted summation specified is

$$\int_{-\infty}^{\infty}\int_{-\infty}^{\infty} g(x_1,x_2)e^{j2\pi(k_1x_1+k_2x_2)}dx_1\,dx_2$$

But this is a Fourier integral, the inverse of that in Theorem 1, and so equal to $G(k_1,k_2)$.

*Huyghens' principle* A classical approach to the study of wave propagation, pioneered by the optical physicists Huyghens and Fresnel, is based on the principle that any point in a wavefront may be considered as a secondary source from which spherical waves radiate, with an amplitude proportional to the field strength at the point. Let us apply this concept to the radiation from an aperture (Figure 3.7.5). Let the aperture be in the plane $x_3=0$, with field strength $g(x_1,x_2)$ as before. Consider a point $P=(p_1,p_2,p_3)$ in front of the radiating aperture. The field at $P$ is the sum of spherical wave components deriving from all points $Q=(x_1,x_2,0)$ in the aperture. Each component as received at $P$ will have
(i) an amplitude proportional to the source strength $g(x_1,x_2)$, inversely proportional to the distance $s$ between $P$ and $Q$ (since the strength of a spherical wave decays with distance) and also having a minor dependence (which we ignore) on the angle between $PQ$ and the wavefront.
(ii) a phase dependent on the path length $PQ$, specifically $2\pi ks$ radians.
In the following theorem we derive the radiation pattern in terms of polar coordinates

$$r=(p_1^2+p_2^2+p_3^2)^{1/2}$$
$$\theta_1=\tan^{-1}(p_1/p_3)$$
$$\theta_2=\tan^{-1}(p_2/p_3)$$

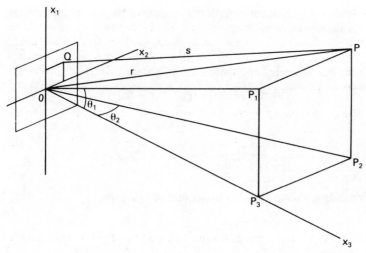

*Figure 3.7.5 Huyghens' principle*

We use approximations valid at distances substantially greater than the aperture size and/or at shallow angles: specifically, the amplitude factor $1/s$ is approximated by $1/r$, and the phase factor $e^{-j2\pi ks}$ is expressed in terms of perturbations from $e^{-j2\pi kr}$.

*Theorem 4*: Let the field in a radiating aperture in the plane $x_3 = 0$ be $g(x_1, x_2)$. Let the distribution of incident radiation on a spherical cap of radius $r$ be $e^{-j2\pi kr} r^{-1} f(y_1, y_2)$ where $y_i = k \sin \theta_i$. Then a first approximation to $f(y_1, y_2)$ is the Fourier transform of $g(x_1, x_2)$:

$$g(x_1, x_2) \Leftarrow G(y_1, y_2) \approx f(y_1, y_2) \qquad (18)$$

and this is asymptotically accurate as $r \to \infty$ while the aperture remains bounded. A second approximation is given by

$$g(x_1, x_2) h(x_1, x_2) \Leftarrow G(y_1, y_2) * H(y_1, y_2) \approx f(y_1, y_2) \qquad (19a)$$

where $h(\ )$ is a quadratic phase shift

$$h(x_1, x_2) = \exp\left\{-j\pi\left(\frac{x_1^2 + x_2^2}{r\lambda}\right)\right\} \qquad (19b)$$

and this is significantly more accurate than the first approximation unless $r \gg (x_1^2 + x_2^2)/\lambda$.

*Proof*  The incident radiation is the sum of Huyghens components over the aperture, namely

$$r^{-1} \int \int g(x_1, x_2) e^{-j2\pi ks} dx_1 dx_2 \tag{20}$$

From the geometry of Figure 3.7.5 it is clear that

$$s^2 = r^2 - p_1^2 - p_2^2 + (p_1 - x_1)^2 + (p_2 - x_2)^2$$

whence

$$s = r \left\{ 1 + \frac{x_1^2 + x_2^2 - 2p_1 x_1 - 2p_2 x_2}{r^2} \right\}^{1/2}$$

Expanding this expression in powers of $x_i/r$ gives

$$s = r - \frac{x_1 p_1}{r} - \frac{x_2 p_2}{r} + \frac{x_1^2 + x_2^2}{2r} + O(x_i^4/r^3)$$

and we can substitute this for $s$ in the integral (20). If we retain only the linear terms, the phase term of the integrand is

$$\exp \left\{ j2\pi k \left( \frac{x_1 p_1}{r} + \frac{x_2 p_2}{r} \right) \right\} = \exp \left\{ j2\pi (x_1 y_1 + x_2 y_2) \right\}$$

and (20) becomes a Fourier integral yielding the result (18). Retaining the quadratic term gives the second approximation (19). The quadratic phase shift is negligible only if $(x_1^2 + x_2^2)/r\lambda \ll 1$, which is equivalent to the condition stated.

The first approximation, usually known as *Fraunhofer diffraction*, is accurate at sufficiently long range: it is identical with the result of Theorem 1 which was derived by superposing plane rather than spherical waves. The second approximation is known as *Fresnel diffraction* and is the usual theory to be applied at shorter ranges.

Comparison of the diffraction patterns (18) and (19) shows that $H()$ acts as a point spread function, in the sense of Definition 3.3.1. It is a circularly-symmetric phase shift

$$H(y_1, y_2) = \frac{-j}{r\lambda} \exp \left\{ j\pi \left( \frac{y_1^2 + y_2^2}{r\lambda} \right) \right\} \tag{21}$$

The general effect of the point spreading is clear from physical considerations. A quadratic phase shift is approximately equivalent to an optical lens: a diverging lens, in the case of expression (19b). A complementary converging lens would bring the pattern $G(y_1, y_2)$ to a focus at range $r$. Thus, in general, patterns viewed at different ranges are defocussed versions of each other.

EXAMPLE  Suppose that we have to measure the far-field polar diagram of a microwave antenna of 3 m diameter, at a wavelength of 3 cm. According to Theorem 4 this must be done at a range of $\geqslant 75$ m: say 600 m, if the phase error is to be kept to $\leqslant \pi/8$. It may be impossible to find a clear range of 600 m in which the field is unaffected by local obstacles. One solution is to measure at a shorter range and then de-convolve the point spread function. The obvious technique for deconvolution is to Fourier-transform, divide out the factor, and re-transform. The problem is that the point-spread effect tends to blur the fine detail such as narrow nulls, and it may be impossible to recover them with an useful accuracy. It is typically found that with aperture width $a$ the troughs around the nulls will vanish for ranges of less than about $a^2/\lambda$, which in the antenna example quoted is about 300 m. An alternative is to calculate the short-range pattern associated with the nominal long-range pattern, and to compare this with experiment.*

EXERCISE  Show that

$$g(x)e^{-j\pi\beta x^2} \Leftarrow \sum_{n=0}^{\infty} \frac{1}{n!}\left(\frac{j\beta}{4\pi}\right)^n G^{(2n)}(y) \qquad (22)$$

(Hint: use Theorem 2.3.7). Use Equation (22) to investigate the radiation patterns from a rectangular aperture. Investigate the convergence of the series at ranges of the order $a^2/\lambda$.

*Diffraction from travelling waves*  In the foregoing discussion, it is assumed that the radiating structure is static. There are at least three practical situations in which this is not the case.

(i) The structure may incorporate a physical travelling wave (as in acousto-optic devices)

(ii) An array may be driven with a time-varying pattern of excitation (as in many types of scanning antenna)

(iii) The whole structure may be in rapid motion (as in airborne systems).

The general method of analysis is to consider a three-dimensional aperture pattern $g(x_1, x_2, t)$ and its transform $G(k_1, k_2, f)$. It is immediately clear that the diffraction pattern has a joint distribution in

---

* For further analysis of Fresnel diffraction, see Born and Wolf (1) and Jull (1).

space and in frequency; indeed, the typical result is a spatial lobe or set of lobes with direction-dependent frequency shift.

The most general case we shall consider is an aperture function moving uniformly along the $x_1$ axis, illuminated by monochromatic radiation, and masked by a fixed aperture (the latter is easily omitted if not required). Further generalisation is not very difficult once the principles are understood.

*Theorem 5*: Let the field of a radiating aperture be modelled as a pattern $g_m(x_1, x_2)$ moving at a uniform velocity $b$ in the positive $x_1$ direction, illuminated at frequency $v$, and circumscribed by a stationary mask $g_s(x_1, x_2)$. The combined angular and frequency spectrum of the radiated wave is

$$\{G_m(k_1, k_2)\delta(f + v + bk_1)\} * G_s(k_1, k_2) \qquad (23)$$

That is to say, the spatial pattern is similar to that of a stationary source, but there is a frequency shift proportional to the component of deflection introduced by the moving element of the aperture.

*Proof*  The aperture function can be written as the product of two factors

$$\{g_m(x_1 - bt, x_2)e^{j2\pi vt}\}\{g_s(x_1, x_2)\} \qquad (24)$$

and the output spectrum is the convolution of their respective transforms. We need to show that the first factor transforms into the first factor of (23). The variable $x_2$ is separable, but in respect of the variables $(x_1, t)$ the travelling wave introduces a skew which transforms into a skewed function of $(k_1, f)$. We can use either Theorem 3.1.5 or the second version of Theorem 3.4.1 to show that

$$g_m(x_1 - bt, x_2) \Leftarrow G_m(k_1, k_2)\delta(f + bk_1)$$

The transform of the sinusoidal excitation is

$$e^{j2\pi vt} \Leftarrow \delta(f + v)$$

(remember that from Theorem 3.7.1 we are using the inverse transform of the aperture function) and so the transform of the first factor of (24) is

$$\{G_m(k_1, k_2)\delta(f + bk_1)\} * \delta(f + v) = G_m(k_1, k_2)\delta(f + bk_1 + v)$$

which gives the required first factor of (23). Note that $\delta(f + bk_1 + v)$ here corresponds to a positive frequency $v + bk_1$.

EXAMPLES  (i) Acousto-optic deflectors. A device widely used for scanning or modulation of beams of light is shown in Figure 3.7.6. A

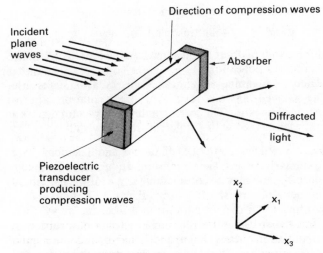

*Figure 3.7.6 Acousto-optic deflector*

transparent crystal is periodically excited by means of a piezo-electric transducer, so that ultrasonic compression waves are propagated along the $x_1$ axis. Compression increases the refractive index of the material, so that a periodic perturbation of optical phase delay fills the optical aperture. This constitutes a *phase grating* which diffracts light in much the same way as other forms of diffraction grating. Taking the ultrasonic wavelength as $A$ (corresponding to grating pitch in our previous examples) the aperture factor $g_m(x_1)$ is

$$g_m(x_1) = e^{j\beta \sin 2\pi x_1/A} \tag{25a}$$

where $\beta$ is the peak phase excursion. By Equation (2.4.26) we can expand this in Fourier series

$$g_m(x_1) = \sum_{n=-\infty}^{\infty} J_n(\beta) e^{j2\pi n x_1/A} \tag{25b}$$

the coefficients being Bessel functions, just as in the theory of frequency modulation sidebands. So the transform is

$$G_m(k_1) = \sum_{n=-\infty}^{\infty} J_n(\beta)\delta(k_1 - n/A) \tag{26}$$

This gives a series of beams like those of the infinite grating in Figure 3.7.4(b) but with different relative amplitudes. Each beam is broadened by virtue of the masking function as in Figure 3.7.4(c). The $n$th order beam is shifted in optical frequency from $v$ to

$$v + nb/A = v + n(\text{ultrasonic frequency})$$

Typically this is a shift of order $10^8$ in a frequency of order $10^{14}$, and is immaterial in most applications.

(ii) Multiple-beam scanning antennas. Some radar systems use electronically-scanned antenna arrays whose excitation approximates to a travelling pulse. The corresponding array factor defines a fan of beams, each tagged with a different frequency shift.

*Modified arrays* The arrays of Definition 2 and Theorem 2 are assumed to comprise many elements, similarly excited. Given an array of elements, there may be considerable scope for the individual treatment of each. In a transmitting array, they may be individually excited according to an overall pattern; in a receiving array, their individual signals may be jointly processed to detect some property of the incident radiation. Many radar and sonar systems use quite elaborate processing, and the design of the array and the signal processing algorithm can hardly be separated. In the present context, we confine our treatment to a simple generalisation of Theorem 2. Within this limitation, the system may be either time-invariant or time-variant.

*Theorem 6*: Let $N$ individual radiating elements located at $(a_i, b_i)$ in the $(x_1, x_2)$ plane be coherently excited, with the amplitude and phase of the $i$th element defined by the complex coefficient $c_i$. Then the angular spectrum of the array is

$$G(k_1, k_2) = G_e(k_1, k_2)G_a(k_1, k_2) \qquad (27)$$

where the array factor is

$$G_a(k_1, k_2) = \sum_{i=1}^{N} c_i e^{j2\pi(a_i k_1 + b_i k_2)} \qquad (28)$$

and $G_e(k_1, k_2) \Rightarrow g_e(x_1, x_2)$ is the angular spectrum of each element.

*Proof* The field in the aperture plane is

$$g(x_1, x_2) = \sum_{i=1}^{N} c_i g_e(x_1 - a_i, x_2 - b_i)$$

$$= g_e(x_1, x_2) * \sum_{i=1}^{N} c_i \delta(x_1 - a_i, x_2 - b_i)$$

The Fourier transform of the second sum is the expression (28), and (27) is the transform of the convolution.

EXAMPLES  (i) The phased array. Consider the linear array whose array factor with uniform excitation is given by (13). Now let the excitation of the $i$th element have a phase delay of $2\pi\psi a_i$. Then

$$g_a(x_1) = \sum_i e^{-j2\pi\psi a_i}\delta(x_1 - a_i)$$

$$= e^{-j2\pi\psi x_1} \sum_i \delta(x_i - a_i)$$

which differs by a factor $e^{-j2\pi\psi x_1} \Rightarrow \delta(k_1 - \psi)$ from the uniformly-excited array. Consequently the angular spectrum is modified by convolution with $\delta(k_1 - \psi)$, which shifts it by $\psi$:

$$G_a(k_1) = \frac{\sin \pi NA(k_1 - \psi)}{\sin \pi A(k_1 - \psi)} \tag{29}$$

(ii) The tapered array. Suppose that the $c_i$ are real, with amplitudes decreasing away from the centre. Then the side lobes are reduced in magnitude.

EXERCISES  (i) Analyse a tapered array with a linear taper. (Hint: consult Theorem 2.4.7 and the following examples.)
(ii) A time-variant system. Consider a linear array of $N$ elements in which a block of $n$ ($\ll N$) elements are excited simultaneously, the block position being traversed rapidly along the array. Investigate this system (a) by using time-varying coefficients $c_i$ (b) by considering the excitation as a travelling pulse and using Theorem 5.

*Polarisation*  The foregoing treatment is entirely in terms of scalar waves, and it remains to be said that extension to vector fields is possible. We revert to the superposition of plane waves used in Theorem 1. Suppose a wave whose axis of propagation is in the $(x_1, x_3)$ plane is polarised with an $e$ vector in the same plane. We can consider the angular spectral function as defining the $e_1$ component. Taking this as unity, there will necessarily be an $e_3$ component of magnitude $-k_1/k_3$, so that the $e$ vector normal to the axis of propagation is of magnitude $k/k_3$. There will consequently be a magnetic field, comprising an $h_2$ component of magnitude $k/k_3 Z_0$. Now consider a wave polarised normally to the plane: there will similarly be components $e_2, h_1, h_3$ related to each other.

Clearly, the description of the aperture field requires two orthogonal components to be specified. Also, the wave impedances in the aperture will depend on the wave polarisation and on the polar diagram of the antenna. These matters are important in the design of antennas and feeds, but they do not change the nature of the major phenomena exhibited by the scalar analysis. In the case of highly directive systems — which covers most applications both in radio and in optics — the quantitative effects are quite small. For example, if a wave is inclined at an angle $\theta$ to the $x_3$ axis, the ratio (wave $e$-vector/aperture $e$-field) differs for two crossed polarisations by a multiplicative factor $\cos \theta$. This is 0.99 for an angle of 8.1° (quite a broad beam, in radio or optics): 0.999 for 2.5°: 0.9999 for 0.8° (a fairly narrow beam in radio practice): 0.99999 for 0.25° ($\approx 5$ mrad, still not an exceptionally narrow beam in optics). So our scalar-wave approach is a valid introduction to the subject of radiation patterns.

# APPENDIX: TABLES OF FOURIER TRANSFORMS

The following tables include only results which are proved or used in this book. They comprise (a) all the general properties which are widely used (b) a selection of specific transforms. For more extensive lists of specific transforms, see the handbooks by Campbell and Foster, Gradshteyn and Ryzhik or Erdelyi. The arrangement of the present table is as follows:

Table 1    General properties in one dimension
Table 2    Specific transforms in one dimension
Table 3    General properties in two dimensions
Table 4    Specific transforms in two dimensions
Table 5    Two-dimensional transforms in polar coordinates

274

**Table 1** GENERAL PROPERTIES IN ONE DIMENSION

|  | *Time domain* | *Frequency domain* |
|---|---|---|
| Definition | $g(t)$ | $G(f) = \displaystyle\int_{-\infty}^{\infty} g(t)e^{-j2\pi ft}\,dt$ |
| Inversion | $g(t) = \displaystyle\int_{-\infty}^{\infty} G(f)e^{j2\pi ft}\,df$ | $G(f)$ |
| Reciprocity | $G(-t)$ | $g(f)$ |
| Scaling | $g(t/T)$ | $|T|G(fT)$ |
| Shifting | $g(t-\tau)$ <br> $e^{j2\pi Ft}g(t)$ | $e^{-j2\pi f\tau}G(f)$ <br> $G(f-F)$ |
| Convolution | $g(t)*h(t)$ <br> $g(t)h(t)$ <br> $\{h(t)\}^n$ <br> $\{h(t)\}^{*n}$ | $G(f)H(f)$ <br> $G(f)*H(f)$ <br> $\{H(f)\}^{*n}$ <br> $\{H(f)\}^{n}$ |
| Differentiation | $g'(t)$ <br> $-j2\pi t g(t)$ | $j2\pi f G(f)$ <br> $G'(f)$ |
| Integration | $\displaystyle\int_{-\infty}^{t} g(x)\,dx$ | $\dfrac{G(f)}{j2\pi f} + \tfrac{1}{2}\delta(f)G(0)$ |
| Repetition | $\text{rep}_T\, g(t)$ | $T^{-1}G(f)\text{rep}_{1/T}\,\delta(f)$ |
| Sampling | $g(t)\,\text{rep}_T\,\delta(t)$ | $T^{-1}\,\text{rep}_{1/T}\,G(f)$ |
| Autocorrelation | $R_g(\tau) = \displaystyle\int_{-\infty}^{\infty} g(t)g(t+\tau)\,dt$ | $|G(f)|^2 = G(f)G(-f)$ |

**Table 2** SPECIFIC TRANSFORMS IN ONE DIMENSION

| Time domain | Frequency domain |
| --- | --- |
| $\delta(t)$ | $1$ |
| $1$ | $\delta(f)$ |
| $e^{-\pi t^2}$ | $e^{-\pi f^2}$ |
| $\operatorname{rect} t$ | $\operatorname{sinc} f$ |
| $\operatorname{sinc} t$ | $\operatorname{rect} f$ |
| $\frac{1}{2}e^{-|t|}$ | $\{1+(2\pi f)^2\}^{-1}$ |
| $U(t)e^{-t}$ | $(1+j2\pi f)^{-1}$ |
| $\delta(t-\tau)$ | $e^{-j2\pi f\tau}$ |
| $e^{j2\pi Ft}$ | $\delta(f-F)$ |
| $\{1-|t|\}\operatorname{rect}(\tfrac{1}{2}t)$ | $\operatorname{sinc}^2 f$ |
| $\frac{1}{2}\operatorname{sgn} t$ | $(j2\pi f)^{-1}$ |
| $U(t)$ | $(j2\pi f)^{-1}+\frac{1}{2}\delta(f)$ |
| $\operatorname{rep}_T \delta(t)$ | $T^{-1}\operatorname{rep}_{1/T}\delta(f)$ |
| $\dfrac{\operatorname{sinc}(2t)}{1-4t^2}$ | $\frac{1}{2}\{1+\cos(\pi f)\}\operatorname{rect}(\tfrac{1}{2}f)$ |
| $\operatorname{sinc} t \cdot e^{-|t|/k}$ | $\dfrac{1}{\pi}\{\tan^{-1}(f+\tfrac{1}{2})2\pi k - \tan^{-1}(f-\tfrac{1}{2})2\pi k\}$ |
| $\cos(\pi t)\cdot\operatorname{rect} t$ | $\dfrac{2\cos(\pi f)}{\pi(4f^2-1)}$ |
| $\left\{\dfrac{\sin \pi|t|}{2\pi}+\dfrac{(1-|t|)}{2}\cos(\pi t)\right\}\operatorname{rect}(\tfrac{1}{2}t)$ | $\left\{\dfrac{2\cos(\pi f)}{\pi(4f^2-1)}\right\}^2$ |
| $U(t)J_n(2\pi t)$ | $\dfrac{1}{2\pi(1-f^2)^{1/2}[(1-f^2)^{1/2}+jf]^n}$ |

**Table 3** GENERAL PROPERTIES IN TWO DIMENSIONS

| | Original domain | Transform domain |
|---|---|---|
| Definition | $g(x,y)$ | $G(u,v) = \displaystyle\int_{-\infty}^{\infty}\int_{-\infty}^{\infty} g(x,y)e^{-j2\pi(ux+vy)}\,\mathrm{d}x\,\mathrm{d}y$ |
| Inversion | $g(x,y) = \displaystyle\int_{-\infty}^{\infty}\int_{-\infty}^{\infty} G(u,v)e^{j2\pi(ux+vy)}\,\mathrm{d}x\,\mathrm{d}y$ | $G(u,v)$ |
| Reciprocity | $G(-x,-y)$ | $g(u,v)$ |
| Scaling | $g(ax,by)$ | $|ab|^{-1}G(a^{-1}u, b^{-1}v)$ |
| Shifting | $g(x-a,y-b)$ | $e^{-j2\pi(au+bv)}G(u,v)$ |
| | $e^{j2\pi(ax+by)}g(x,y)$ | $G(u-a,v-b)$ |
| Separation | $g(x).h(y)$ | $G(u).H(v)$ |
| Convolution | $g(x,y)*h(x,y)$ | $G(u,v).H(u,v)$ |
| | $g(x,y).h(x,y)$ | $G(u,v)*H(u,v)$ |
| Differentiation | $\dfrac{\mathrm{d}}{\mathrm{d}x}g(x,y)$ | $j2\pi u G(u,v)$ |
| | $\dfrac{\mathrm{d}}{\mathrm{d}y}g(x,y)$ | $j2\pi v G(u,v)$ |
| | $-j2\pi x g(x,y)$ | $\dfrac{\mathrm{d}}{\mathrm{d}u}G(u,v)$ |
| | $-j2\pi y g(x,y)$ | $\dfrac{\mathrm{d}}{\mathrm{d}v}G(u,v)$ |

**Table 3** (contd.)

| | Original domain | Transform domain |
|---|---|---|
| **Repetition** | $\text{rep}_{X,Y}\, g(x,y)$ | $(XY)^{-1} G(u,v)\text{rep}_{1/X,1/Y}\,\delta(u,v)$ |
| **Sampling** | $g(x,y)\,\text{rep}_{X,Y}\,\delta(x,y)$ | $(XY)^{-1}\,\text{rep}_{1/X,1/Y}\,G(u,v)$ |
| **Rotation** | $g(x\cos\theta + y\sin\theta,\ -x\sin\theta + y\cos\theta)$ | $G(u\cos\theta + v\sin\theta,\ -u\sin\theta + v\cos\theta)$ |
| **General linear transformation** | $g(ax+by,\ cx+dy)$ | $\dfrac{1}{|ad-cb|}G\!\left(\dfrac{du-cv}{ad-cb},\ \dfrac{-bu+av}{ad-cb}\right)$ |

278

**Table 4** SPECIFIC TRANSFORMS IN TWO DIMENSIONS

| Original domain | Transform domain |
|---|---|
| $\delta(x,y)$ | 1 |
| $\delta(x)$ | $\delta(v)$ |
| $e^{j2\pi(ax+by)}$ | $\delta(u-a,\ v-b)$ |
| $\text{rect}(x,y)$ | $\text{sinc}(u,v)$ |
| $e^{-\pi(a^2x^2+b^2y^2)}$ | $(ab)^{-1}e^{-\pi(u^2/a^2+v^2/b^2)}$ |
| $\delta(x)\,\text{rep}_Y\,\delta(y)$ | $Y^{-1}\,\text{rep}_{1/Y}\,\delta(v)$ |
| $\text{rep}_{X,Y}\,\delta(x,y)$ | $(XY)^{-1}\,\text{rep}_{1/X,1/Y}\,\delta(u,v)$ |

**Table 5** TWO-DIMENSIONAL TRANSFORMS IN POLAR COORDINATES

| Original domain | Transform domain |
|---|---|
| $g(r)$ | $2\pi\displaystyle\int_0^\infty g(r)J_0(2\pi qr)r\,dr$ |
| $2\pi\displaystyle\int_0^\infty G(q)J_0(2\pi qr)q\,dq$ | $G(q)$ |
| $g(r)e^{jm\theta}$ | $(-j)^m e^{jm\phi}2\pi\displaystyle\int_0^\infty g(r)J_m(2\pi qr)r\,dr$ |
| $\text{circ}(r/a)$ | $\dfrac{aJ_1(2\pi aq)}{q}$ |
| $\delta(r-a)$ | $2\pi aJ_0(2\pi aq)$ |
| $e^{-\pi r^2}$ | $e^{-\pi q^2}$ |

# REFERENCES

Abramowitz, M. and Stegun, I., *Handbook of Mathematical Functions*, National Bureau of Standards (1964)

Adams, M. J., *An Introduction to Optical Waveguides*, Wiley (1981)

Aitchison, J. and Brown, J. A. C., *The Lognormal Distribution*, Cambridge University Press (1957)

Bailey, N. T. J., *The Elements of Stochastic Processes, with Applications to the Natural Sciences*, Wiley (1964)

Barker, R. H., 'Synchronising of binary digital systems', chap. 19 of W. Jackson (Ed.): *Communication Theory*, Butterworth (1953)

Barrett, J. F. and Lampard, D. G., 'An expression for some second-order probability distributions and its application to noise problems', Trans. IRE **IT-1**, 10–15 (1955)

Bartlett, M. S., *An Introduction to Stochastic Processes*, Cambridge University Press (1955)

Beckmann, P., *Probability in Communication Engineering*, Harcourt Brace & World (1967)

Blackman, R. B. and Tukey, J. W., 'The measurement of power spectra from the point of view of communication engineering', *Bell Syst. Tech. J.* **37** (Jan. and March 1958). Reprinted in book form by Dover.

Bode, H. W. and Shannon, C. E., 'A simplified derivation of linear least square smoothing and prediction theory', *Proc. IRE* **38**, 417–425 (1950)

Born, M. and and Wolf, E. *Principles of Optics*, 4th edn., Pergamon Press (1970)

Bracewell, R., *The Fourier Transform and its Applications*, McGraw-Hill (1965)

Broyden, C. G., *Basic Matrices*, Macmillan (1975)

Campbell, G. A. and Foster, R. M., *Fourier Integrals for Practical Applications*, Van Nostrand (1948)

Cattermole, K. W.
  (1) *Principles of Pulse Code Modulation*, Butterworth (1970)
  (2) 'Efficiency and reciprocity in pulse amplitude modulation', *Proc. IEE*, **105B**, 449–462 (1958)

Cattermole, K. W. and O'Reilly, J. J.
  (1) *Problems of Randomness in Communication Engineering*, Pentech Press (1984)
  (2) *Optimisation Methods in Electronics and Communications*, Pentech Press (1984)

Chernoff, H., 'A measure of asymptotic efficiency for tests of a hypothesis based on a sum of observations', *Ann. Math. Stat.*, **23**, 493–507 (1952)

Cooley, J. W. and Tukey, J. W., 'An algorithm for the machine calculation of complex Fourier series', *Math. Computation*, **19**, 297–301 (1965)

Courant, R. and Hilbert, D., *Methods of Mathematical Physics*, Interscience (1953)

Cox, D. R. and Miller, H. D., *The Theory of Stochastic Processes*, Methuen (1965)

Cramer, H., *Mathematical Methods of Statistics*, Princeton University Press (1946)

Davenport, W. B. and Root, W. L., *Introduction to the Theory of Random Signals and Noise*, McGraw-Hill (1958)

Dresher, M., 'Moment spaces and inequalities', *Duke Math. J.*, **20**, 261–271 (1953)

Edwards, A. W. F., *Likelihood*, Cambridge University Press (1972)

Erdelyi, A., *Tables of Integral Transforms*, McGraw-Hill (1954)

Feller, W.,

(1) *An Introduction to Probability Theory and its Applications*, Vol. 1 (2nd ed) Wiley (1957)

(2) *An Introduction to Probability Theory and its Applications*, Vol. 2, Wiley (1966)

Fisher, R. A.

(1) *Contributions to Mathematical Statistics*, Wiley (1950)

(2) 'On the mathematical foundations of theoretical statistics', *Phil. Trans. Roy. Soc.*, A, **222**, 309–368 (1922)). Reprinted in (1).

Franks, L. E., *Signal Theory*, Prentice-Hall (1969)

Gallagher, R. G., *Information Theory and Reliable Communication*, Wiley (1968)

Gradshteyn, I.S. and Rhyzhik, I. M., *Table of Integrals, Series and Products* (4th edn.) Academic Press (1965)

Hacking, I., *Logic of Statistical Inference*, Cambridge University Press (1965)

Hartley, R. V. L., 'Transmission of information', *Bell Syst. Tech. J.* **31**, 751–763 (1928)

Helstrom, C. W., *Statistical Theory of Signal Detection*, Pergamon Press (1968)

House, K. E., 'Filters for the detection of binary signalling: optimisation using the Chernoff bound; *Trans. IEEE*, **COM-28**, 257–259 (1980)

Hunt, B. R., 'Digital Image Processing', Chapter 4 of A. V. Oppenheim (Ed.): *Applications of Digital Signal Processing*, Prentice-Hall (1978)

Jahnke, E. and Emde, F., *Tables of Functions*, Dover (1960)

Johnk, C. T. A., *Engineering Electromagnetic Fields and Waves*, Wiley (1975)

Jull, E. V., *Aperture Antennas and Diffraction Theory*, Peter Peregrinus (1981)

Jury, E. I., *Theory and Application of the z-transform Method*, Wiley (1964)

Lampard, D. G., 'Some Theoretical and Experimental Investigations of Random Electrical Fluctuations', Ph.D. dissertation, University of Cambridge (1954)

Lancaster, H. O.

(1) 'The structure of bivariate distributions', *Ann. Math. Stat.*, **29**, 719–736 (1958)

(2) 'Correlations and canonical forms of bivariate distributions', *Ann. Math. Stat.*, **34**, 532–538 (1963)

Landau, H. J. and Pollak, H. O., 'Prolate spheroidal wave functions, Fourier analysis and uncertainty', *Bell Syst. Tech. J.* **40**, 65–84 and **41**, 1295–1336

Lever, K. V. and Cattermole, K. W., 'Quantising noise spectra', *Proc. IEE*, **121**, 945–954 (1974)

Lighthill, M. J., *Introduction to Fourier Analysis and Generalised Functions*, Cambridge University Press (1958)

Loeve, M., 'Sur les fonctions aléatoires stationnaires du second ordre', *Revue Sci.*, **83**, 297–303 (1945)

Maxwell, J. C., *A Treatise on Electricity and Magnetism*, (1st ed. 1873: 3rd ed. 1891), reprinted by Dover in two volumes (1954)

Miller, K. S., *Multidimensional Gaussian Distributions*, Wiley (1964)

Nyquist, H., 'Certain topics in telegraph transmission theory', *Trans. AIEE*, **47**, 617–644 (1928)

Oppenheim, A. V. and Schafer, R. W. *Digital Signal Processing*, Prentice-Hall (1975)

Parzen, E., *Stochastic Processes*, Holden Day (1962)

Pearson, D. E., *Transmission and Display of Pictorial Information*, Pentech Press (1975)

Ramo, S., Whinnery, J. R. and Van Duzer, T., *Fields and Waves in Communication Electronics*, Wiley (1965)

Rice, S. O., 'Mathematical analysis of random noise', *Bell Syst. Tech. J.* **23**, 282–332 and **24**, 46–156 (1944–5)

Saltzberg, B. R., 'Intersymbol interference error bounds with application to ideal band-limited signalling, *IEEE Trans.*, **IT-14**, 563–568 (1968)

Sansone, G., *Orthogonal functions*, Interscience Publishers (1959)

Sarmanov, O. V. and Bratoeva, Z. N., 'Probabilistic properties of bilinear expansions of Hermite polynomials', *Theory of Probability and its Applications*, **12**, 470–481 (1967)

Schwartz, L., *Théorie des Distributions*, 2nd edn. Hermann (1966)

Shannon, C. E., 'Mathematical theory of communication', *Bell Syst. Tech. J.* **27**, 379–423 and 623–656 (1948). Reprinted in Shannon and Weaver.

Shannon, C. E. and Weaver, W., *The Mathematical Theory of Communication*, University of Illinois Press (1949)

Silvey, S. D., *Statistical Inference*, Penguin (1970)

Slepian, D. and Pollak, H. O., 'Prolate spheroidal wave functions, Fourier analysis and uncertainty', *Bell Syst. Tech. J.*, **40**, 43–64 (1961)

Sneddon, I. N., *Special functions of Mathematical Physics and Chemistry* (1961)

Snyder, D. L., *Random Point Processes*, Wiley (1975)

Tranter, C. J., *Bessel Functions with some Physical Applications* (1968)

Van Der Pol, B. and Bremmer, H., *Operational Calculus based on the two-sided Laplace Integral*, Cambridge University Press (1959)

Ville, J. A. and Bouzitat, J., 'Note sur un signal de durée finie et d'énergie filtrée maximum', *Cables et Transmission*, **11A**

Wald, A., *Statistical Decision Functions*, Wiley (1950)

Watson, G. N.
(1) *Theory of Bessel Functions*, 2nd edn., Cambridge University Press (1958)
(2) 'Notes on the generating functions of polynomials: Laguerre polynomials', *J. London Math. Soc.* **8**, 189–192 (1933)

Whittle, P., *Probability*, Penguin (1970)

Wiener, N., *The Interpolation, Extrapolation and Smoothing of Stationary Time Series*, Wiley (1949)

Woodward, P. M., *Probability and Information Theory, with Applications to Radar*, Pergamon Press (1953)

Wozencroft, J. M. and Jacobs, I. M., *Principles of Communication Engineering*, Wiley (1965)

Yao, K.
(1) 'Quadratic-exponential moment error bounds for digital communication systems', *Conference Record, 10th Asilomar Conf. on Circuits, Systems and Computers*, pp. 99–103 (1976)
(2) 'Error probability of asynchronous spread spectrum multiple access communication systems', *IEEE Trans.*, **COM-25** (1977)
(3) 'Moment space error bounds in digital communication systems', in J. K. Skwirzynski (Ed.): *Communication Systems and Random Process Theory* (1978)

Yao, K. and Tobin, R. M., 'Moment space upper and lower bounds for digital systems with intersymbol interference', *IEEE Trans.*, **IT-22**, 65–74 (1976)

# Index